Ancient Landscapes, Pastoral Visions

Samuel Palmer to the Ruralists

Anne Anderson, Robert Meyrick, Peter Nahum

Ancient Landscapes, Pastoral Visions
Samuel Palmer to the Ruralists

Exhibition dates:
Southampton City Art Gallery 18th April-22nd June 2008.
Victoria Art Gallery, Bath 26th July-7th September 2008.
Victoria Art Gallery, Bath 13th September-19th October 2008, *The Ruralists*.
Falmouth Art Gallery 20th September-1st November 2008.

SOUTHAMPTON CITY COUNCIL®

Punter Southall GROUP

PETER NAHUM At The Leicester Galleries

Friends of Southampton's Museums Archives and Galleries

Fred. Olsen

TABRETTS Fine Art Ltd

NADFAS 40TH ANNIVERSARY

Ancient Landscapes, Pastoral Visions
Samuel Palmer to the Ruralists

Anne Anderson, Robert Meyrick, Peter Nahum

ACC EDITIONS

ISBN 978-1-85149-569-6

British Library Cataloguing-in-Publication Data
A catalogue record for this book is available from the British Library

Design by Agata Maja Żurkiewicz / Officina Libraria, Milan, Italy

Printed in Italy by Geca Spa, Cesano Boscone (Milan), for the Antique Collectors' Club Ltd., Woodbridge, Suffolk IP12 4SD, UK

Contents

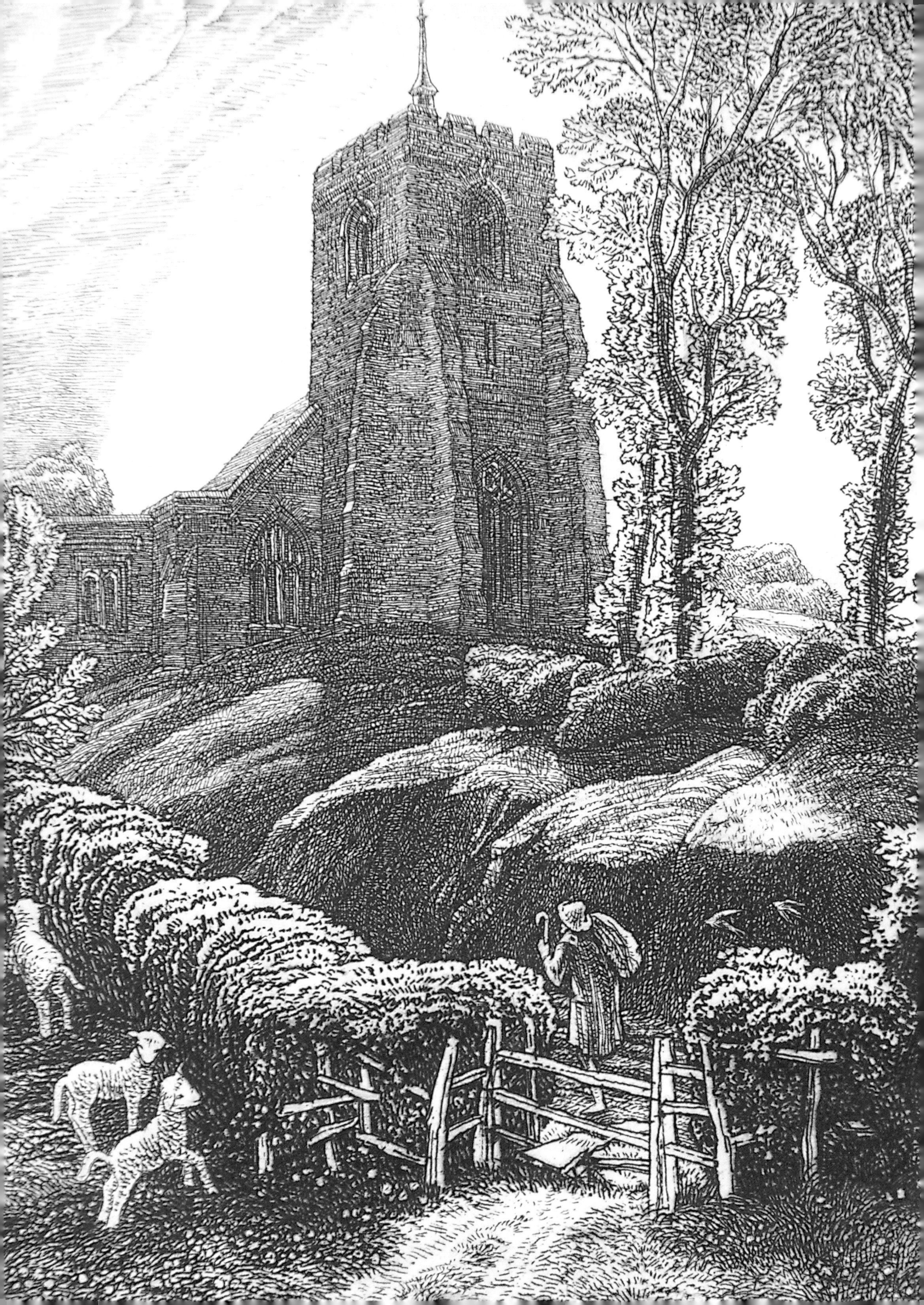

Foreword

Southampton City Art Gallery's present strong reputation can be attributed for the most part to its permanent collection, built up in a relatively short space of time from the early 1930s. Though it can broadly tell the story of the development of western art from the Renaissance to the present day, the outstanding element is British twentieth century and contemporary art. The emphasis is very much on the modern movement. Of this international phenomenon, a lineage can be traced from its birth in France with Impressionism through various figurative and abstract movements to Conceptualism and Post-Modernism.

The distinct and singular British School, however, has grown side-shoots at various stages, often referencing native traditions. Britain has always produced influential, non-conformist and idiosyncratic artists such as Stanley Spencer and Cecil Collins who refuse categorisation. The strands of pastoral landscape and sentiment in British art, from William Blake and Samuel Palmer onwards, have stood outside modernism for obvious reasons. They remain however a compelling alternative viewpoint and that such ideas held allure for progressive painters like Paul Nash, John Piper and Graham Sutherland as well as others including the Ruralists, attest to their potency and relevance in the modern age.

The origins of 'Ancient Landscapes – Pastoral Visions' dates to September 2005 when Graham Ovenden came to Southampton from his home in Cornwall to open a special anniversary exhibition organised by Dr Anne Anderson of Southampton Solent University. 'Southampton School and College of Art: A Celebration of 150 Years of Artistic Success' traced the achievements of that institution (housed in 1939 with new City Art Gallery) and its students from Sir Hubert von Herkomer to Graham Ovenden and others. It was there that Graham, a local boy, confirmed his life's vocation, nurtured by his inspirational teacher, Jim Sellars. The latter's evocative and intensely observed landscapes of the Test Valley reveal inner visions of the Palmer tradition and as a tribute we have dedicated a small gallery at Southampton to his work to accompany our exhibition.

Combining historic and contemporary work of related and recurring themes for 'Ancient Landscapes – Pastoral Visions' was the brainchild of Anne Anderson and Graham Ovenden. I am enormously indebted to Anne for her tireless endeavours in researching and curating the show, and to Graham for his enthusiastic support and guidance. I would also like to thank them, Peter Nahum and Robert Meyrick, for their eloquent and informative catalogue essays.

We are immensely grateful to our lenders, public and private, without whose generosity the exhibition would not have been possible. In addition we thank the Antique Collectors' Club for publishing this catalogue and the exhibition's sponsors, Stuart M. Southall, Punter Southall Group, Fred Olsen, Peter Nahum, Friends of Southampton's Museums Archives and Galleries and the National Association of Decorative and Fine Art Societies, Hampshire and the Isle of Wight, for their kind and valuable contributions.

The pastoral landscape tradition remains strong in the West Country and the exhibition travels to the Victoria Art Gallery, Bath and Falmouth Art Gallery. We are grateful to Jon Bennington, Brian Stewart and their colleagues for their assistance and participation.

Tim Craven
Curator
Southampton City Art Gallery

Author's Foreword

This exhibition grew out of the celebrations held in 2005 to mark 150 years of the Southampton School and College of Art. Researching the complex history of this institution it soon became clear that although Southampton has never generated a 'school of painters', it has provided the educational means to enable talented students to 'get on'. Amongst Southampton's successful 'boys' can be numbered Sir Hubert von Herkomer, Edward Gregory and Graham Ovenden, although almost one hundred years separates their time at the school and college. Graham Ovenden, who was born in Alresford and raised in Southampton, went on to the Royal College of Art where he met Peter Blake. In 1975 Ovenden, now married and living in Cornwall and Peter Blake joined forces with David Inshaw and the Ann and Graham Arnold to form the Brotherhood of Ruralists. It was Laurie Lee, the author of *Cider with Rosie*, and admirer of the Brotherhood, who evidently first coined the name 'Ruralists' but the idea of retreating from London's smog to recapture a lost vision of a disappearing rural England was certainly not new; Samuel Palmer's coterie found Shoreham in the 1820s. But the Ruralists do seem to have captured the spirit of the 1970s, with their escape from London to the West Country in search of a 'less complicated life-style' and their desire for a sense of community. They were after the 'Good Life'.

The last time the Ruralists were seen as a group in Southampton (at the University Art Gallery) was in 1978 – thirty years ago. Christopher Martin writing about the Ruralists in 1991 considered them to be in their 'autumn'; you might say I discovered them in their 'winter'. But now seems an appropriate time to look back, to locate where the Ruralists fit in the sweep of 20th century British art. Jerrold Northrop Moore's *The Green Fuse: Pastoral Vision in English Art 1820-2000* (Antique Collectors' Club, 2007) has provided much inspiration; it was at Graham Ovenden's instigation, and with his help, that this exhibition on the English Pastoral tradition has been realised. Graham's enthusiasm for the project has been untiring; he has introduced me to new painters and new writers. His knowledge of art and music is exhaustive; he is quite a rarity, being a graduate of both the RCA and the Royal Academy of Music. Like his Victorian heroes Graham is a polymath or even a 'renaissance man'. This exhibition is a tribute to his 'vision'. It is also hoped that the show will be a fitting accolade to over thirty years of Ruralist collaboration, with many works, from private collections, brought together and discussed for the first time. I would like to thank all the private lenders who have made this possible. I would particularly like to thank Stuart M. Southall for all his support, as both a lender and benefactor of the exhibition. I would also like to thank all the artists who have given their time, their works and have been generous with their copyrights. Finally I would like to thanks Tim Craven and Esta Mion-Jones at Southampton City Art Gallery.

There are many coincidences at work here; the seven original Ruralists included two couples called Graham and Ann (although one was an Anne). Graham Arnold and Peter Blake are the same age; both born in 1933. Graham Arnold taught David Inshaw and Peter Blake taught Graham Ovenden; both are exactly ten years younger. Arnold was himself taught by John Minton. Arnold and Blake both attended the RCA at the same time, although they only formed a passing acquaintance. On the wider stage of English art, Cecil Collins celebrates his centenary (he was born in 1908); Vaughan Williams died fifty years ago, in 1958. With the celebration for the 150th Anniversary of Elgar's birth last year, it seems an auspicious time to revaluate the English landscape tradition in the 21st century.

Taking as its starting point the 1926 exhibition of Samuel Palmer's work at the Victoria and Albert Museum, the exhibition traces the English tradition through Paul Nash, the Class of 21, the Neo-Romantics and the Ruralists. Four major themes have been identified to explore the Romantic response to the British countryside. *Pastoral Visions* examines Palmer's legacy, with works that show an overt debt to his idyllic landscapes suffused with piety. *In Search of England* focuses on the countryside and the 'great tree' as the embodiment of our national character. *Ancient Landscapes* considers the significance of prehistoric sites and primeval landscapes; connoting continuity and timelessness, they remind us of our 'roots'. The *Nocturne*, a favourite of Palmer, Nash and the Ruralists, offers the mysterious light of the moon, the supernatural mood heightened by owls and ghostly phantoms. The exhibition concludes with the work of James Sellars (1927-2000), mentor of Graham Ovenden and influential lecturer at the Southampton College of Art, who introduced his students to Palmer's 'Valley of Vision'.

This exhibition travels to the Victoria Art Gallery, Bath (the Ruralists coalesced at Wellow), where, for reasons of space, the works are divided into two complementary shows, one devoted to the Ruralists. A selection of works then moves to Falmouth Art Gallery (the Ovendens live in Cornwall); I would especially like to thank Jon Benington at Bath and Brian Stewart at Falmouth for making this possible. I would also like to thank all the sponsors of the exhibition; Stuart M. Southall, Punter Southall Group, Fred Olsen, Peter Nahum at the Leicester Galleries, NADFAS Hampshire and the Isle of Wight and FOSMAG.

Anne Anderson
February 2008

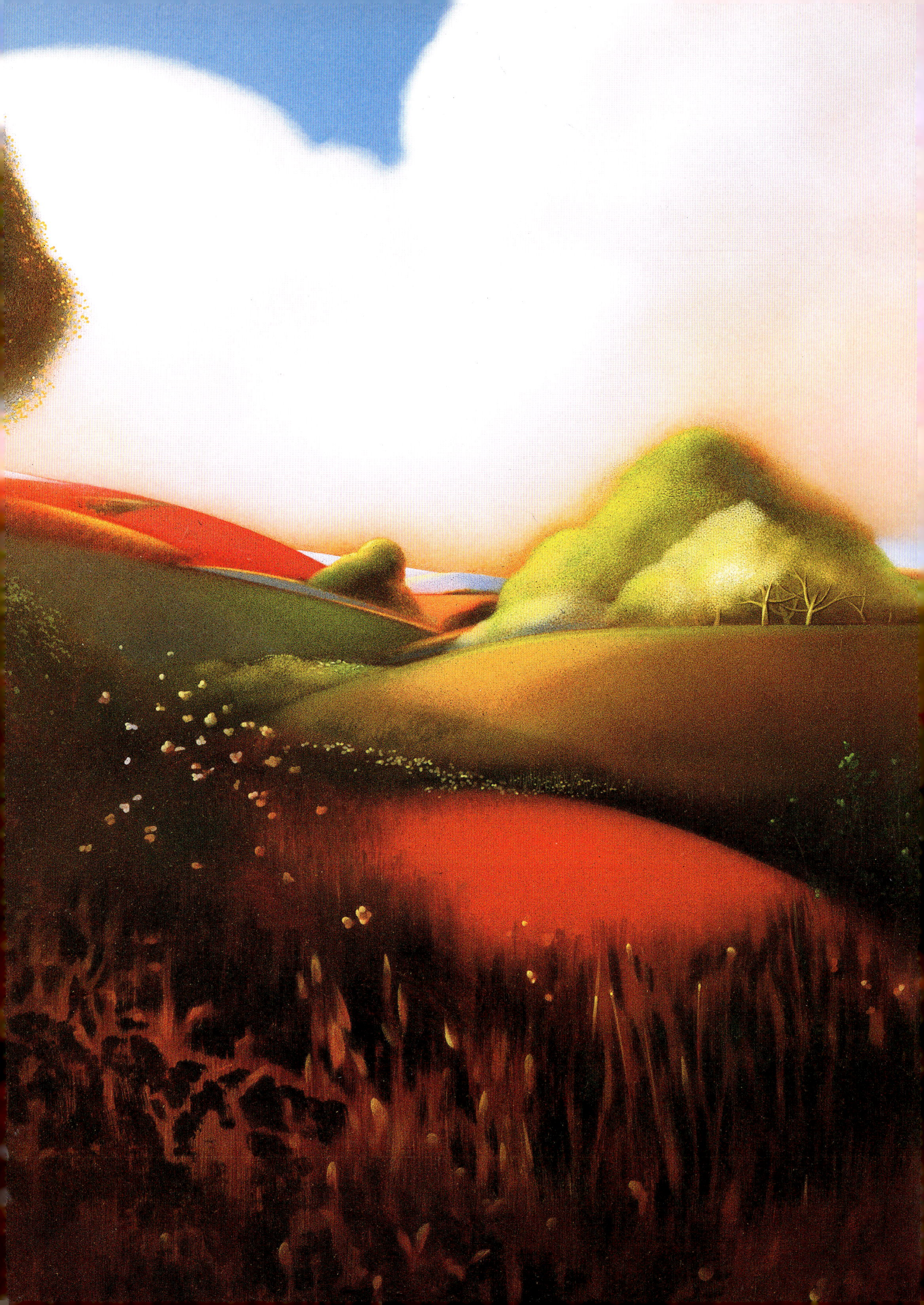

Ancient Landscapes, Pastoral Visions: Motifs and Meanings

Anne Anderson

Samuel Palmer: Vision and Landscape, an exhibition held at the British Museum in 2005-2006, highlighted the influence of Samuel Palmer (1805-1881) and the 'Ancients', the young disciples of the elderly William Blake (1757-1827), on the development of landscape in the post-First World War era. Writing in 1946, Michael Ayrton (1921-1975) concluded, 'It is Palmer, more than any other individual draughtsman, who influences the landscape drawing of the younger generation today'.[1] Palmer's intensity was communicated to a younger generation through *An Exhibition of Drawings, Etchings and Woodcuts by Samuel Palmer and other disciples of William Blake* held at the Victoria and Albert Museum in 1926, with F.L. Griggs, the master-printer of Chipping Campden, acting as a mediator, re-strking Palmer's seminal etchings. Graham Sutherland (1903-80) particularly seized on Palmer's etchings, which offered him a wholly new beginning, a turning point not dependent on 'progressive' French art but rooted in the 'English vision'. Ayrton was also determined to inoculate his contemporaries against the 'French flu', and make them uphold their own native traditions. The English way stressed 'mystical and poetic realism' over French 'succulence of surface, classical elegance and the sensual enjoyment of paint for its own sake'.[2] The impact of the war itself, reflected in a new feeling for nature and mysticism, must be held to account for the Neo-Romanticism of the next two decades. Paul (1889-1946) and John Nash (1893-1977) John Piper (1903-92), John Craxton (1922-), John Minton (1917-57) and Eric Ravilious (1903-42) would all fall, to a greater or lesser extent, under the sway of Palmer's vision. These artists established a 'characteristically English' approach to landscape painting, capturing the eerie moods of nature and preserving rural values seen to be increasingly eroded by commercial pressures and globalisation.

In the aftermath of the Second World War these pressures clearly escalated, but it was not until the 1970s that a group of artists coalesced to take on the mantle not only of the Ancients but also of the Pre-Raphaelite Brotherhood (1848-1853). John Everett Millais (1829-96), Dante Gabriel Rossetti (1828-1882) and William Holman Hunt (1827-1910) had regained their erstwhile positions in the artistic canon by the late 1960s, their art apparently offering a springboard much as Palmer's had done in the 1920s. The Brotherhood of Ruralists embraced the Victorian revival and Neo-Romanticism of the 1970s, embodying the very spirit of the era with their retreat from London to the West Country in search of a 'less complicated life-style' and their desire for a sense of community; their utopia imagined a shared life allowing more time to paint! This collective of seven artists, Graham (1932-) and Ann (1936-) Arnold, Graham (1943-) and Annie Ovenden (1945-), Peter Blake (1932-) and his then wife Jann Haworth (1942-) and David Inshaw (1943-), debuted at the Royal Academy in 1976: (Fig. 1)

> 'They are a group, though separate in techniques and talent. A brotherhood, and sisterhood, closely bound by their sympathies...They came together in 1975 to rediscover the countryside and to re-settle their souls.'[3]

Palmer has become a symbol of 'Romantic escapism'; should the Ruralists be viewed in the same way? Is their vision antiquated and outmoded or are they the inheritors of the English pastoral tradition, which privileges humanism, nationalism and the literary? This tradition has been denounced for its insularity

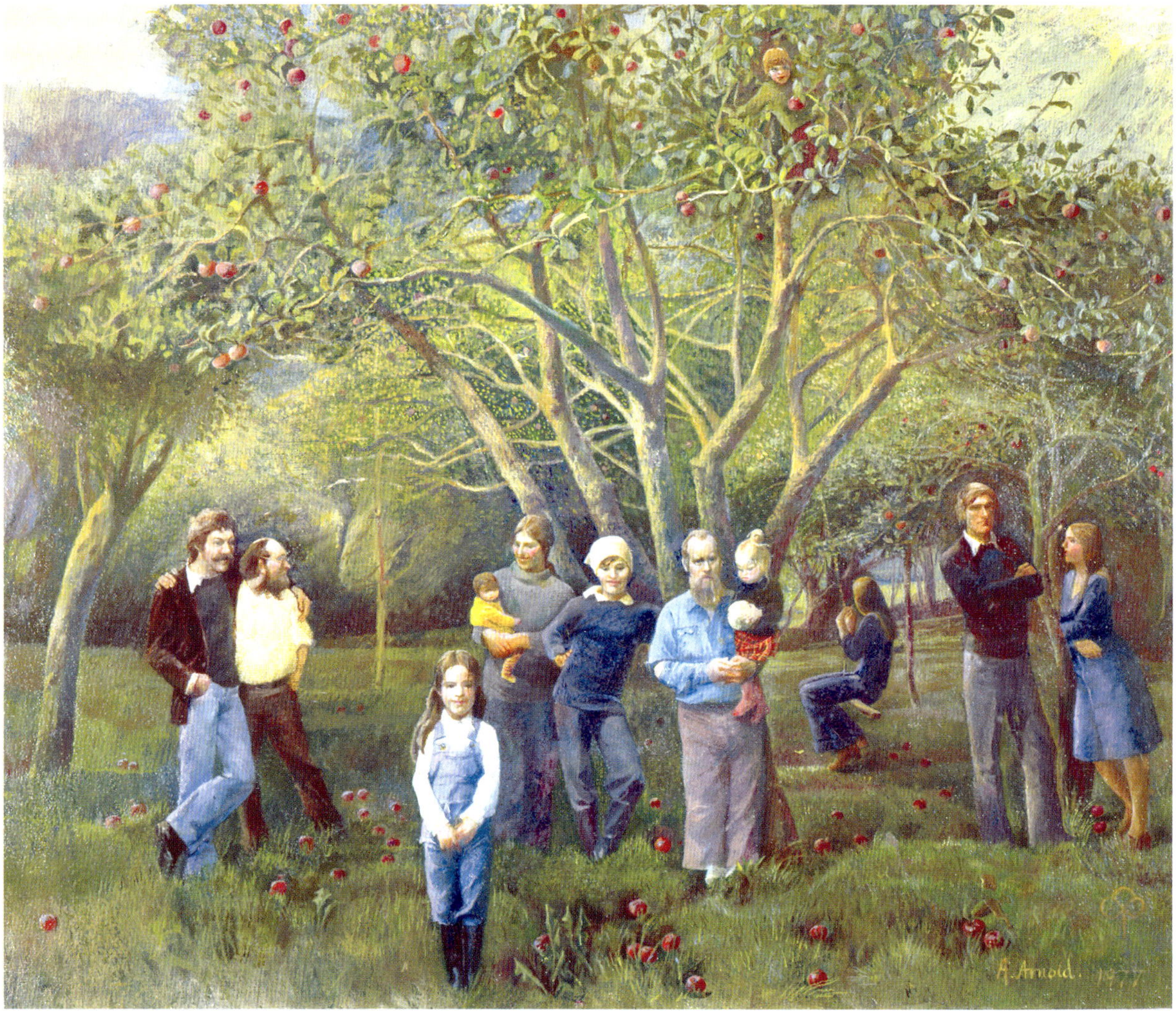

Fig. 1. Ann Arnold (1936-)
The Brotherhood of Ruralists at Coombe, 1977
oil on canvas, 460 x 560 mm
private collection

and apparent disregard of contemporary issues. This halcyon view of life in the countryside masks anxieties, the threat of urban development, the infiltration of roads and railways and the erosion of local identity. Yet, ironically, Sutherland's etching have been viewed as 'signs of the times', being 'the "still small voice" after too much of the "big noise"' [4] In the 21st century the 'big noise' is still there but the 'small voice' has become louder with regard to 'green' issues. There a lingering desire to recapture a lost innocence, to return to a time before the proverbial Fall. The Ruralists access a 'state of grace' through the eyes of the child, with works that share the 'intense child-bright close-view of the natural world that still thrives outside the concrete pack-ice of cities'.[5] Such works are unashamedly nostalgic, even sentimental, in taking us back to our own childhood experiences, evoking 'an overriding sense of yearning for a 'Paradise Lost', whether it is for a prelapsarian English Arcadia, or for lost youth and unspoilt beauty'.[6] John Betjeman (1906-84) and John Piper gladly accepted the label of nostalgic since, as Piper declared 'nostalgia for something means love for it, and if that is intense then it is worth having'.[7] Philip Larkin wrote approvingly of Betjeman, 'If the spirit of our century is onward, outward and upward, the spirit of Betjeman's work is backward, inwards and downwards'.[8] The same words could be applied to Graham

Ovenden, who still wears the hat bequeathed to him by Betjeman. As editor of the Shell Guides to the English counties (Paul Nash wrote and illustrated the *Shell Guide to Dorset* in 1935), Betjeman helped to foster the myth of the 'real' England, 'feeding our nostalgia for a pre-industrial, pre-Reformation past as unreal as those little visions of a pastoral Paradise made by Palmer in Shoreham'.[9]

This exhibition sets out to examine the conundrum of being 'reactionary' and 'contemporary' within the context of the English Landscape tradition. It builds on recent research and exhibitions to examine the phenomenon of Pastoralism in the 21st century[10]. As Sutherland asserted,

> 'Painting, it is true, can often be the equivalent of lyric poetry…Often what is meant by poetical painting shows itself variously in, say, a love of the ideal, a transfiguring and melancholy light, an ominous overtone, or a forced atmosphere of fantasy.' [11]

But the artist goes on to speak of 'poetry in another and greater sense-poetry which enlightens the significance and nature of things. Poetry also which makes things hold more significance than their original meaning, and which defines their essence'. Graham Ovenden strives to create visual poetry in this sense, expressed most eloquently in *Orchard Moon* (1984, Cat. 123) and *All Hallows* (*The Sea Cathedral*) (1983; Cat. 90), which relates to a Walter de la Mare short story. Such works hold deep personal significance, as well as expressing 'universal truths', using the particular to reflect on wider experience: 'Romantic art deals with the particular…is the result of a vision that can see in these things something significant beyond ordinary significance: something that for a moment seems to contain the whole world; and, when the moment is past, carries over some comment on life or experience besides the comment on appearances'.[12] *The Sea Cathedral* 'rests on the land's end facing the ocean. In the distance a shaft of light beams down on the ocean. The church…is a symbolic focus at the very edge of a view that separates land from sea and sky. The scene has the same mysterious air of presence created by many of his other works'.[13] Is this evocative configuration of land, sea and sky a symbol of eternity, perhaps the promise of a life hereafter? Yet the precipitous Cathedral, threatened by the sea, 'cliff clung, looming lonely', is rather troubling, even sinister. Ovenden is not crudely specific; rather we are offered an enigma, an intimate blending of art and beliefs, which are personal, unorthodox and mystical. *Orchard Moon* is especially Palmer-like, with its luminous moon floating on vaporous white clouds. The eye is taken through the folds of the landscape, a natural tunnel extending to the horizon where the moon rises and casts its slivery light. The image is peaceful but melancholic, suggestive of loss. There are inevitably three apple trees, one being less mature, almost child-like. The religious significance of the Trinity immediately springs to mind, while apple trees recall Palmer's *Magic Apple Tree*, painted during the Shoreham period, as well as a time of innocence before the Fall. Using a device borrowed from Caspar David Friedrich (1774-1840), the great German Romantic painter, the V of the valley is reflected in an inverted V that rises above the moon. These old symbols for woman (the Mons Venus) and man strengthen our belief that we are in Eden or Paradise. The image could be a *pictura poesis* or a poetic picture, a concept that has a long western tradition extending back to the Venetian painter Georgione.

The practice of appending poetic excerpts to landscapes was permitted at the Royal Academy, following Sir Joshua Reynolds' assertion that, 'A landskip [*sic*] …conducted under the influence of a poetical mind, will have the same superiority over the more ordinary and common views as Milton's *Allegro* and *Penseroso* have over a cold prosaik [*sic*] narration or description'.[14] Literary associations were used to elevate landscape to a higher intellectual level. William Blake (1757-1827) and Dante Gabriel Rossetti went further than simply borrowing from their literary counterparts, being both painters and poets; Paul Nash also strove for recognition in both art forms, while Piper achieved success as a poet-painter, publishing two volumes decorated with his own vignettes. It was Blake who bound the two arts together:

'Poetry consists in bold, daring and masterly conceptions; and shall painting be confined to the mere sordid drudgery of facsimile representations of merely mortal and perishing substances, and not be, as poetry and music are, elevated into its own proper sphere of invention and visionary conception?' [15]

As a poet and painter, Graham Ovenden's work relates to both the literary and artistic English romantic tradition, and like Blake he has experimented with combining visual images and poetry (Fig. 2). Paul Nash still valued Poetry and Sentiment despite the prognostications of Roger Fry (1866-1934), the influential art critic, who did his best to convince the English school that the only way forward was through Cezanne and the cultivation of 'significant form'. Fry was vehemently opposed to 'subject' let alone literary associations. For Fry, who took his lead from French Post-Impressionism and Cubism, there was no such thing as 'hidden meaning', rather painting, based on an initial visual sensation, should be 'pure', 'disinterested', un-literary, formal and appeal to a separate 'aesthetic emotion'.[16] Both Fry and Clive Bell negated what an artist was trying to say, which was mere 'arty' anecdote. This outlook scorned figuration and representation in favour of abstraction. The geometric and mechanical were preferred to the organic; evidently the virtues of beauty, harmony and grace were outmoded. The poet-critic T.E. Hulme (1883-1917) championed the 'desire for austerity and bareness, striving towards structure and away from the messiness and confusion of nature and natural things'.[17] The 'urge to empathy', to foist personal responses onto unfeeling nature, faith in the subjective vision and man's instinct to look for God, were resoundingly quashed. More recently conceptual art has brought back the 'idea', but has negated the work itself:

'In an era of extreme formal aesthetic experimentation that has embraced such notions as the concept behind a work of art is more valuable that the work itself, or is in fact the work, landscape has not been recognised as a vital field of contemporary art. It has on the one hand either been regarded as the provenance of the outdated and unfashionable or the domain of the amateur watercolourist. In fact the strong romantic association between English art and the natural world is often unjustifiably viewed as a provincial and at best idiosyncratic concern.' [18]

Yet the desire to imbue landscape with emotional significance has persisted; being the native tradition, 'Going in for nature' is hard to suppress. Graham Ovenden has evolved his own landscape vision, being able to evoke the reality of the natural world through draughtsmanship, luminosity and prismatic colour, as well as a deep feeling for the spirit of a place (Cat. 108). His colours are rich and deep, the emotive colours of the Pre-Raphaelites, which evoke the sensual mystery of Nature: 'They are visionary or romantic colours with symbolic qualities: essentially they are poetic'.[19]

The Romantic impulse resurfaced in the years immediately following the First World War, and during the Second World War. Essentially a 'mode of feeling' or 'an attitude of mind', Romanticism comes to the fore in times of stress and anxiety; the artist Keith Vaughan believed he was 'living in a Romantic era because the essence of Romantic art is conflict, the struggle to organise chaos and reconcile opposites'.[20]

Simon Martin contends that 'at such points in history, romantic artists have sought refuge from the harsh reality of the present, painting landscapes of the mind, rather than actual landscapes'.[21] Essentially introspective and nostalgic, Romanticism relies on memory and associations. For John Minton (1917-1957), looking back to Blake and Palmer made a connection with a 'lost' England, fulfilling 'a certain need of this time...of the dignity and nobility of man, that was once in this island, in the golden songs of Shakespeare and the pastoral lyricism of Purcell. Blake reminded them, of something we have lost, perhaps forever'.[22] Those caught up in the hostilities had to be reminded that they were fighting for 'Englishness',

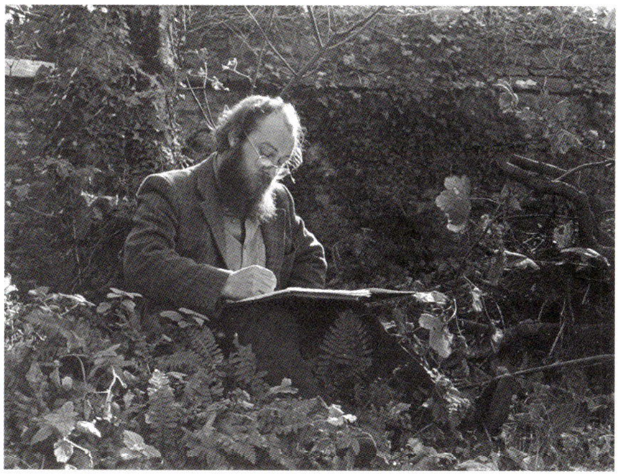

Fig. 2. Graham Ovenden drawing at Morwenstow Cornwall

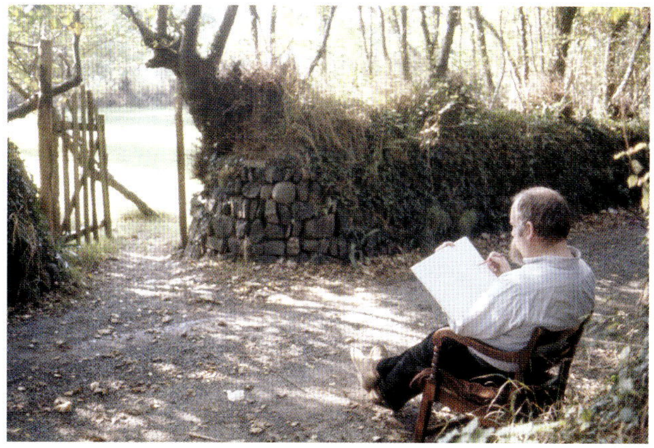

Fig. 3. Peter Blake drawing at Coombe, Cornwall

especially in the face of such terrible losses. Paul Nash befriended the writer Edward Thomas (1878-1917, Cat. 60), whose work has been credited with having 'a freshness and fragrance as characteristic as that of an English day' but Thomas was killed in Flanders at the age of thirty-seven.[23] This 'quiet watcher of the countryside' was swept up in the Great War and transformed into a 'man of action and a soldier', as well as a poet. Despite his reputation as a war poet, Thomas made his name 'in prose which has the essential quality of poetry'.[24] *The Heart of England* (1906) reveals his love of the English countryside:

> 'For him the English countryside held everything needed for the satisfaction of the appetites of man, whether physical, mental, or spiritual. He loved the English country...for its peaceful smallness; for that brooding quiet which hovers over the unfrequented spot where a lane mounts a stile to lose itself in a disused field-path; for the intimacy of its woods; for the still security of its little valleys nestling happily between the low, smooth hills; for its pale sunshine; its unexpected rains, and for its changeful skies. His life and thoughts lay among the simple things which have their roots in the distant and forgotten past.' [25]

Thomas preferred the village church to the cathedral, a simple folk-song to classical music; he wrote about the everyday and 'the common life of the open air': 'But never has the common and ordinary been rendered more thrillingly beautiful than by the pen of Edward Thomas...His prose...is an inspiration to all those whose eyes are not sealed to the wonders of the daily detail of the countryside, and he brings back to the contemplative reader something of childhood's contentment and joy in the seemingly small and trivial'.[26] Thomas vividly describes nature:

> 'For a minute only, in one shadowed wood that faced the departing night, all the birds sang together stormily and hardly moving from the sprays on which they slept, with something of the night in their voice... The young hazel boughs bent at the top with fresh leaves that were so beautiful and frail that they seemed but just to have been persuaded to stay and give up winged life... Wild cherry leaves and flowers mingled like lovers so young that the boy rivals the girl in tenderness.' [27]

Evidently, Thomas's writings need to be approached in a 'spirit of sympathy and meditation', as they capture 'the strongly beating heart of England itself; an essence, as it were, which makes our own countryside essentially different from that of any other place in the world'.[28]

In capturing the 'freshness and fragrance' of an 'English spring day', Thomas was following in the footsteps of Richard Jefferies (1848-1887), whose spiritual autobiography, *The Story of My Heart* (1883, Cat. 54) describes 'the very spirit of the English scene in a universal way': 'It is a hymn to visible beauty, singing of the green world of leafy woods, hedgerows or lush meadows, to the colour of the sky, and to the immemorial appeal of the sea'.[29] Jefferies passionate prose reveals his deep love of the English countryside:

> 'It was in his blood and it shaped his vision of the loveliness of nature. It was in the West Country that he first became conscious of the beauty of the earth. How *could* he forget the countryside that had known and responded to his early dreams, which had quickened his brooding imagination, and made him its child, free of its spacious fields and downs?'.[30]

The son of a farmer, Jefferies, despite 'intermittent' schooling, became 'a highly educated person, with a quite unusual range of information'.[31] This enabled him to embark on a career as a reporter, joining *The Wilts and Gloucestershire Standard*. His early attempts at fiction were indifferent but *Greene Ferne Farm* (1880), *The Dewy Morn* (1884) and *Amaryllis at the Fair* (1887) display his strengths as a novelist. But it was as a writer of English country life, its scenes, people, and ways, that Jefferies is remembered. "The Pageant of Summer", in *The Life of the Fields*, is considered one of his most successful 'pictures, painted with a lavish brush, bright with the colours of the English landscape and the joys of the open air'[32] :

> 'I cannot leave it; I must stay under the old tree in the midst of the long grass, the luxury of the leaves, and the song in the very air. I seem as if I could feel all the glowing life the sunshine gives and the south wind calls to being. The endless grass, the endless leaves, the immense strength of the oak expanding, the unalloyed joy of finch and blackbird; from all of them I receive a little...The exceeding beauty of the earth, in her splendour of life, yields a new thought with every petal. The hours when the mind is absorbed by beauty are the only hours when we really live...These are the only hours not wasted – these hours that absorb the soul and fill it with beauty. This is real life, and all else illusion, or mere endurance. Does this reverie of flowers and waterfall and song form an ideal, a human ideal, in the mind? It does...To be beautiful and to be calm, without mental fear, is the ideal of nature. If I cannot achieve it, at least I can think it.' [33]

'Jefferies's England' clearly appealed to Edward Thomas, whose definitive biography *Richard Jefferies: His Life and Work* was published in 1909. John Powell Ward, both a literary academic and poet, places Edward Thomas in the 'The English Line' descending from Wordsworth to Philip Larkin. This lyrical English tradition includes John Clare, the 'peasant poet', Thomas Hardy and Robert Frost. The so-called Georgian Poets of the First World War era – Rupert Brooke, W.H. Davies, Walter de la Mare and John Masefield – followed the example of Wordsworth, by capturing the native landscape in plain language with attention to natural detail. Broadly speaking English Line poetry is:

> '...characterised by a melancholy moodiness, a certain elusiveness of its material...and a sense of the presence of the familiar and everyday as the only things – if even those – that can be relied on at least to be present. A greyness and colourlessness fills the present, making for a yearning for the past, childhood and what is lost more generally... It is commonly lyrical, which is its attraction; but equally inward and subjective, as though that elusive subject... is forever the poet's own feelings, thoughts, fears and disturbances.' [34]

This type of poetry is commonly spoken in the first person, suggesting that humanity is broadly the same everywhere. Essentially democratic in outlook, it is 'hard on the rich, compassionate towards the poor, and saying that despite great material difference all are capable of feeling and suffering the same things'.[35] Finally, the language used is often called 'simple' or 'ordinary', having the directness of speech; Wordsworth's 'words are themselves thought and feeling', his sole aim being 'to express mind and emotion themselves' [36]:

> 'The Rainbow comes and goes,
> And lovely is the Rose;
> The Moon doth with delight
> Look round her when the heavens are bare;
> Waters on a starry night
> Are beautiful and fair,
> The sunshine is a glorious birth.' [37]

These lines (10-16) are from Wordsworth's most famous long poem *Ode: Intimations of Immortality*, in which dejection and fear are born from the loss of childhood happiness and security. Childhood is going to slip further and further away but there is pleasure in expressing this loss. This mix of melancholy and pleasure, arising from the need to go right down into the depths of one's feelings, the 'mind's abyss', is typical of the English Line. Pain has to be endured to achieve 'self-knowing'; for Keats pain and pleasure were intermingled 'simply because joy is already slipping away as you enter it'. A.E. Houseman (1859-1936) dwells on a vanished world of childhood, the lost paradise, in his most famous poetical work, *A Shropshire Lad* (1892). His 'blue remembered hills' encapsulate this sense of loss:

> 'Into my heart an air that kills
> From yon far country blows:
> What are those blue remembered hills,
> What spires, what farms are those?
>
> That is the land of lost content,
> I see it shining plain,
> The happy highways where I went
> And cannot come again (ASL XL).'

John Powell Ward calls Houseman 'the poet of pain', his vision narrowed down to 'a single image of the unspoken grave'; 'his memory has a terseness... It is written in the basic lexicon of sadness, loss, love, tears, trees and graves, but with exact execution'. [38] With Houseman we have come a long way from 'the gentle, fertile, natural scene, which normally is the dwelling place of the English melancholic poet'.[39] Jefferies's poetical prose celebrates life, being sensuous, although merged and mingled with the spiritual, even religious. As a 'poet of humanity', his aim was to communicate a 'higher ideal': 'He allied himself to Nature, and still plays his part in her office of granting health, and hearty pleasure, and consolation, and the delights of the senses and of the spirit, to men'. [40]

Pastoral lyricism has its roots in the *Idylls* of the Greek bucolic poet Theocritus (*c*.308-*c*.240 BC) and the *Eclogues* of the Roman poet Virgil (70-19 BC). [41] The traditional form of pastoral elegy evokes an idyllic view of rural life, celebrating the fecundity of nature with fruit laden trees and fields of ripening corn. Once associated with Christianity, the Pastoral acquired a spiritual dynamic, Christ being presented as the Good Shepherd. Milton is the most famous exponent of the Christianized pastoral, though William Blake also subscribed to the form in his *Songs of Innocence and Experience* (1789-94). It was Blake's wood engravings for the *Pastorals of Virgil* (1821) that transplanted this bucolic imagery from classical Arcadia to the English countryside, initiating a tradition that stretches from Samuel Palmer to Paul Drury, Graham Sutherland and Robin Tanner in the 1920s. England was transformed into 'God's green acre', but with a lingering sense of a pagan past; Pan, the goat-footed god is transformed into a keeper of flocks. There is rarely any sign of the harsh realities of rural life; 'the overriding sensation is of man's communion with nature'.[42] In Arcadia man lives in sacred reverence with the soil; for Henry Peacham, in *Minerva Britannia* (1612), rustic life was above all a 'proclamation of the stupendous benevolence of the Creator'. [43] The quintessential English scene evokes a 'humanist happy valley' of 'rolling hills safely grazed by fleecy flocks and cooled by zephyrs moist and sweet'. This idealised view, embodying a whole world of associations and sentiments, has been transmitted to us through paintings, engravings, photographs and posters, designed to summon loyalty to this 'temperate, blessed isle'.[44] Arcadian traditions, 'Pan's fertile realm populated with nymphs and satyrs' or God's promised land, trail 'the memories of generations behind them'[45] Paul Nash, David Nash and Andy Goldsworthy have tried to distance themselves from such reminiscences with 'found' sculptures, driftwood from the seashore or tree stumps and limbs, drawing on the natural processes of nature. While decidedly minimalist, and beautiful, such work rarely escapes from its implicit connotations; we cannot deny that the landscape is a 'text on which generations write their recurring obsessions'.[46] While the Arcadian idyll has been revealed as just a 'pretty lie', cloaking man's abuse of his environment, we still long for the time when man was part of nature, rather than its exploiter.

Palmer employed the shepherd/poet or 'Man of Melancholy' to intercede on behalf of the viewer in this bonding with nature. Contemplative reflection led to melancholy, signifying not 'low spirits' but rather 'the capacity to muse on subjects other than the petty preoccupations of this world'.[47] In his companion poems on the theme of melancholy (*Il Penseroso*) and mirth (*L'Allegro*), John Milton (1608-74) evoked 'Such sights as youthful Poets dream/ On Summer eves by haunted stream'.[48] The melancholic sought to 'walk alone in some solitary grove, betwixt wood and water, by a brook side, to meditate upon some delightsome and pleasant subject…to melancholize, and build castles in the air, to go smiling to themselves'.[49] The secluded spot offered respite and solace, or 'time out', captured in James Thomson's (1700-48) *Ode on Solitude*:

'Oh! let me pierce thy secret Cell
And in thy deep recesses dwell
Perhaps from Norwood's oak-clad hill
When meditation has her fill,
I just may cast my careless eyes
Where London's spiry turrets rise,
Think of its crimes, its cares, its pain
The shield me in the woods again.'

The country as a place to retire to has been a constant of modern British sensibility. But even in the sequestered, safe harbour of the pastoral, death cannot be excluded; nature constantly reminds us of the passing of time, the changing of the seasons, of the cycle of life. The English melancholic impulse comes from the classical epithet *Et in arcadia ego*, read not as 'And I have dwelt in Arcadia too', but 'Even in Arcadia I, Death, am present'. Erwin Panofsky recognises this meaning, long forgotten on the Continent, as underpinning the English or 'insular' tradition, enacted in the retention of *memento mori*, such as the red poppies of Flanders. [50] 'Sweet sadness' comes from recognising the omnipotence of Death; surrounded by burgeoning life we remember that death comes to all. It follows that the pastoral has always been a favoured mode for elegy, 'written out of sympathy for the deaths of others, the act of speaking makes the speaker highly conscious of his own frail mortality and the brevity of his time'[51] (Cat. 126). But as the pastoral favours perennial flowers, it also betokens immortality and remembrance.

The English tradition in poetry and painting seeks Blake's 'green and pleasant land', a long-lost rural England that is correlated with the innocence of childhood; during times of uncertainty and upheaval, both personal and national, it has come to the fore. Thus Virgil, in the *Georgics*, 'sang of the care of fields, of cattle, and of trees, while great Caesar thundered in war by deep Euphrates'.[52] The pastoral acts as both an antidote to war and an ironic foil. War 'belongs to the demonic world, and no one engages in it or contemplates it without implicitly or explicitly bringing to bear the contrasting "model world" by which its demonism is measured'.[53] Griggs *Memory of Clavering* (1934) was conceived in the spring of 1918, whilst hearing the distant sound of guns from the Western Front across the English Channel. English writing has been steeped in 'a highly sophisticated literary pastoralism' and 'a unique actual ruralism', according to Paul Fussell: 'What other nation supports through all the vicissitudes of modern economics and politics a periodical like *Country Life*, devoted very largely to the excitation of rural nostalgia?'.[54] In Britain 'the townsman envies the villager his certainties and...has always regarded urban life as just a temporary necessity. One day he will find a cottage on the green and "real values"'.[55] It has been suggested by Raymond Williams, that this 'special British ruralism' is partly the result of Colonialism and Imperialist exile; England as 'home' is a memory and an ideal. Moreover, with industrialisation and urbanisation coming so early, the British needed 'what Empson calls "the permanent tradition of the country": an idea of themselves as indeed a people with immemorial rural roots and of a spiritual disposition that is at home among tall trees, clear streams, hunting fields and sheepfolds, ricks, roses and hedgerows'.[56] For the British, nature is, as Wordsworth and Palmer revealed, a 'stay' against the chaos of industrial and urban life. Simon Schama argues that the 'irresistible cycle of vegetation, where death merely composted the process of rebirth' also offers us the promise of 'immortality'.[57] From childhood, our view of nature is loaded with complicated memories, myths and meanings: 'Before it can ever be a repose for the senses, landscape is the work of the mind. Its scenery is built up as much from strata of memory as from layers of rock.'[58]

While many of us find comfort and refuge in our urban gardens, 'the greensward as a remnant of an old pastoral dream',[59] we still long to escape to the countryside and recover those 'real values'; we imagine more time with our families and a sense of belonging. Most of us have to wait until our retirement to live the dream but the Brotherhood of Ruralists escaped into a world of shared artistic ideals. The Ruralists favour 'landscapes of the mind', with a strong literary thread running through many works by Graham Arnold and Graham Ovenden (Fig. 4). Personal favourites include Shakespeare (the Ruralists illustrated the Arden Shakespeare Covers), Thomas Hardy, Richard Jefferies, Edward Thomas and A.E. Houseman. Ann Arnold has illustrated the work of the 'peasant' poet John Clare, best known for *The Shepherd's Calendar*.

Ann Arnold was introduced to Hardy at the age of seventeen, while at Art School; she and Graham spent their honeymoon in Cornwall, sharing Hardy's poems:

> 'Hardy evokes the feeling that "now" is merely the latest manifestation, the tip of the branch, other twigs will grow to replace them. So one's awareness of time and place and eternity; of now and here, are caught and held. All these things I would like in my paintings. There is little topographical reference to Hardy's places because their particularity is replaced by my own'.[60]

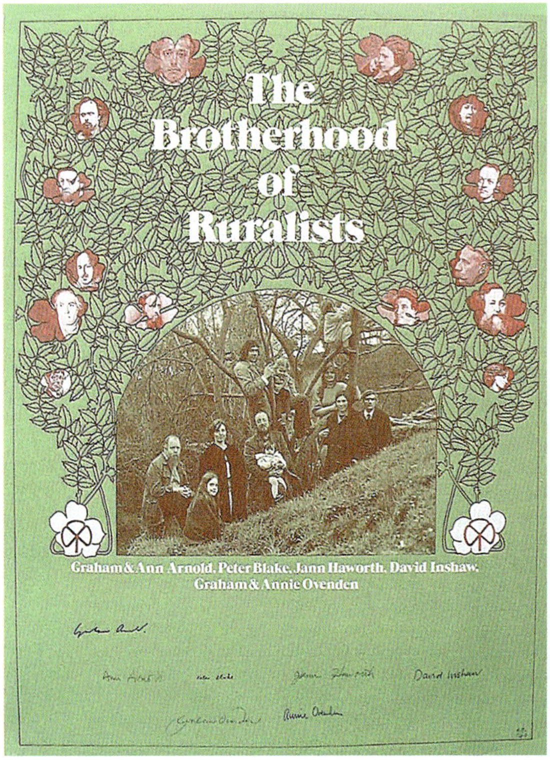

Fig. 4. The Brotherhood of Ruralists Heroes
Shakespeare, William Blake, Samuel Palmer
Dante Gabriel Rossetti, William Morris, Elgar…

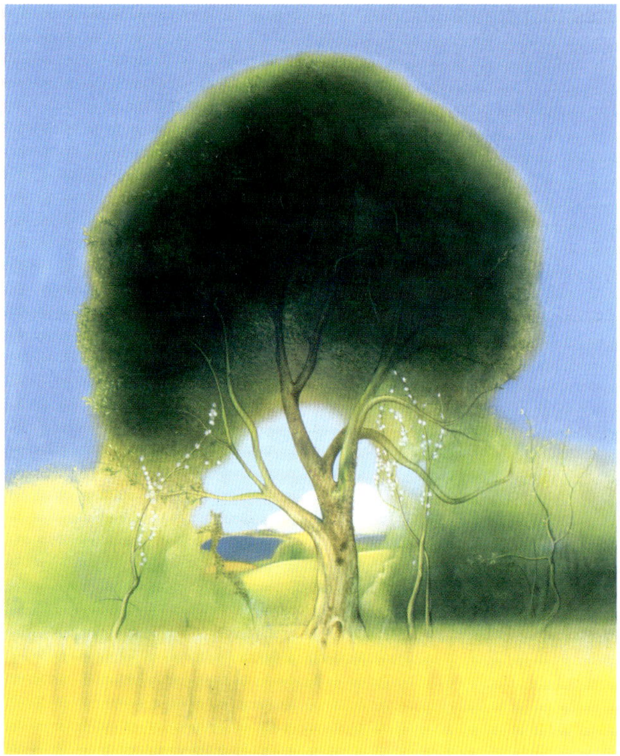

Fig. 5. GRAHAM OVENDEN (1943-)
The Great Tree
oil, 465 x 394 mm, private collection

Graham Ovenden, artist, poet, musician, craftsman, designer, photographer and writer, has also drawn on Hawker of Morwenstow[61] (the Ruralists went on 'painting holidays' together at Coombe, near Morwenstow [Fig. 3]), Gerald Manley Hopkins, John Betjamin, Walter de la Mare and the music of Elgar. Laurie Lee, who has written personal tributes to the Ruralists and Graham Ovenden, notes this interconnection of word and image, which could itself be seen as the 'English line': they 'reaffirm in their work the serenity and lyricism of nature without overlooking the deeper strains of magic, mystery and myth'.[62] Their paintings offer a complexity of meaning, often deeply personal, from childhood memories to lost loves. There are 'steadfast obsessions', from specific landscapes, David Inshaw's Wessex and Annie Ovenden's Barley Splatt, her home in Cornwall, to Graham Ovenden's quest for a spiritual communion with nature. Man's lingering mark on the landscape frames the recognition of the brevity of life: 'nature's repetitive death, its breathing rise and fall, symbolised in the forlorn, flower-decked form of Ophelia'.[63] There is often a sense of 'passing', with 'long shadows running across old humps of grass- the light's farewell to a day and an age'.[64] There is that inevitable melancholy, a sentiment to be found in so much English rural poetry and landscape painting. In the face of progress, nature appears vulnerable and fragile but we know it is not; there is resilience and rejuvenation. Continuity can be found in the ancient landscapes of Wessex and Cornwall 'where the light seems to strike older and more sacred grounds' and the lingering signs of human habitation, 'sleeping mounds and graves'; 'a world of spirits, shapes and ancient voices that reverberate back to the caves'. [65] (Cat. 98) Affirming the English pastoral tradition, to understand the Ruralists it is necessary to tease out worlds of 'private mystery' and recognise landscapes infused with the sublime or 'sense of divinity.'

Schama argues that we need to rediscover our landscape traditions, a 'rich deposit of myths, memories, obsessions'.[66] Meaning is now often concealed by the commonplace, obscuring the antiquity and complexity of these traditions; *Ancient Landscapes, Pastoral Visions* aims to recover the myths and memories that lie beneath the surface. The cliché of the 'cathedral grove' masks a long history of associations between pagan tree idolatry and the distinctive forms of Gothic architecture. Tree worship evolved through the Christian Tree of Life and the Cross to the implicit association of evergreens with eternal life, as seen in the works of Caspar David Friedrich and Vincent Van Gogh, thereby fulfilling the desire to find in nature a consolation for our morality. Groves of trees, with their promise of annual renewal, became a fitting place for our earthly remains; springing from the crest of a hill we recognise such clumps as sites of worship and reverence since antiquity (Nash, *Landscape with Rooks* or *Wittenham Clumps* 1913-14 Cat. 43a); 'so the mystery behind the commonplace turns out to be eloquent on the deepest relationships between natural form and human design'.[67] Landscape myths and memories endure, shaping our perceptions; national and personal identity is inextricably linked to our 'homeland'.

Whereas Palmer painted village life and labour, seeking a sense of community threatened by 'progress', Sutherland, Nash, Piper and the Ruralists have also been drawn to the longevity and mystery of ancient sites still imbued with a spiritual aura. Palmer's *Lonely Tower* (1867-68, Yale, and 1881, Huntington), in its final form probably the artist's last work, touches on these themes, including not only Milton's solitary philosopher in his crumbling tower but also 'antique relics'. *The Lonely Tower* (Cat. 15) was deeply personal, containing coded references to the death of Thomas More, Palmer's beloved son, such as the waning moon that marks the time of his death. The landscape is based on Leith Hill, Surrey, a landmark close to the spot where Thomas More Palmer died. Reflecting the artist's state of mind, the image communicates 'poetic loneliness', the viewer being asked to contemplate 'not the loneliness of the desert, but a secluded spot in a genial pastoral country, enriched also by antique relics, such as those so-called Druidic stones'.[68] These mysterious prehistoric stones can be seen on the horizon, at the base of the hill, under the crescent moon. These relics point to a primordial past, those spirits and voices that reverberate back in time. Stonehenge, Avebury, Silbury Hill and the White Horse, Uffington, which have been venerated over the centuries, provide a spiritual dynamic that underpins the romantic conceptualisation of the British landscape. In seeking the 'almost pagan mystical qualities of the landscape', Graham Ovenden has shown a similar interest in the 'mystical resonance of pagan monuments and symbols'.[69] In *Spring Morning, Wiltshire* (1984, Cat. 108) dawn is breaking over three monoliths, whose forms are echoed in three fully leafed trees; all is bathed in a vaporous gloom with a nimbus of light hovering on the horizon. The Trinity, a recurrent figure in Ovenden's work, lays Christian symbol over the pagan past, suggesting a resurrection or rebirth of life. *The Tower of Babel* (1984/5, Cat.17), a large monolith that acts as a symbolic focus, has more explicit religious connotations. In *Sentinels of Silbury* (1982, Cat. 100) the indeterminate time, half-day/half-night, evokes 'a mood or presence that is part of the scene and part of the imagination of the artist. Whether one calls it romanticism or mysticism, it is an integral part of Ovenden's vision':

> 'We see the deep rich colours before light fades from twilight and night dominates the sky. The dormant world of the woodland in the foreground leads to the central focus of the painting, which is a dark looming Silbury Hill. Yet the painting's focus is not just Silbury Hill. The clouds floating above the hilltop meet at an apex in the distance that fixes the focus of attention at a point almost behind the summit. In fact the painting emphasizes by means of visual focus a presence that is intangible. The presence is at once part of the scene and is almost something else that lies beyond the material reality of the scene, the mysterious sentinels of the painting's title.' [70]

Ovenden is certainly attracted to the 'supernatural'. While Wordsworth and Palmer conjured up a benevolent Mother Nature, Tennyson called her 'red in tooth and claw'. Romantics have plundered the realms of nightmares, the subconscious, the macabre, madness, eroticism, and death, as seen in Henry Fuseli's infamous *Nightmare* (1781) and Mary Shelley's *Frankenstein* (1818): 'The insights they brought back from their communions with Nature were that she was either wilfully vicious, or implacably indifferent'. [71] These opposing views of nature, as benign or malign, were also utilised by the Neo-Romantics; Graham Sutherland made a dramatic switch from the gentle to the sinister response in 1929. *Pastoral* (1930, Cat. 1) marks this change in direction as, despite its title, the image is far from elegiac in mood. Roberto Tassi has described it as a 'tragic landscape'.[72] The gnarled tree stump, the overarching, distorted trees and ominous shadows give this etching an underlying sense of menace. Such undertones can also be detected in Sutherland's *Entrance to a Lane* (1939, Tate Britain) and *Green Lane* (1945, Cat. 37); they are overt in Michael Ayrton's *Entrance to a Wood* (1945, The Arts Council of Great Britain) which 'with its bayonet-sharp branches barring a tunnel to sunlight must be seen as a kind of war picture'.[73] Paul Drury's *Michelham Yews, III* (1950, Cat. 38) is equally prickly and menacing, with its split log resembling the open jaws of a crocodile guarding the entrance to the tunnel. As in Ayrton's *Entrance to a Wood* we are barred from the light at the end of the tunnel. In these works landscape becomes a vehicle for 'disturbing moods'; 'There have always been two kinds of arcadia: shaggy and smooth; dark and light; a place of bucolic leisure and a place of primitive panic'.[74]

For the Ruralist's, nature still possesses ambiguities, with light playing on form to create shadow and mystery; 'Ruralism is no less sensible to this disquieting interplay than it is to the prismatic ecstasy of the natural world'.[75] Graham Ovenden's *The Residence of the Philosopher Kempe* (1984, private collection) is one of his most powerful works in its use of rich, evocative but disquieting colour, with the sensual beauty of the purple light that hangs on the mountain. Walter de la Mare's short story, *Mr Kempe*, tells the frightening experience of an uninvited visitor to Kempe's remote dwelling, buried deep in an impenetrable forest. Once inside the sinister and decayed 'straggling gabled house' we are transported back to the world of the Elizabethan metaphysical poets, for Kempe was 'possessed, I gathered, by one single aim, thought and desire. All these years of his "retirement" had apparently been spent in this one quest- to prove Man's possession of a "Soul"'.[76]

Once Nature was anthropomorphised, as 'a gentle teacher' or a 'cruel mistress', it was a short step to attributing human emotions to natural phenomena. Ruskin condemned this projection of moods and feelings on to flowers, trees and clouds as the 'pathetic fallacy': 'a falseness in all our impression of external things'.[77] But the Romantic soul fancies itself as a tree, flies with the birds and sinks with the moon. Nash sided with Wordsworth's mythology, 'which has been of the very greatest importance in English culture', validating the 'systematic animation of the inanimate which attributes life and feeling to non-human nature'.[78] Feeding his imagination on Rossetti and Romantic novels, the young Paul Nash saw trees as people: 'he began to project his sexual longings on to softly rounded landscapes and skies across which moon-faced women trailed their hair (*Vision at Evening*, 1911, V&A).[79] Yorke describes Nash as 'fixated on breast-like hillocks and saw three elm trees in terms of naked women'. Nash himself declared:

> 'I lived the drama of the nocturnal skies, falling stars, moonrise, storms and summer lightening. I shared with Samuel Palmer an appetite for monstrous moons, exuberance of stars. This strange greed may have been aroused by seeing pictures of Blake, for, oddly enough, I did not set eyes on Palmer's designs until five or six years later.' [80]

The elm trees became the Three Graces and Wittenham Clumps (Cat. 43a) two breast-like hillocks, were 'the pyramids of my small world' [81]:

> 'I sincerely love and worship trees and know they *are* people and wonderfully beautiful people- much more lovely than the majority of the people one meets. Again, I turned to the landscape

not for the landscape sake but for the "things behind," the dweller in the innermost: whose light shines thro' sometimes. I went out to try and give a hint in my drawings of those sometimeses'.[82]

Trees, upright and limbed, were an obvious symbolic substitute for people, especially for an artist looking to charge landscape with significance even though empty of figures. Evidently, Nash attempted to 'paint trees as if they possessed a moral goodness and wisdom derived from their observations of our human follies'.[83] He sung their praises in verse:

'O dreaming trees, sunk in a swoon of sleep
What have ye seen in these mysterious places?
What images? What faces?
What unknown pageant thro' these hollows moves
At night? What blood-fights have ye seen?
What scenes of life and death? What haunted loves?'[84]

This is certainly an instance of Ruskin's 'pathetic fallacy'; 'All this mooning around playing at pantheism in Metroland was finished for ever by the brutal experiences which befell him on the Ypres Salient in 1917'.[85] Yet Nash did not abandon trees, rather they were transformed into the 'found objects' and 'unconscious archetypes' of Surrealism. In Romney Marsh he discovered a weathered log that he likened to a Henry Moore sculpture in its combination of figure and landscape features. Entitled *Marsh Personage* it was exhibited at the 1936 London *Surrealist Exhibition*, which Nash helped to organise: 'Soon Nash was searching for other logs and flints he could personalise in his pictures as Monsters, Minotaurs, Presences or Equivalents'.[86] (Cat. 64) Pagan myth recognised the hollowed tree as the tomb of slaughtered gods, encased within the bark awaiting release to initiate a new cycle of life. Surrealism sanctioned unexpected juxtapositions, between a stone gate-post and the moon (*Pillar and Moon*, 1932-42, Tate Britain) or a tree stump and a tennis ball (*Event on the Downs* ,1934, Government Art Collection); Nash managed to fuse the English way with Continental Modernism- principally Surrealism and Abstraction- which he declared were the ' two most powerful expressions of the modern spirit'.[87] In *November Moon* (1942, Cat. 131) mushrooms have grown to the size of cars; 'Call it, if you like, a transcendental conception; a landscape of the imagination'.[88] Surrealism also allowed Nash to let two disparate scenes flow into each other; in *Circle of the Monoliths* (1937-8, Leeds Museums and Art Galleries) the land dissolves into a sea bisected by First World War trenches. Reading *The Golden Bough* and Sir Thomas Browne's *Urne Burial* provided yet more obtuse and esoteric symbols, which 'he scarcely understood himself, but which all helped him endow landscape with layers of significance'.[89] Images from his boyhood dreams came back to haunt him: 'ladders, steps, scaffolds, open doors and spiralling sunflowers speak of his yearning for flight into the "peopled sky". Ultimately, his pictures told him, it was the call of death he was painting'. [90]

Trees, full grown and sapling, singly or in groups of three (*Trinity*, Peter Nahum, Cat. 123a) are a recurring subject in Graham Ovenden's paintings. They offer a 'prismatic experience; the radiant glow of the colourful foliage of these trees is often represented as a ball of colour'. [91] They are painted with tenderness, with a 'clear sensual delicacy'. Trees are often the central motif as in *The Druid's Grove* (1983), *The Burning Bush* (1975) and *The Great Tree* (1978 and 2004). *The Druid's Grove* stresses the tree as an eternal mystical emblem; the megalithic henge and stone circle have their primordial origins in groves of trees. Nash's attachment to the 'breast-like' Wittenham Clumps (Cat. 43a), twin hills at Sinodun near Wallingford, Oxfordshire, not only recognises the all-encompassing relationship with the 'Great Mother' but also observes the veneration of specific sites through succeeding generations. The Clumps, Nash's most favoured site, mark a sanctified place, a long barrow and an Iron Age fortification, which have been respected through time: 'I felt their importance long before I knew their history. It was the look of them that told most, whether on sight or in memory. They were the Pyramids of my small world'.[92] Although nature has reclaimed these sites, the clearly delineated thicket of trees is a marker, respected by generations who have worked the land. These trees communicate, visually and through collective memory, the continuity of occupation and worship from ancient pagan deities to Christianity, the pillars and spanning arches of Gothic architecture being conceived as a forest canopy. In *Salisbury Cathedral from the Bishop's Grounds* (1823, Frick, New York) John Constable frames the Cathedral with an arch of trees; the link between God and Nature is made explicit. In effect the Cathedral is an ossified forest; conversely the Great Tree embodies the Gothic organic structure.

Ovenden's *The Communion of Trees* (1980) shows two trees bending to form an arch, creating a tunnel to a glowing valley beyond; a glimpse of paradise? A similar device is used in *The Autumn Apple Tree* (1976) and in *The Great Tree* (1978, private collection, Fig. 5), where we look through a porthole into a world beyond. Saplings blossom to either side of *The Great Tree*, protected by its canopy of foliage, analogous to a mother figure; the tree emanates a halo-like aurora, emphasising its divinity. A sapling in *The Valley towards the Moors* (1978) is not only child-like but also Christ-like. *The Great Tree* defies the seasons, compressing the life cycle, so we have the blossoming saplings, the full leaf of the tree and young corn ripening in the background; a pantheistic fecundity is allied to a sense of time standing still, which condenses nature into this one iconic tree. The Divine is thus expressed through natural forms. Ovenden argues that his art, and that of the Ruralists, is closer to the Flemish *primitifs* (Van Eyck, Memling) of the 15th century, than to the Romantics, with its 'clear objective transcendentalism'.[93] Ovenden is still 'searching for what underlies the heightened reality', commending fellow Ruralists Peter Blake and Graham Arnold for their ability to 'imbue simple objects with mystery and wonder'. Blake has likened himself to a tree:

> 'I am a tree, so to speak. The trunk is fairly straight and represents traditional figurative painting. Where my art has left to go on different excursions there are branches like Pop art, wood engraving and Ruralism. They all may look unalike but they come off the same stem. What I am working at now is in direct line with what preoccupied me years ago; the same fantasies.' [94]

While searching for 'England', the Ruralists, like Palmer, were also seeking themselves, reconciling personal relationships and finding emotional strength in the 'group'. The Ruralists constantly photographed each other, in 'fond groups or singly, revealing a close, sometimes, wry awareness of each other'.[95] This need to find kindred spirits finds its predecessors in the Ancients and the Pre-Raphaelite Brotherhood but there are other less formal groupings and associations that underline the significance of the collective. The Class of 21 saw Graham Sutherland (1903-1980) and his fellow students at Goldsmiths' College of Art, Paul Drury (1903-1987), Edward Bouverie Hoyton (1900-1988), and Robin Tanner (1904-1988) searching for 'landscapes that had remained unchanged for centuries' on the outskirts of London, taking them into Sussex and Palmer's Kent.[96] Together they visited Shoreham, even adopting the singular costume of the Ancients, cloaks and wide brimmed hats: 'Emulating Palmer, the young printmakers etched idyllic rural landscapes that conjure a vanished world of purity and goodness', A.E. Houseman's 'land of lost content'. Meyrick concludes: 'There is a prevailing nostalgia in their rendering of a rural way of living considered to be at risk. Their etchings depict what is for many an ideal of English village life, untainted by progress' .[97] (Cat. 22)

Shared enthusiasms took Sutherland and John Craxton (1922-) to Pembrokeshire in 1943:

'It was in this country that I began to learn painting. It seemed impossible here for me to sit down and make finished paintings "from nature"... I found that I could express what I feel by paraphrasing what I saw...I felt just as much part of the earth as my features were part of me. I did not feel that my imagination was in conflict with the real, but reality was a dispersed and disintegrated form of imagination.' [98]

Entrance to a Lane (1939, Tate Britain) and *Green Lane* (1945, Cat. 37) demonstrate Sutherland's 'paraphrasing' of nature, his thorn-inspired heads owing something to Picasso. These skewer-like forms influenced Michael Ayrton (1921-1975) who met Sutherland in Pembrokeshire in 1945. However, in Ayrton there is a 'demonic restlessness and a spiritual unease' that prevents him 'achieving Palmer's calm visions of England before the Fall'.[99] In terms of artistic groupings, Sutherland and Ayrton are now numbered amongst the Neo-Romantics, a body of artists that includes Paul Nash, John Piper, John Minton and John Craxton but this was not a brotherhood and there was no manifesto. The appellation was created by the critics and applied in 1942. Some have argued, including John Piper in his *Romantic British Artists* (1942) there is no such thing as Neo-Romanticism, seeing a continuation or survival rather than a revival of the sentiments expressed as Romanticism since *c.*1789. Piper's continuing tradition stretches back through Rossetti, for whom Nash had a predilection, Palmer, Blake, Turner, Constable, Cozens to Richard Wilson. It is argued that Romanticism reflects a state of mind, induced by major social and cultural changes such as the French Revolution and the First World War. At these times man turns 'inward' and seeks affirmation of the 'divine' as a guiding, essentially benevolent, force. Nature comes to the fore, not only as solace in times of stress but also as the manifestation of God' work. Blake struggled to see 'A World in a Grain of Sand / And Heaven in a Wild Flower'; while Wordsworth heard Great Pan himself 'low-whispering through the reeds'. The appeal of the Neo-Romantics was 'to mystics and particularly to pantheists who feel a fraternity or even a unity, with all living things, to those with the sense sublime of something more deeply infused. Their work can be considered the expression of an identification with nature'.[100]

Neo-paganism, seen especially in the work of Edward Calvert (1799-1883), went hand in hand with Primitivism and the belief that the peasant's connection with the natural world was stronger than the urban labourer's (Cat. 5); by 1851 the urban population exceeded the rural population. The well-heeled 'townee' saw nature from afar, from the distance of the city with all its comforts and amenities; Samuel Palmer conceded, 'Rural poetry is the pleasure ground of those who live in cities'.[101] An inevitable nostalgia for the uncontaminated countryside led to an idealisation of rural life. Evidently the peasant might be less sophisticated but surely he was in tune with nature and thereby closer to God. Wordsworth certainly took this view: 'in that condition the essential passions of the heart find a better soil in which they can attain their maturity, are less under restraint, and speak a plainer and more emphatic language... because in that condition the passions of men are incorporated with the beautiful and permanent forms of nature'.[102] The social cohesion of family and village life stood in sharp contrast to the fragmentation and alienation of urban existence. The pace of life in the countryside was slower; there was more time to 'stop and think' and be 'at peace'. The Ancients, the brotherhood of young artists, which included Palmer, George Richmond (1809-1896) and Edward Calvert, found their enchanted valley at Shoreham, near Sevenoaks, Kent. Here Palmer developed the theme of an ideal pastoral existence, a unity of church, social order and the countryside. *Coming from Evening Church* (1830, Tate Britain) shows a procession of villagers making their way home from church. *A Hilly Scene* (*c.*1824-6, Tate Britain) shows a church steeple embedded in the landscape: 'But the main character is nature, in its wholeness and divineness, measured out in slightly stiff renderings of effulgently leafy bushes, glimmering birches, massive oaks and gnarly rocks, and in occasional moments of breathtaking ambiguity. In *Late Twilight*, a crescent moon overlooks a dark farm while floating on a horizon of glowing white that probably denotes clouds, but also reads as a vast beneficent sea separating heaven and earth'.[103] The peasantry were blissfully unaware that they resided in Arcadia or that in tilling the field or herding the sheep they were nearer to the Great Creator. This Romantic, essentially patronising, image of rustic bliss permeates the Victorian era and even persists in the 20th century, expressing itself not only in landscape painting but also in the Arts and Crafts Movement; peasant culture, regional customs and crafts, were thoroughly mythologized. The repeated claim that 'ancient man was superior to modern man' earned the Ancients their name.

The Ancients clearly idealised rural life and the dignity of labour, there being little sign of poverty, drudgery or hardship in their images of the countryside. The beauty of nature cancelled out the misery of living in antiquated housing and coping with the elements. Palmer provided his followers with a stock of motifs, the hamlet nestling in the 'secret valley', the 'bright cloud' and the glowing sunset, thatched cottages and country churches, fields and stooks of corn, the shepherd tending his flock under a star-lit night and the weary ploughman wending his way home at the end of the day, the rising sun, crescent moon and evening star. Apple trees laden with fruit point to nature's fecundity, while the opening of the fold intimates not only the start of a new day but also an awakening or reaffirmation of faith (Cat. 6). For Palmer nature required interpretation to 'reveal the Paradise to come behind the shimmer of appearances. It is an exalted role for the painter to seek'.[104] Romanticism endowed the artist with vision, a clearer sight of worlds beyond. In the 21st century such notions seemed hackneyed or pretentious. Yet the Ruralists, and especially Graham Ovenden, have taken on the mantle of the artist-visionary-prophet. The forms of nature do not require an exact rendering; rather they can be paraphrased or intensified in order to communicate an idea. That idea is essentially the relationship of Man and Nature, with Nature standing in for God. The validity of a work is invested in how well it communicates its subject to the viewer; we are required to look below the surface of the paint to comprehend the deeper meaning, Wordsworth's 'something far more deeply interfused'.

After 1850, following his marriage and travels in Italy, Palmer returned to the pastoral elegies of his youth. His work culminated in a series of richly coloured watercolour illustrations to Milton and Virgil, intended for printing; *The Bellman* (1879, Cat. 18), *The Lonely Tower* (1879 Cat. 15) and *Opening the Fold* (1880, Cat. 6) belong to this group. Although beautiful, these works fail to recapture the zeal of his youth at Shoreham, where the Ancients cultivated an artistic community: 'We were brothers in art, brothers in love, and brothers in that for which art and love subsist – the Ideal – the Kingdom within'.[105] Like the Ruralists, the Ancients were a community of 'equals'. The collective was a means of making a protest, of critiquing society; the Ancients viewed their era as morally degraded, 'The Past for Poets, the Present for Pigs', while the Ruralists, their art denounced as 'old fashioned', sought to challenge the art establishment. Both groups were 'disaffected'. The Ancients were party to the 'conservative intellectual movement of the 1820s that was arguing for a reassertion of traditional values to counter the detrimental social effects of "progress"'.[106] Forming in 1975, the Ruralists were vanguards of the Green Movement, going in search of the Good Life, a 'conservative' reaction to the despoliation of the natural world. To a certain extent both Ancients and Ruralists opted out, seeking to establish 'the alternative lifestyle of the creative individual'. Even after the fragmentation of the Ruralists, Graham and Annie Ovenden cultivate the communal spirit at Barley Splatt, itself a testimony to Arts and Crafts ethics (much of this Gothic fantasy, based on the architecture of Pugin and Burges, was built with Graham's own hands). It must also be said that neither Ancients or Ruralists spearheaded a new direction in the art of their times; conversely they can be lauded for 'going their own way' or 'doing their own thing':

'The work of Graham Ovenden provides a significant instance of an artist, who despite the fashions of recent years, has assiduously pursued his own aesthetic concerns, resulting in a body of landscape work that is not only a vital addition to the landscape tradition but a wholly original synthesis of his own imaginative vision and aesthetic values.'[107] In so doing they have contributed to a continuum in English art- the Romantic thread that can be traced through the Ancients, the Class of 21, the Neo-Romantics to the Ruralists and even beyond; 'the romantic vision, the relation of the natural to the mystical or aesthetic vision, which was celebrated by artists from Blake up until the Neo-Romantic revival in the 1940s, is reflected in Ovenden's own landscape vision'.[108] The mid 1980s, with the long awaited display of the Tate's Turners in the Clore Gallery and a major exhibition of Neo-Romantic art of the 1940s at the Barbican, promised a resurgence of interest in the British romantic vision and a return to 'an art that deals with myth, symbol, the figure, landscape and representation'.[109] But it was not until 2005, when Gillian Carnegie's (1971-) paintings were included in the Turner Prize competition, that a modern landscape was hung on Tate Britain's walls.

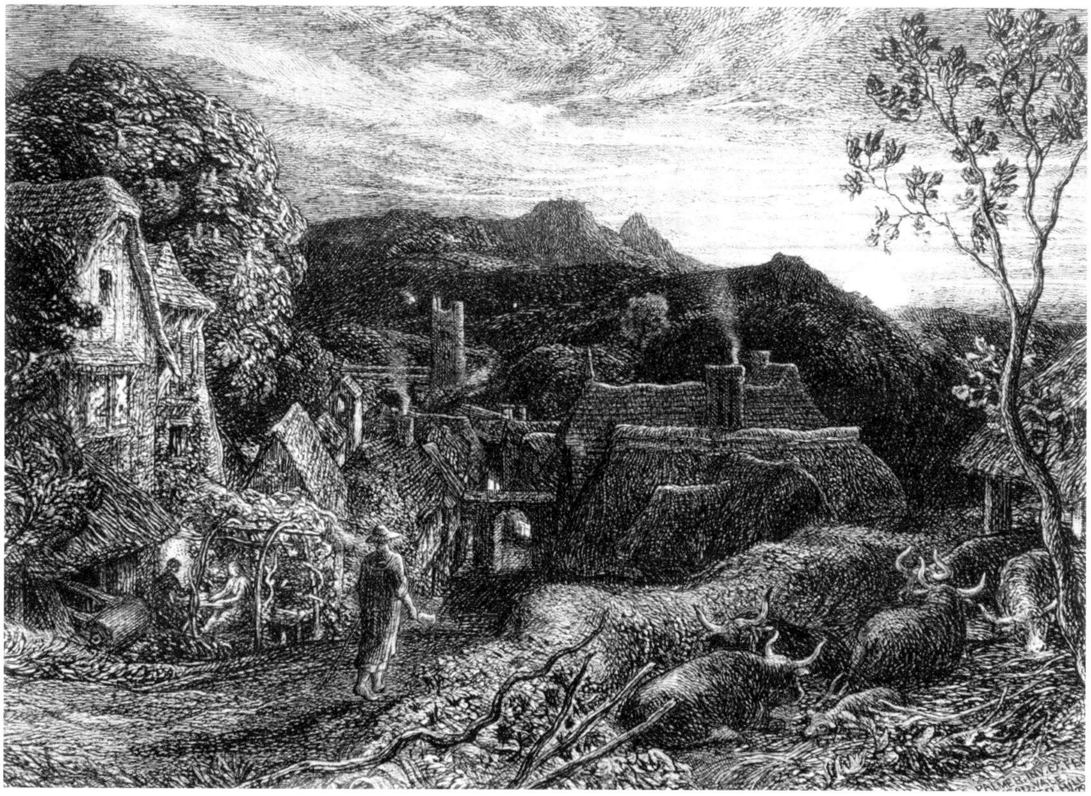

18. Samuel Palmer (1805-1881)
The Bellman from Il Penseroso, 1879
etching on paper, 167 x 233 mm
Stuart M. Southall

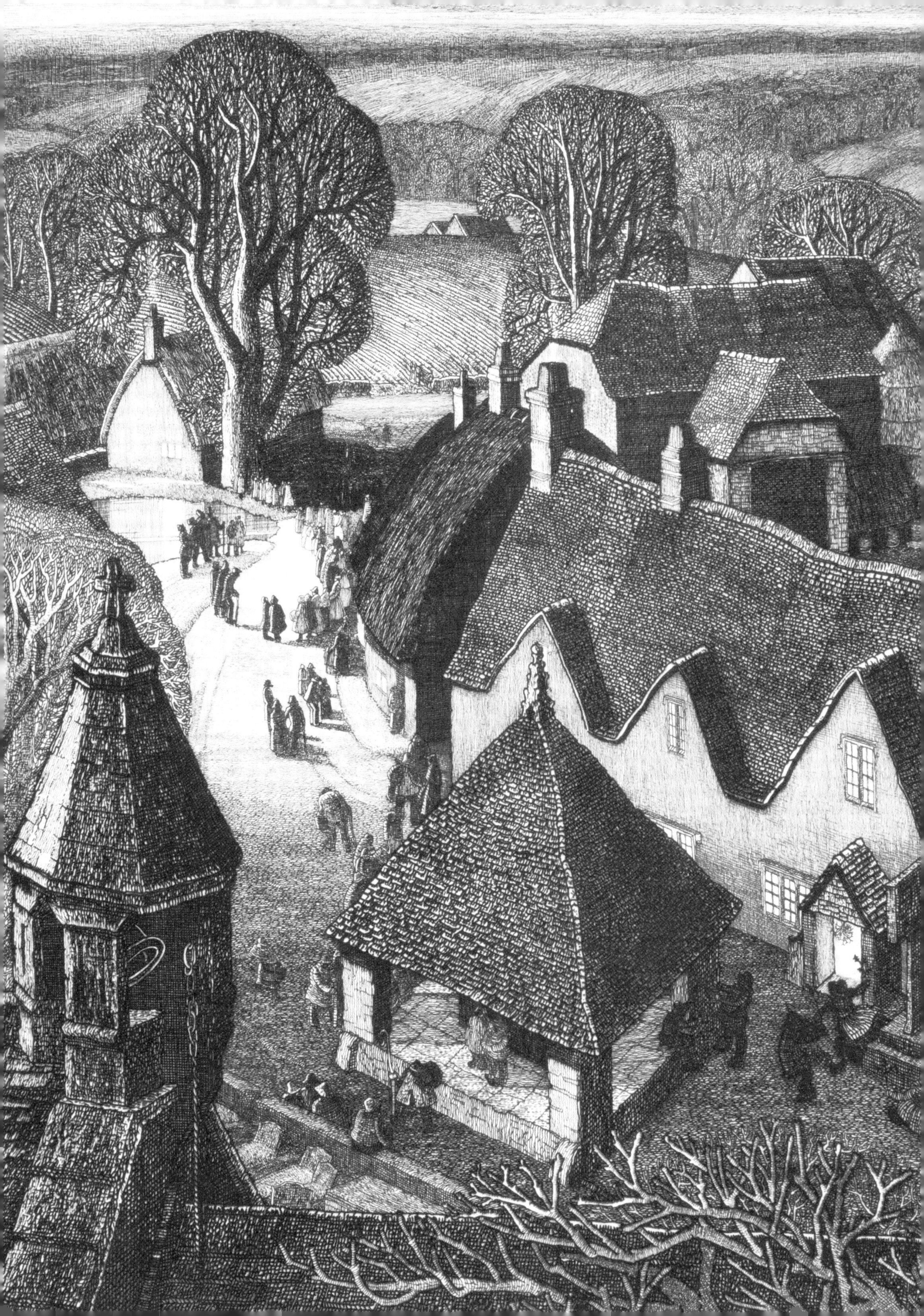

Pastoral Revisions:
'Little Englandism' in British Printmaking, 1915-1935

Robert Meyrick

Ancient churches in overgrown graveyards. Shepherds tending livestock in the meadow. Fields tilled by ox-drawn ploughs. Corn reapers at harvest time; farmsteads and thatched cottages, coaching inns and village green. Each conjures up an England of bygone days – a rural, peaceful England, where labour was as honest as it was hard, where man was at one with nature and where, in the eyes of many, the Church was all embracing. In the years following the Great War, the public sought comfort in such visions – or revisions – of Englishness, and artists found a ready audience for their views of picturesque villages, vernacular architecture, and pastoral scenes of life in the countryside. Their works captured a quintessential 'Olde England' of harvest festivals, maypoles and Christmas carollers for the dream of which thousands had recently laid down their lives. As one contemporary reviewer remarked, 'recent experiences' had created a 'keener sense of England and, consequently, a keener appreciation' for artists who, without 'deliberately cultivating the national spirit,' were about to make 'Little Englandism' become 'respectable.'[1]

Having fallen under the spell of Blake and Palmer, etchers working in the 1920s and 1930s – F.L. Griggs, Graham Sutherland and Joseph Webb among them – became especially attuned to the English landscape tradition. They travelled the countryside in pursuit of Britain's architectural heritage: medieval farms, tithe barns, and parish churches. Their approach to landscape tended to be conservative and nostalgic, recalling a golden age and a way of life perceived to be under threat as a consequence of suburbanisation and the expansion of road and rail networks. In 1920, Griggs's exhibition of etchings and drawings at the XXI Gallery in London was recommended as an opportunity to enjoy a 'moment of escape in fancy, from noisy streets and newspapers, into the peaceful countryside yet left to us in our homeland.'[2]

Amid social, political and economic upheaval, printmakers of the 1920s and 1930s found themselves divided by aesthetic ideologies. Some, like Edward Wadsworth and C.R.W. Nevinson, chose to confront the changing world and reflect it in their work, using new media and alternative subjects. By comparison, landscape artists like Sutherland expressed themselves in terms of the past. Drawn from observation, memory and imagination, their etchings are intimate in scale and imbued with a feeling for place that characterises a great deal of British landscape painting and literature. Their pastoral revisions hark back to the days of Elizabethan poet Christopher Marlowe, whose 'Passionate Shepherd' promised his love the pleasures that 'valleys, groves, hills, and fields, / Woods or steepy mountain yields', to sit with her 'upon the rocks / And see the shepherds feed their flocks, / By shallow rivers, to whose falls / Melodious birds sing madrigals.'

Poets and artists of the 1920s and 1930s would also draw upon the rich seam of childhood experience, yearning for Blake's pre-industrialised 'green and pleasant land' or mourning the 'land of lost content' and 'blue remembered hills' recounted in A E. Housman's *A Shropshire Lad* (1896, Cat. 62 and 63). Housman's description of life in the countryside and young men meeting early deaths had struck a chord during World War I, as later would Dylan Thomas, whose *Fern Hill* (1945) recalled the idyllic landscape the poet experienced as a child, being 'young and easy under the apple boughs, / about the lilting house and happy as the grass was green'. Therein lie subconscious expressions of national identity that, not surprisingly, are particularly forceful at times of national crises and international isolation. Palmer had experienced the Swing Riots of 1830, the uprising of agricultural workers in south and east

England, and he keenly felt the uncertainty in Europe following the Franco-Prussian War of 1870-71. Griggs, Sutherland, Edward Bouverie Hoyton and Paul Drury had lived through the Great War; and two decades later, as Europe would again be plunged into turmoil, a new generation of British painters – John Minton, Keith Vaughan, Michael Ayrton, John Craxton and John Elwyn – would come under Palmer's influence and find consolation in the English Romantic landscape tradition.

A predominant force in British landscape painting, Romanticism has been stylistically divergent in its expression; yet it always possesses a distinctive emotive quality. Whereas Turner inspired awe with his grand seascapes, his contemporaries Blake and Palmer worked on a rather more intimate scale. The origin of their particular strain of Romantic landscape art can be found in Blake's tiny wood engravings for Robert Thornton's *Imitation of Virgil's First Eclogue* (1821, Cat. 3). These visionary illustrations became a seminal force for generations of British Romantic artists. There is a distinct dreamlike quality in their strange and claustrophobic settings, their mood and character amplified by moonlight. To Palmer they were:

> '…visions of little dells, and nooks, and corners of Paradise; models of the exquisitest pitch of intense poetry. [...] Intense depth, solemnity, and vivid brilliancy only coldly and partially describes them. There is in all such a mystic and dreamy glimmer as penetrates and kindles the innermost soul, and gives a complete and unreserved delight, unlike the gaudy daylight of this world.'[3]

In pursuit of Virgil's shepherd Tityrus, who reposes under a spreading beech tree in Arcadia as he 'meditates the woodland muse on slender oat', a group of idealistic young artists, the self-styled 'Ancients' – Palmer, Edward Calvert and George Richmond – consciously set out to produce a type of Romantic art that differed from the grand canvases of Constable and Turner. More inspiring than imposing, it was closely aligned with the spiritual landscapes of Blake. The influence of Blake's Virgil illustrations on Calvert is evident in his exquisitely detailed copperplate engraving *The Sheep of His Pasture* (1828, Cat. 4), whose strayed sheep grazing along a river at sunrise take on the allegorical significance of Christian symbolism. John Piper noted that Romantic art:

> '…is the result of a vision that can see […] beyond ordinary significance: something that for a moment seems to contain the whole world; and, when the moment is past, carries over some comment on life or experience besides the comment on appearances.'[4]

Having witnessed the rick burnings and the destruction of threshing machines that were symptomatic of the widespread discontent among agricultural workers in Kent, Palmer imagined a mythical England where farmhands ploughed with oxen and walked home singing by moonlight. The farming methods shown in etchings like *The Early Ploughman* (1861) were already outdated in Palmer's day. In his later etchings, Palmer returns to the pastoral ideals of his Shoreham period. There is 'a sheen of pastoral religiosity' over what David Lillington has called an 'escapist response to the dark satanic mills.'[5] Etched after an 1867 watercolour of a shepherd and his love contemplating the night sky, *The Lonely Tower* (1879) has as its literary source Milton's *Il Penseroso*: 'Or let my lamp at midnight hour / Be seen in some high lonely tower / Where I may oft outwatch the Bear.' Such lofty sentiments, however, stood in stark contrast to the commercial value of etchings during that period. Palmer was dismayed at being unable to achieve realistic prices for the labour involved, complaining that he could get 100 guineas for a small drawing that took him a fraction of the time he spent on an etching.

By the end of the nineteenth century, etching had become a respectable practice for artists. Original yet affordable, modern etchings came to be seen as a symbol of refinement. The so-called 'Etching

Revival' culminated in the 1920s with an unprecedented market for contemporary prints. For collectors and connoisseurs there was an abundance of publications on both historical and contemporary print practice, from *Print Collectors' Quarterly* to *Fine Prints of the Year*. The growing demand and the promise of commercial success led many artists to turn to printmaking. Young etchers could secure contracts with London's most regarded print publishers and look forward to solo exhibitions in the West End. Graham Sutherland was still a student when he staged his first exhibition at the XXI Gallery; Joseph Webb was twenty-five when his one-man show opened at P. & D. Colnaghi in Old Bond Street, and Edgar Holloway just seventeen when Molly Bernhard Smith, the indefatigable proprietor of the XXI Gallery, mounted his first exhibition of etchings and watercolours.

Writing in 1919, Charles Marriott regretted that art had become too London-centric and was no longer 'rooted in the common life of the people'; for 'Bond Street is not the whole of art any more than Covent Garden is the whole of agriculture.' He believed that the 'real basis of both art and architecture is labour'. Griggs would exemplify the importance of labour in art made by 'men and women who obviously took pleasure and pride in craftsmanship.' He reworked his plates over a long period; *Maur's Farm* developed through eight states between 1913 and 1924. The buildings he etched are 'directly products of a flourishing village life' built on agriculture, and only by reviving earlier 'conditions of life and the habit of unhasting, unresting labour' can such crafts flourish anew.[6] Though figures are seldom present in Griggs's etchings, the buildings themselves 'recall the life that produced the architecture'[7] (Cat. 86).

Illustrator of thirteen volumes of Macmillan's *Highways and Byways* travel guides that popularised him among younger artists, Griggs made his first etchings in 1896. Not until 1912, however, did he etch what he considered to be his first serious plate – *Sutton*, a romanticised view of St Andrew's Church on the Isle of Ely. It would set the tone for his subsequent prints, in which Griggs elaborated and reassembled architectural elements to envision new and fantastic structures. The sensation of place is strong; but compared to Palmer's warmth, Griggs's etchings of Gothic cathedrals and medieval buildings, largely devoid of human presence, are rather austere and at times funereal. The air is stifling and seemingly incapable of supporting human life. 'Everyone seems to be indoors at prayers,' one reviewer observed, in settings 'sadly hinting at voices from forgotten graves.'[8] Whereas Palmer identified with the individuals he depicted, Griggs valued their collective achievements, his figures being principally in service of the composition.

Griggs mourned what he perceived as the loss of a better world founded on rural and Christian values, a world rooted in the strong sense of community as it existed in the villages. In 1903, he had moved to Chipping Campden in Gloucestershire. He was involved in the Arts and Crafts Movement in the Cotswolds and, through his foundation of the Campden Trust, he became actively engaged in the preservation and conservation of old buildings. 'It is too much to hope that, even after this war, we shall recover England, the real England, of the Tudor period,' remarked an *Evening Standard* reviewer, 'but Mr. Griggs does manage to suggest the firm, fair, and well-ordered conditions of those days are possible in modern life.'[9] As a student in 1896, Griggs had encountered Palmer's etchings in a volume of *The Eclogues of Virgil*. Twenty years later he would engage in a correspondence with A.H. Palmer, the artist's son, and collaborate with Martin Hardie, Frank Short and the Cotswold Gallery to publish a final edition from five Palmer plates. His knowledge and enthusiasm for these works would turn Griggs into a mediator of Palmer's artistic ideologies for a new generation of young etchers. In search of advice and instruction Sutherland, Drury, Tanner and Webb all visited his studio in Gloucestershire.

As impressionable students at Goldsmiths' School of Art, Sutherland, Drury, Tanner and Edward Bouverie Hoyton witnessed the resurgence of interest in Palmer's work. Lawrence Binyon's book *The Followers of Blake* was published in 1925; a year later, the Cotswold Gallery issued the new editions from Palmer's plates just prior to the Victoria and Albert Museum's exhibition *Drawings, Etchings and Woodcuts by Samuel Palmer and other Disciples of William Blake*. The poetic and emotional quality of Palmer's landscapes appealed to Sutherland and his contemporaries, one of whom, William Larkins, introduced his fellow students to an impression of Palmer's *The Herdsman's Cottage* (etching, 1850) that he had found in a bookshop on Charing Cross Road. Sutherland recalled that he 'was amazed at its completeness, both emotional and technical.' The students visited Shoreham and 'even wore cloaks in imitation of the Ancients.' To Sutherland, it seemed 'wonderful that a strong emotion' like Palmer's could 'change and transform the appearance of things.' He knew his 'obsession was a young man's passion, an adolescent flame, which was bound to end in one's "first death". Nevertheless, the idea of the way in which emotion can change appearances never left [him]'.[10]

Visiting the Garden of England where a century earlier Palmer had found inspiration for his 'Valley of Vision', Sutherland began a series of small plates in emulation of Palmer: rural subjects with cottages, country churches, autumnal cornfields, stooks of corn and starry skies. In 1926, he and Drury arranged to visit Chipping Campden where Griggs taught them to mix inks, demonstrated his wiping techniques, and took impressions from their plates, including Sutherland's *Lammas* (etching, 1926, Cat. 23). Griggs imparted his enthusiasm for Palmer's works, both for their technique and their emotional power.

Sutherland's first Palmeresque plate was *Cudham, Kent* (etching, 1924), followed by *Cray Fields* (etching, 1925, Cat. 8) with its enormous evening star and setting sun. In the *Village* (etching, 1925, Cat. 19), his finest print in this idiom, a woman kneels in the foreground with a basket of potatoes beside a harrow and plough. The furrowed field and hedgerow guide the eye past barns and oast houses to a twilit sky where birds gather before roosting and against which the tower of a church is silhouetted: every inch is densely etched, each of the myriad marks imbued with passion. For *Lammas*, like the equally reverent *May Green* and *Michaelmas* that followed, Sutherland appropriated Palmer's mark making and borrowed motifs from Blake and the Ancients to commemorate Lammas Day on which the bread baked from new grain is consecrated. Sutherland's *Pecken Wood* (etching, 1925) and Drury's *After Work* (etching, 1926) present a halcyon vision of rural life in which weary villagers return home at the end of a long day carrying sheaves or faggots of firewood. Palmer aside, these works had their origins in Pre-Raphaelite landscape painting extolling the virtue of working the land, an attitude popularised in the latter half of the nineteenth century.

An evening student at Goldsmiths' and a contemporary of Sutherland, Tanner, too, was an admirer of Palmer and Griggs. As suggested by the titles – Easter, Harvest Festival, November, Autumn, and Christmas – Tanner's etchings of his native Wiltshire record the cycle of the seasons as celebrated in religious and pagan festivals. *Christmas* (etching, 1929, Cat. 20) was begun on a 'night of perfect moonlight' in October 1928. Tanner was 'working through the small hours' near the ancient market cross in Castle Combe as 'moonlight lay in sheets of silver so bright and constant.' He remained constant to his pastoral vision until his death, insisting that his etchings were not merely 'pleasant pastorals' but a 'protest' at the 'destruction of Britain' due to the encroachment of modern life. [11]

Commenting on Sutherland's watercolours and etchings exhibited at the XXI Gallery in 1928, *The Times* appreciated their literary associations and invited readers to 'think of an art which is the graphic form of pastoral poetry,' an art whose rich catalogue of imagery makes it 'poetically significant to the imaginative mind.'[12] Noting that Sutherland had achieved the 'noble solemnity and dignity' of Palmer and Calvert, a critic writing for the *Times of India* nonetheless feared that, despite their 'quiet poetry and irresistible appeal', an alignment with literary traditions would 'condemn them in the eyes of the sternest of critics.'[13] A critic for *Apollo* appreciated Sutherland's 'successful efforts to escape from the orthodox etching line', yet expressed himself concerned about the artist's 'mannerism', arguing that his referencing of Palmer's technique had become rather too 'monotonous'.[14] Sutherland's 'tendency to introspective composition, the building up of scenes from his own memories and those of others' was 'becoming dangerous.' His works had become a 'trifle aweary for lack of natural inspiration and the spontaneous impulse of individual treatment.' He was 'apparently too much obsessed by the outlook and methods of Samuel Palmer and F. L.Griggs.'[15] A reviewer for

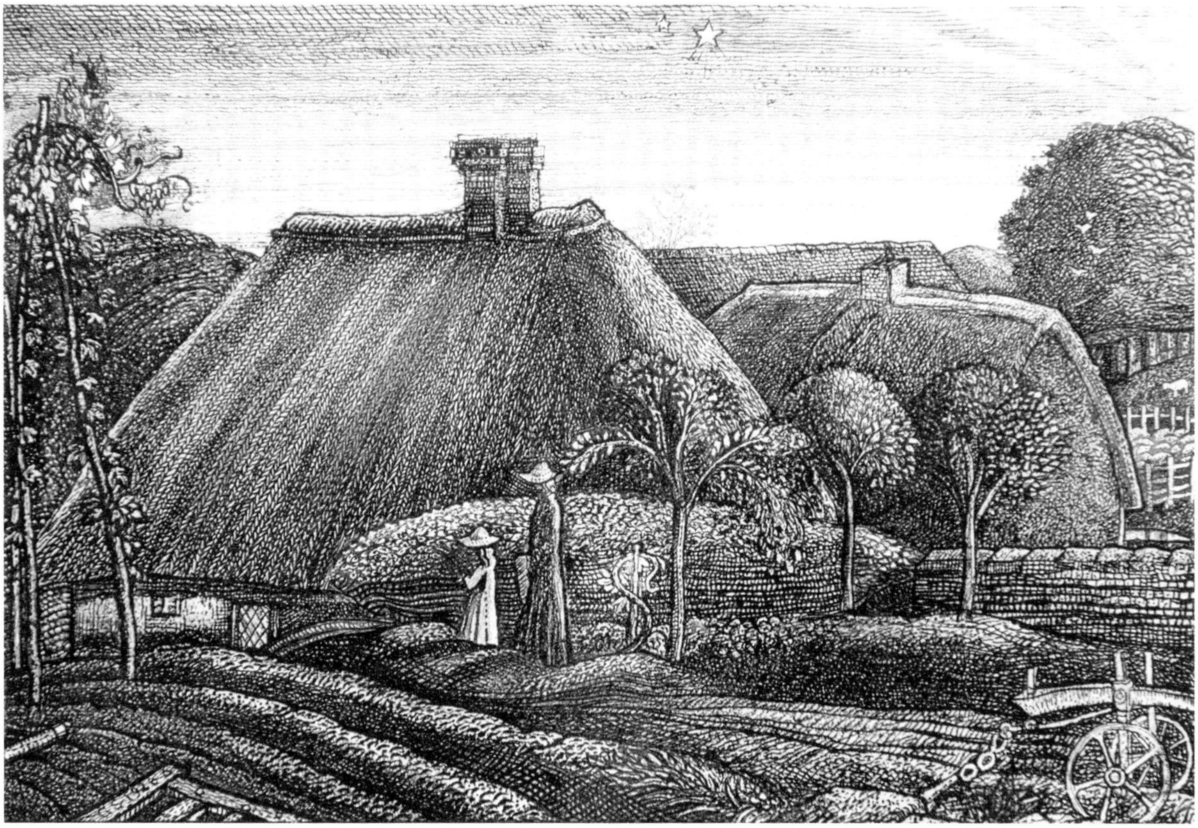

23. Graham Vivien Sutherland (1903-80)
Lammas, 1926
etching on paper, 110 x 162 mm
Stuart M. Southall

The Scotsman concurred that, in Sutherland's latest etchings and drawings, 'the deep elegiac poetry of Palmer's work and his careful and reverent craftsmanship' had been absorbed but were 'repeated without much variation.'[16] The article goes so far as to suggest that the 'Shorhamesque' etchers had had their day, for 'unlike the Jesse tree, artistic trees seldom bear their supreme fruit last.' A decade had passed since the end of the Great War. Britons were rebuilding their lives and the sentiments expressed by Griggs, Sutherland and their contemporaries were no longer shared quite as widely and keenly. 'Little Englandism' seemed outmoded.

After 1929, Sutherland's etchings were appreciably less indebted to Palmer and the influence of Paul Nash is apparent. The simplification of form and composition foreshadow his work in Pembrokeshire during the mid-1930s after he abandoned etching in favour of painting. This was as a consequence of adverse criticism, a depreciation in sales, and the realisation that his appropriation of Palmer's technique and iconography had led him into a cul de sac. In *Wood Interior* (etching, 1929/30, Cat. 46) and *Pastoral* (etching, 1930, Cat. 1), Sutherland no longer celebrated the harmony of a bygone world; anxious forebodings take the place of earlier Christian sentiments. His trees are no longer leafy and compact, foliage writhes like tentacles, the twisted roots and large rotting stump in the foreground contributing to a sense of disease. While its title *Pastoral* alludes to a Palmeresque idyll, decay and death take the place of nature's fertility, of tranquillity and beauty.

Opening up in 1924, the market for contemporary etchings peaked between 1925 and 1927, then went into sharp decline following the Wall Street crash in October 1929. Subscribers were forced to withdraw their orders, leaving dealers, publishers and artists to experience the fallout. Few etchers who had

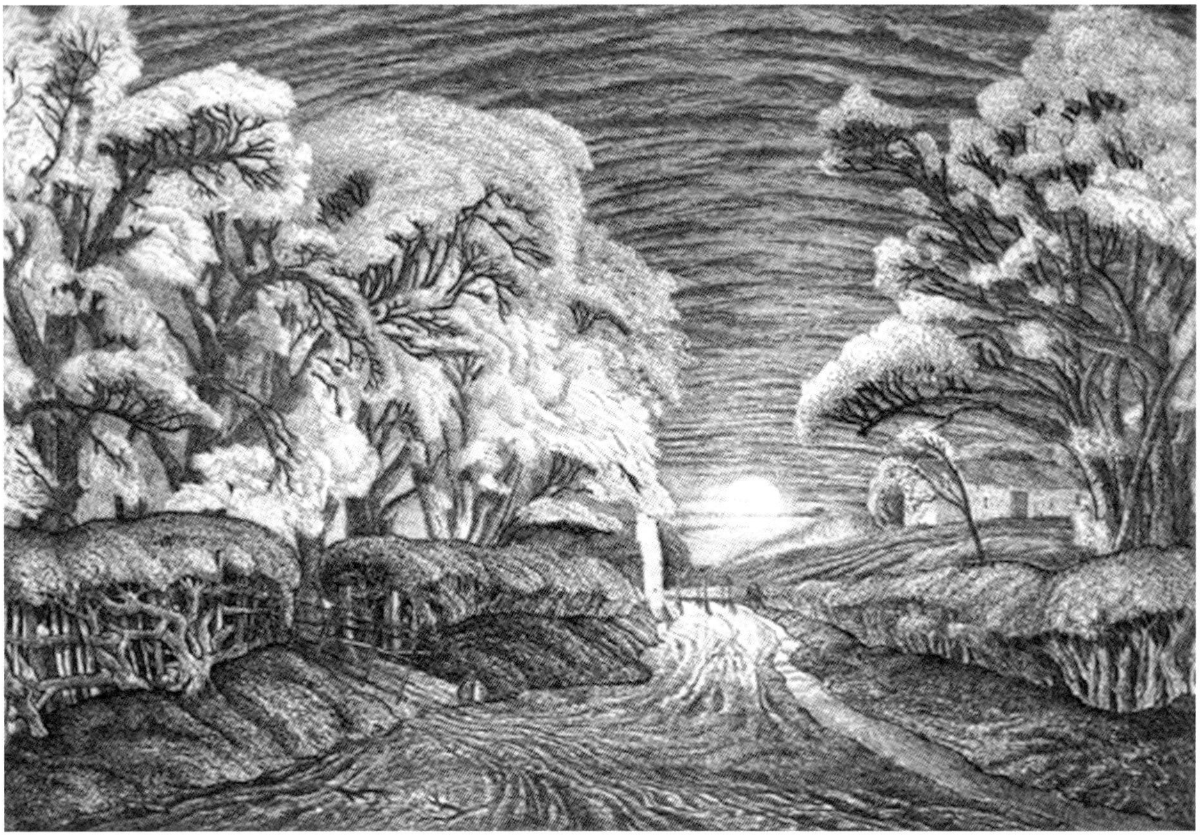

125. Joseph Webb (1908-1962)
Pippin Lane, 1938
etching on paper, 172 x 240 mm
Stuart M. Southall

enjoyed success in the 1920s remained active throughout the 1930s. Most gave up etching in favour of painting and design. Published annually between 1923 and 1938, *Fine Prints of the Year* charts the rise and fall of the market in Britain and the United States. Malcolm Salaman's 1933 editorial lamented that the 'etching market had fallen on meagre times'; by 1934, the 'great and beautiful art of etching' appeared to be 'temporarily out of favour'. In 1938, Campbell Dodgson noted that 'some of the most distinguished etchers and engravers have suspended their activity in the field of graphic art in favour of the more remunerative practice of painting'.[17] Artists like Webb and Edgar Holloway had arrived too late on the scene to prosper from the opportunities that once existed.

At an early age, Webb began etching imaginary, medieval-inspired barns and cathedral-like structures. The best of his fine-wrought landscapes – the iconic *Rat Barn* and *Dream Barn*, *Asylum* and *Prison* – demonstrate sound draughtsmanship, technical virtuosity and a sure understanding of the medium. In 1929, Webb visited Chipping Campden where Griggs not only demonstrated his wiping, printing techniques and use of old papers – taking impressions of *Rat Barn* and *Dream Barn* – but imparted to Webb an enthusiasm for the emotional power of Palmer's art. *The Shepherd's Haven* (etching, 1929, Cat. 27) resonates with pastoral poetry, the work of Palmer and Calvert, and prints by Webb's contemporaries Sutherland, Drury and Tanner. A young shepherd cradling a lamb approaches an ecclesiastical- looking barn, its doors open and interior lighted – clear allusions to the 'Good Shepherd' and 'Lamb of God'. Sharing Griggs's love of ancient buildings, Webb conveys similar religious and mystical concerns; what sets his etchings apart from the work of his contemporaries, however, is their mystery and intense longing for a spiritual refuge beyond this world. Like Blake, Webb considered himself a mystic-visionary and radical thinker. In Blake's compositions, Webb saw that realism could be secondary to spirituality – the landscape a vehicle, its physical appearance transformed.

Webb was passionate about the British countryside. On his travels to Gloucestershire, south east Wales, Lincolnshire and the West Sussex coast he never failed to be 'absorbed and enthralled'.[18] In the summer of 1931, he was in Buckinghamshire, drawing sites with literary associations. *Stoke Poges* (etching, 1931, Cat. 126), for example, shows the graveyard and twelfth century church of St Giles where Thomas Gray is believed to have set his 'Elegy Written in a Country Graveyard' (*c.*1742-50). An impression of the first state of the etching bears the inscription 'Where heaves the turf in many a mouldering heap,' a line from the poem. *Streamend* (etching, 1936, Cat. 22) depicts a quiet rural scene, a nostalgic interpretation of the ford at Water End, a small Hertfordshire village on the banks of the River Lea. A horse-drawn cart crosses the river. The brick chimneys and gables of the sevententh century Water End Farm are visible above the large barn. Both the farm and church have been imported by Webb to improve the composition. *Pippin Lane* (etching, 1938, Cat. 125), one of several nocturnal subjects that he etched immediately before the War, marked Webb's return to the pastoral idiom of his darker, deeply bitten plates.

At Harrow, Webb's comment was sought by young Edgar Holloway, who 'really came to grips with etching' when, in 1932, Webb taught him 'that it was necessary to have the courage to etch right through the plate if required.'[19] Holloway had just encountered Webb's work at first hand in London, after moving there with his parents. It was through prints by Griggs, Sutherland, Drury and Webb that he came to appreciate Palmer. Throughout the summer of 1932, Holloway worked on six plates under Webb's guidance. He began to etch his plates densely and moved away from the predominantly linear and summary methods that had characterised his earlier output. He was encouraged not to rely solely on exact representation. *Eastcote* (etching, 1932), for example, was altered at Webb's suggestion to create a composite view by positioning the village church in the distance beneath the arch of a pigeon cote at the entrance to a farm at Northolt. *Self Portrait No. 6* (etching, 1932) was discussed with Webb at his studio. It was one of Holloway's first copper plates to be taken through several stages of biting, grinding and re-polishing in order to build up an intensely detailed surface.

In January 1936, Holloway shared a small cottage on Netteswell Common in Essex with Scottish artist William Wilson. They bought an etching press and spent days travelling the countryside drawing and painting. At dusk, as late evening light fell over the farm buildings and the remains of an Augustinian Priory, Holloway painted *Latton Priory, Exterior*, which also became the subject of one of his etchings (Cat. 88). It was followed by *Latton Priory, Interior* (etching, 1936 Cat. 89), depicting part of the fourteenth century structure forming a barn. Along with *Bosses Farm* and *Brockles Farm*, etched the same year, these works show the influence of Wilson, who sought to create a 'mood' with his etchings.

Although Holloway began exhibiting when it was no longer possible to make a living solely as an etcher, he was fortunate to have entered printmaking at a time when artists could still establish their reputations as etchers. Despite the market decline, he continued to make prints until 1947. In 1949, under the influence of Eric Gill's writings, he abandoned fine art to become a letterer, joining the Guild of St Joseph and St Dominic on Ditchling Common. He made no further etchings until his retirement. In 1990, following resurgence of interest in prints from the inter-war years, including his own work, he returned to the pastoral idiom in *Orchard Moon* (Cat. 122), which depicts an old orchard at Burnt House Bostal near Ditchling. Like *The Bride* (Cat. 81) and *Wolstonbury* (Cat. 77), it was etched after watercolours he had painted of the South Downs in 1982. They are more deeply lyrical, Neo-Romantic interpretations of landscape, concerned with expressing the spirit of place, detail being pared down to the essential elements of a scene.

Coined in 1942 by critic Raymond Mortimer, the phrase 'Neo-Romantic' was meant to capture a phenomenon that is difficult to define as a movement. As Malcolm Yorke points out, the Neo-Romantics 'issued no manifesto, had no subscription list, no joint exhibitions, no agreed meeting place, no leaders, no appointed spokesmen and no agreed programme.'[20] While Neo-Romanticism is often described as an archetypal English art form, not all its principal exponents were English: Robert Colquhoun and Robert MacBryde were Scots and Ceri Richards was Welsh, and for the English artists the Welsh landscape itself provided inspiration. Stylistic and regional differences notwithstanding, it is a so-called 'kindred spirit' and an attitude towards landscape that ties certain artists together. They shared a similar vision and sensitivity toward the 'power of the landscape', their scenes, whether real or imagined, reflecting the loneliness of wartime isolation.

By 1938, as war in Europe seemed increasingly likely, artists focussed once more on pastoral subjects and nocturnal views. Inspired by Sutherland's Welsh landscapes, a younger generation of painters – whom we now associate with the Neo-Romantics – turned to the countryside. Sutherland had first visited Pembrokeshire in 1934 and returned there to paint throughout his life. Among the artists to join him there was John Craxton, who visited the 'little England beyond Wales' in 1943. Sutherland taught him 'the importance of invention', to achieve a 'distillation of the landscape rather than an actual portrayal.'[21] There is little in Craxton of the optimism and tranquillity resonant in the work of earlier pastoralists. Instead, the atmosphere of his ink drawings *Poet in Landscape* (1941) and *Dreamer in Landscape* (1942, Cat. 66) is melancholy and anxious. A similarly dark and sombre landscape is Minton's haunting *Recollection of Wales* (ink, 1944, Cat. 94), drawn from memory and imagination. Its long undulating road, sweeping into sharp perspective toward the horizon, the shady enclosed spaces, and the angularity of line owe much to Sutherland's paintings of south west Wales. 'What distinguishes Neo-Romanticism from traditional romanticism,' Peter Woodcock suggests, is an 'element of darkness, dissolution, an almost pagan reverie breaking through the ruins of post-industrialism.'[22]

Closer to the Palmeresque idiom, Minton's *Landscape with Harvester Resting* (ink and wash, 1944 Cat. 28) depicts a farmhand reclining beside a stook of corn, the new moon suggesting a cosmic bearing on youth's existence. The drawing takes its subject from Palmer's *The Valley Thick with Corn* (1825), which at the time belonged to Peter Watson, arts benefactor and patron of the Neo-Romantics. Before it was reproduced in the literary magazine *Horizon* in November 1941, Craxton got to see Palmer's sepia drawing in Watson's London flat, along with works by Picasso and Sutherland. Craxton became immediately convinced to adopt Palmer's overall working of the picture surface and infuse his drawings with tension. In Palmer's work, both Craxton and Minton discovered how landscape could become an emotive vehicle capable of conveying religious and spiritual ideals through an imaginative transformation of observed nature.

John Elwyn's *The Stillness of the Roots* (ink and watercolour, 1944 Cat. 76), with its lone figure enveloped in the shade of gnarled and towering trees, resonates with Craxton's eerie nocturnal scenes. The natural elements of Elwyn's *Elm Roots on the Banks of the Taff* (ink and watercolour, 1946) have a presence beyond the literal, and the atmosphere is heightened by blood-red smoke-laden skies. Like the works of Sutherland, Elwyn's interpretation of natural forms was affected by the experience of Surrealism. Elwyn also admired Edward Burra's paintings of strange natural objects set against disturbing surrealist landscapes. In true Romantic spirit, Elwyn later wrote:

> 'However important the appearances of things may be it is the reaction to these appearances in oneself that is to me of value in painting. If one responds to the mood of the surrounding countryside, if one can become aware of the pulsating earth around one, one can get nearer to the essence, the *genius loci* of the place. To arrive at that point and to be able to express the

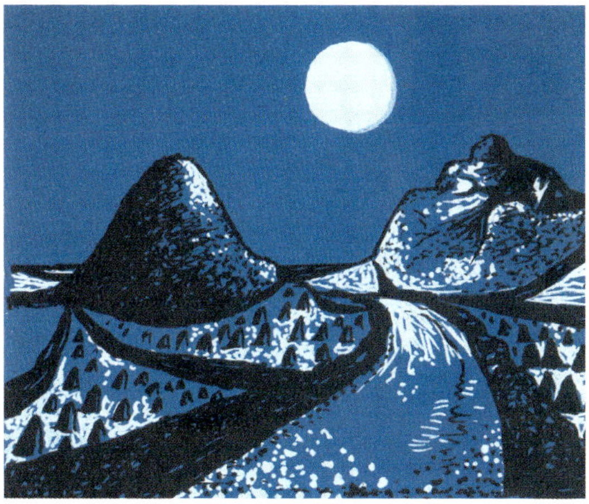

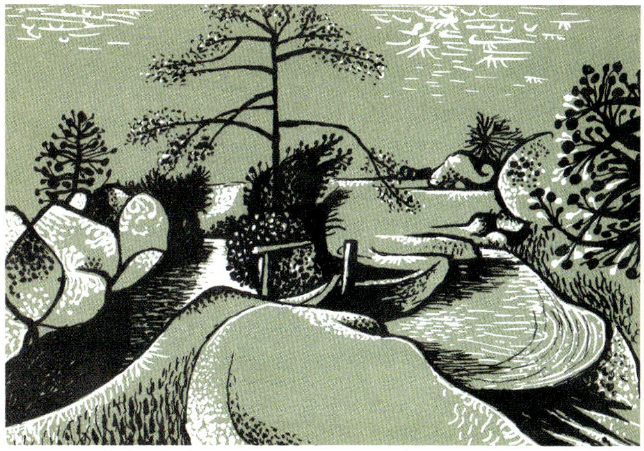

67. John Craxton (1922-)
The Poets Eye
anthology chosen by Geoffrey Grigson with 16 lithographs by John Craxton, 1944
Anne Anderson (Book: Case)

> experience of environment and convey it on to a canvas is what I would like to achieve. It should be a personal and individual synthesis of the chosen subject.'[23]

Towards the end of the War, Neo-Romantic art reached a still wider audience when several young painters turned to book illustration and contributed to popular illustrated anthologies – among them *Britain in Pictures*, *New Writing and Daylight*, *New Excursions into English Poetry*, and Frederick Muller's poetry series *The Poet's Eye* (Craxton, 1944 Cat. 67), *English, Scottish and Welsh Landscape 1700-1860* (Piper, 1944 Cat. 120), *Soldier's Verse* (William Scott, 1945), *Poems of Death* (Ayrton, 1945) and *Poems of Sleep and Dream* (Robert Colquhoun, 1947). In 1947, Paul Elek inaugurated the 'Camden Classics' series and commissioned illustrations from Keith Vaughan (*The Adventures of Tom Sawyer*, 1947) and John Minton (*Treasure Island*, 1947). Minton's line drawings for Alain-Fournier's *The Wanderer* (1947) are a milestone in Neo-Romantic book illustration. Originally published in 1913 as *Le Grande Meaulnes*, *The Wanderer* was conceived as a series of sensations and impulses. This sorrowful story of seventeen-year-old Augustin's quest for his lost love appealed to Minton's sensibilities as the embodiment of the Romantic ideal.

Insisting on innovation and originality, most post-war artists and critics rejected a drawing on the past as escapist, insular and reactionary. Yet Elwyn was not ashamed to have a 'parochial mind.' Like his contemporaries, he found inspiration in a familiar environment. He sympathised with Benjamin Britten for whom 'the important things are the local things.'[24] Today, the transformation of the British landscape and the changes imposed on our traditional way of life are as much of a concern as they were for the contemporaries of both Palmer and Sutherland. The 'spirit of place' is 'deeply embedded in our national consciousness,' Woodcock argues. 'Every new motorway is questioned, every ancient wood fought for. The old Neo-Romantic world has long gone, but the dream persists.'[25] More than a commercial catering to the demand for nostalgic retreats and recreations of a bygone way of life, 'Little Englandism' lives on in the British psyche as a valid struggle for continuity and assurance.

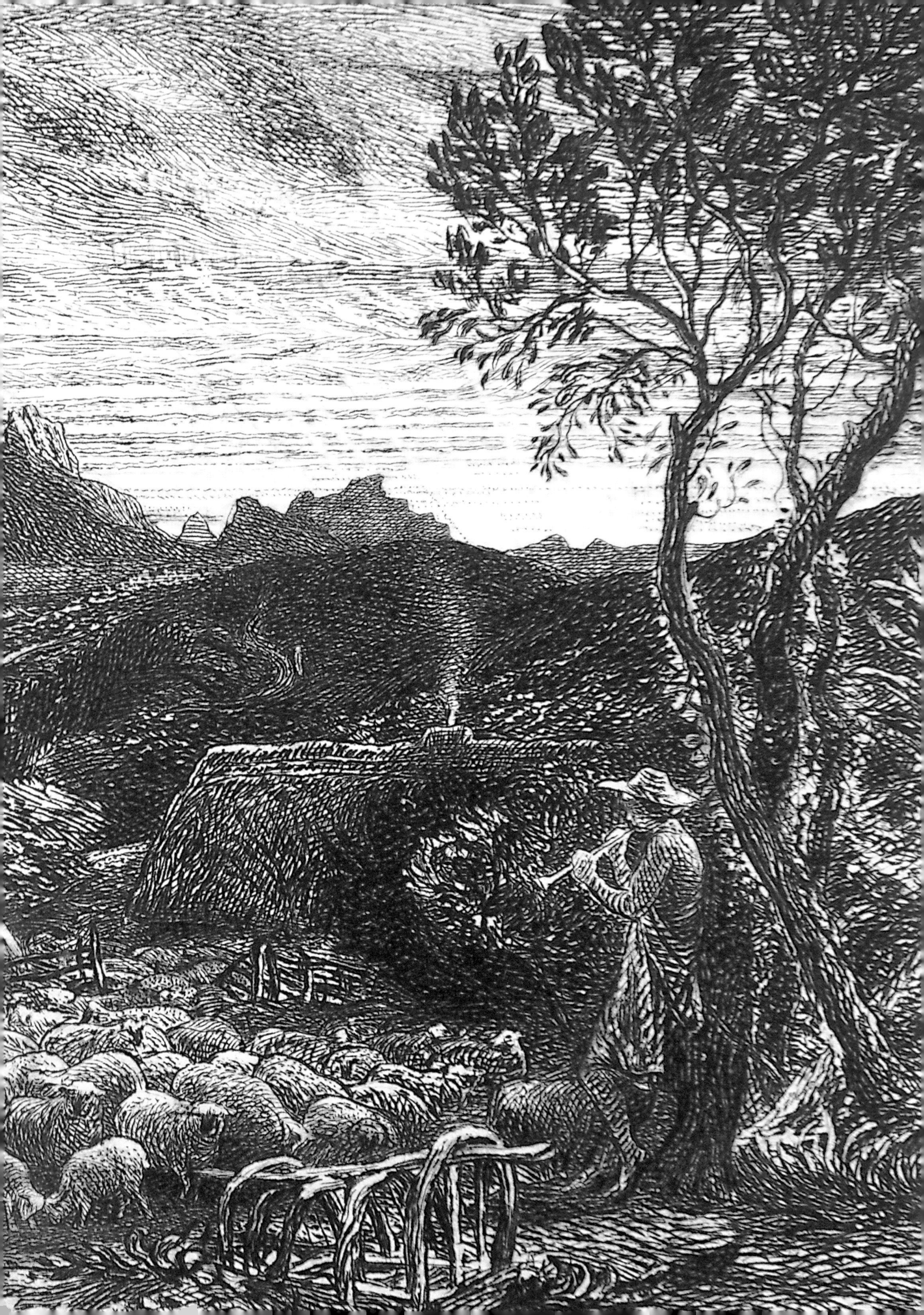

Pastoral Visions

Given his influence, it is ironic that Blake can hardly be classed as a landscape painter; it was his series of seventeen woodcuts commissioned to illustrate Thorton's *Virgil* (1821) that had a crucial impact. These tiny works, packed with emotional feeling, Blake's 'ecstatic vision', provided a point of departure for Palmer:

> 'They are visions of little dells, and nooks and corners of Paradise; models of the exquisite pitch of intense poetry. I thought of their light and shade, and looking upon them I found no word to describe it. Intense depth, solemnity, and vivid brilliancy only coldly and partially describes them. There is in all such a mystic and dreamy glimmer as penetrates and kindles the inner-most soul, and gives complete and unreserved delight, unlike the gaudy daylight of this world.'[1]

To Calvert and Palmer, the woodcuts 'revealed a path which they could follow in freedom' [2], also confirming Palmer's conviction 'that the only way to see was to see religiously'.[3]

Samuel Palmer was the quintessential Romantic artist, intense, moody, troubled and interesting. Yet he was also conservative in his outlook, deploring the 1832 Reform Bill and Catholic emancipation: 'he firmly turned his easel away from the rick-burning, machine-smashing peasantry of Kent to paint mythical England where the yokels ploughed with oxen , strolled home signing hymns by moonlight and happily worked in fecund landscapes'.[4] Palmer's 'Imaginative Art', being highly personal, often failed to find buyers. Like his mentor, William Blake, Palmer viewed the English countryside with a spiritual fervour; for him Shoreham was a magical place, his outlook being more optimistic than Blake's. Here under the influence of his friends Calvert and Richmond he produced his most inspired works. But the idyll was comparatively short-lived, with Palmer moving back to London in 1835. Marriage to John Linnell's daughter, in 1837, necessitated a more commercial outlook and naturalistic rather than visionary works. Sadly, not fully appreciating their artistic value, his surviving son, A.H. Plamer, destroyed the early intense, mystical landscapes that had survived in the artist's studio. Works of the Shoreham period, largely painted for the artist's own portfolio, are consequently very rare; they were a revelation, both in conception and technique, at the 1926 Victorian and Albert Museum exhibition, *Drawings, Etchings and Wood-cuts by Samuel Palmer and other Disciples of William Blake*. [5] Robin Tanner recorded his encounter with Palmer's poignant self-portrait, now in the Ashmolean, Oxford: 'never before, I thought, had a man's portrait so mirrored his work. I knew that the Shoreham drawings, so heavily charged with feeling, could only have emerged from such a poet'.[6]

Palmer's vision was rekindled by a commission from Leonard Rowe Valpy, John Ruskin's solicitor, who encouraged the artist to develop a theme of his own choice, thus enabling Palmer to paint a cycle of landscapes based on Milton's *L'Allegro* and *Il Penseroso* (1645). This project occupied Palmer's last years, remaining uncompleted at his death. By the 1860s Palmer's vision had deepened, ecstasy and enthusiasm being replaced by a more meditative mood. F.G. Stephens contrasted Palmer's styles, likening the earlier to Keats and the later to Tennyson: 'Like many of Tennyson's poems, the later watercolours and etchings certainly have a rich and tenebrous melancholy'.[7] The Milton watercolours, together with their related etchings, are now regarded as Palmer's greatest 'post-Shoreham' achievements. The other major project that filled Palmer's last years was his translation of Virgil's *Eclogues*, in which he hoped to communicate more of the 'pastoral essence' of Virgil than other translators. He was advised that the project would only be worth pursing if it was illustrated. Consequently, Palmer worked on etchings for this publication until his death: 'They take a long time for the very reason that I am longing to see them done, and known that the shortest and only way is to aim at no mechanical finish and to put only touches of love'.[8] Although only partially completed, it was posthumously published in 1883.

Concurrent with the V&A exhibition was a plan to reprint Palmer's etchings from the original plates still in the possession of A.H. Palmer. Sir Frank Short, long-time President of the Society of Painter-Etchers, was the first to take new impressions but the success of the enterprise rested with Frederick Landseer Maur Griggs (1876-1938), the most brilliant living technician. Griggs had also absorbed Palmer's artistic ideals: 'only the great, poetic etcher of beautiful old Campden has fully succeeded in imagining what these conceptions of the Virgil etchings are'.[9] Griggs had loved Palmer's works since childhood, this veneration being reflected in his own drawings and etchings from the First World War to the Depression; despite these years of destruction and uncertainty Griggs continued to 'etch a medieval pastoral England where all was peace; labour was sweet, dignified, and its own reward; and the Catholic church spread its canopy over all'.[10] This 'anachronistic day-dream world' and nostalgic Catholicism appealed to Graham Sutherland and his fellow students at Goldsmiths' College, Paul Drury, Robin Tanner, William Larkins and Edward Bouverie Hoyton. The Class of 21, the year in which Drury entered Goldsmiths', became outstanding etchers, a print-making technique then enjoying a revival.[11] Palmer's *The Herdsman's Cottage* proved a catalyst for the group in 1924:

> 'The day on which one of our band, William Larkins, brought a small Palmer etching which he had found in Charing Cross Road was a turning point…I was amazed by its completeness, both emotional and technical. It was unheard of at the school to cover the plate almost completely with work and quite new to us that the complex variety and multiplicity of lines could form a tone of such luminosity.' [12]

Sutherland also recalled: 'I liked Palmer drawings of the early years… because as a young man I was drawn to a strongly romantic, and so it seemed, independent approach to nature from which I was always drawing'.[13] Captivated by the 'emotional and technical' completeness of Palmer's work, Sutherland went in search of more; in the Tate, Sutherland was struck by the early watercolours acquired in 1922; 'The best of the Shoreham drawings, the very best, were unsentimental. The landscapes were daring, and were drawn from unexpected viewpoints: *The Girl in the Ploughed Field* (*Landscape: A Girl Standing*, *c.*1826, Tate Britain) astonished me with its total disregard for conventional composition. The drawing is almost what we call today naif'.[14] Although Sutherland's attachment to Palmer only lasted a short time, he fiercely advocated allegiance to the English tradition:

> 'Between the years 1927 and 1930 I was very conscious of the English tradition and very aggressive about it. I used to think, for instance, of Samuel Palmer as being essentially the English Van Gogh, which is not so far-fetched in retrospect, because of course he painted suns and moons and so on.' [15]

The etchings of the 'Class of 21' recapture the emotional intensity of Palmer's Shoreham days, seen in Sutherland's *Village* (1925) and *Lammas* (1926), which celebrates a religious festival on the first day of August, when loaves baked from new grain are consecrated affirming the continuing sway of the Christian Calendar on daily life in the countryside. Tanner's *Christmas* (1929) depicts a perfect English village, based on Castle Coombe in Wiltshire. Sketched from the church tower, Tanner recalled 'working through the small hours' as 'moonlight lay in sheets of silver so bright and constant that we drew as easily as by day'.[16] The light of the moon is eerie but not malevolent. The magical light of Palmer's *The Bellman* (1879), the glowing evening sky suffused with a sense of reverence, is rekindled in Sutherland's *Cray Fields* (1925), with the radiating sun, setting behind hop-poles. This luminosity also testifies to knowledge of Griggs's work, as seen in *St Ippolyts* (1927), with its dramatically backlit church. The rising evening star 'creates the suggestion of a passing moment of poetic intensity', [17] while the labourers heading home elicit a sense of well-being or contentment after 'a job well done'. For artistic effect the times of day most favoured were sunrise, heralding the dawn, and sunset, evoking closure and a feeling of peace. To complete the effect, a lark ascends at dawn, while a nightingale betokens the coming of night; Milton's *L'Allegro* has its lark *and Il Penseroso* its nightingale.

With the spirit of Pan still haunting the English pastoral, it comes as no surprise that some artists hoped that the 'little people' still survived, hidden under dock leaves or nestling in primroses. As arch-romantics and dreamers the Victorians needed fairies to escape the intolerable reality of living in a materialistic and scientific age. They also saw a belief in fairies and folklore as part of the disappearing customs of country life. Thomas Hardy feared 'Village tradition, a vast amount of unwritten folklore, local chronicle, local topography and nomenclature, is absolutely sinking, has nearly sunk, into eternal oblivion'.[18] In response to this erosion of local identity, the Folklore Society was founded in 1878. Fairy painting also offered the Victorian artist a chance to explore taboo subjects, a world of dreams and nightmares in which sex, nudity, violence and even drugs could be tackled under the guise of respectable art. Fairies, benign or malevolent, are a tributary of the pastoral tradition, flowing into the literary stream through the works of Shakespeare, Spencer and Milton. Shakespeare's *A Midsummer Night's Dream* and *The Tempest* inspired many of the greatest fairy paintings. *Grimm's Fairy Tales*, published in 1824 and Hans Christian Anderson's *Fairy Tales*, which appeared in the 1840s, fuelled the Victorian fairy craze. One of the first practitioners was William Blake, who claimed to have seen fairies in his own garden:

> 'I was walking alone in my garden, there was a great stillness among the branches and the flowers, and more than common sweetness in the air; I heard low and pleasant sound, and I know not whence it came. At last I saw the broad leaf of a flower move, and underneath saw a procession of creatures the size and colour of green and grey grasshoppers, bearing a body laid out on a rose-leaf, which they buried with songs and disappeared. It was a fairy funeral.' [19]

Blake produced a number of watercolours on fairy themes, including *Oberon, Titania and Puck with Fairies Dancing* (*c.*1785, Tate Britain), which may have inspired his namesake to take up the theme. Given Peter Blake's (1932-) crucial role in the emergence of Pop art in the 1960s, his reinvention as a Ruralist in the following decade may at first sight seem incongruous but Blake entered Arcadia with the fairies. *Titania*, the Queen of the Fairies, was first shown at the Royal Academy Summer Exhibition in 1976, the same year the Brotherhood of Ruralists first exhibited as a group. Blake's fairies are solid and real (*Fairy*, Cat. No. 32): 'he conveys a magical sense through a combination of knowingness and innocence. Titania...combines the body of a young, sexually mature girl-woman with a candid face that is not in the least ethereal'.[20] Blake manages to combine sexual maturity and otherworldly innocence: 'Like the nymphs in classical mythology and Blake's urban strippers, she is a figment of male fantasy, poised eternally between innocence and desire, childhood and womanhood, apparently available yet essentially out of reach.[21] Vaizey describes Blake's fairies as 'full-blooded', dressing 'fantasy in reality'; 'he is a believable surrealist. His fairies are both creatures of the flesh and creatures of fantasy'. [22]

At the end of the 1960s Blake and his then wife Jann Haworth decided to leave London for the country, becoming by definition 'ruralists'. Enter 'Alice in Wonderland', Ophelia and the fairies, concomitant not only with ruralist life but also parenthood; Juliet Liberty Blake had arrived in 1968. In search of a rural 'Shangri-la' Blake moved his family to a converted railway station at Wellow, near Bath. Rural solitude went hand-in-hand with going back to basics, canvas and paint; creating a new trend by being 'backward' rather than ahead of art trends: 'People are so busy *not* doing the traditional art subject...I am now doing them and suddenly, it's extraordinary, one's broken down a new barrier'.[23] By 'being about a hundred years out of date, his "new" approach was a playful gibe at the art world's obsession with advancement'.[24] But life in the country divorced the sociable Blake from his stimulating circle of friends; fortunately new associates were on the horizon. An admiration for David Inshaw took him to Devizes; Blake had invited Inshaw to exhibit at a show he was putting on for the Bath Festival of 1974. Picking up Inshaw's work he met Graham Arnold, who had also made his escape to Wessex. Graham Ovenden, Blake's erstwhile student, and his wife Annie, had found their haven in Cornwall. The Blakes invited all their ruralist friends to dinner on 21st March 1975 (it was Inshaw's birthday) and from this convivial party the Brotherhood of Ruralists was born. A Brotherhood paid homage to the Pre-Raphaelite Brotherhood (1848-53), seven artists, including Millais, Holman Hunt and Rossetti, who exhibited a similar sensibility for nature, realism and the past. There was no manifesto, just shared enthusiasms:

> 'Simply, our aims are the continuation of a certain kind of English painting; we admire Samuel Palmer, Stanley Spencer, Thomas Hardy, Elgar, cricket, English landscape, the Pre-Raphaelites, etc...Our aims are to paint about love, beauty, joy, sentiment and magic. We still believe in painting with oil paint on canvas, putting the picture in a frame and, hopefully, that someone will like it, buy it and hang it on their wall to enjoy.' [25]

In an interview with Sir Alistair Johnston in September 1999, Graham Ovenden discussed the motives and inspirations behind his Ruralist vision. An ideal bound up with a 'mystic Arcadia' and the 'girl-child', where the origins of English landscape painting are to be found in Celtic and Christian Pantheism:

> '...back to the roots of Sir Gawain and the Green Knight, further, the first English poets, then taking its progression through. Its summits being William Blake and Samuel Palmer, ending up in this century with Paul Nash, Spencer, and artists of a like nature.'

Marina Vaizey sums up the Ruralists:

> 'They shared not style, but sympathy, and attracted an unusual amount of both praise and adverse criticism. They took their annual holiday together. They were in a sense omnivorous, and in that sense Victorian; they saw visual imagery almost as a seamless whole, able to connect disparate images. They were not retrograde but reactionary in a non-pejorative sense. An intense attention to detail, and to the reconciliation of disparate worlds, was often a feature: dream-like paintings (by David Inshaw), compilations and collages (by Graham Arnold) and a remarkably empathetic understanding of the countryside (by Ann Arnold), were among the characteristics of the Ruralists... All were involved in the imaginative world of the Victorians.' [26]

Blake's involvement, he devised the hang for the Ruralist debut at the Royal Academy, guaranteed a public interest (Blake had been elected an associate member of the RA in 1974, being elected a full Royal Academician in 1981). A BBC film about the Ruralists by John Read, *Summer with the Brotherhood*, was aired in 1977. In 1983 Blake invited the Brotherhood, by then dissolving, to contribute to his Tate Gallery retrospective, a wall of paintings on *The Definitive Nude.* Blake's ruralist sojourn ended with his return to the metropolis in 1979, but he can still be occasionally found at Barley Splatt, the Ovenden's Cornish home, where one can imagine fairies at the bottom of the garden.

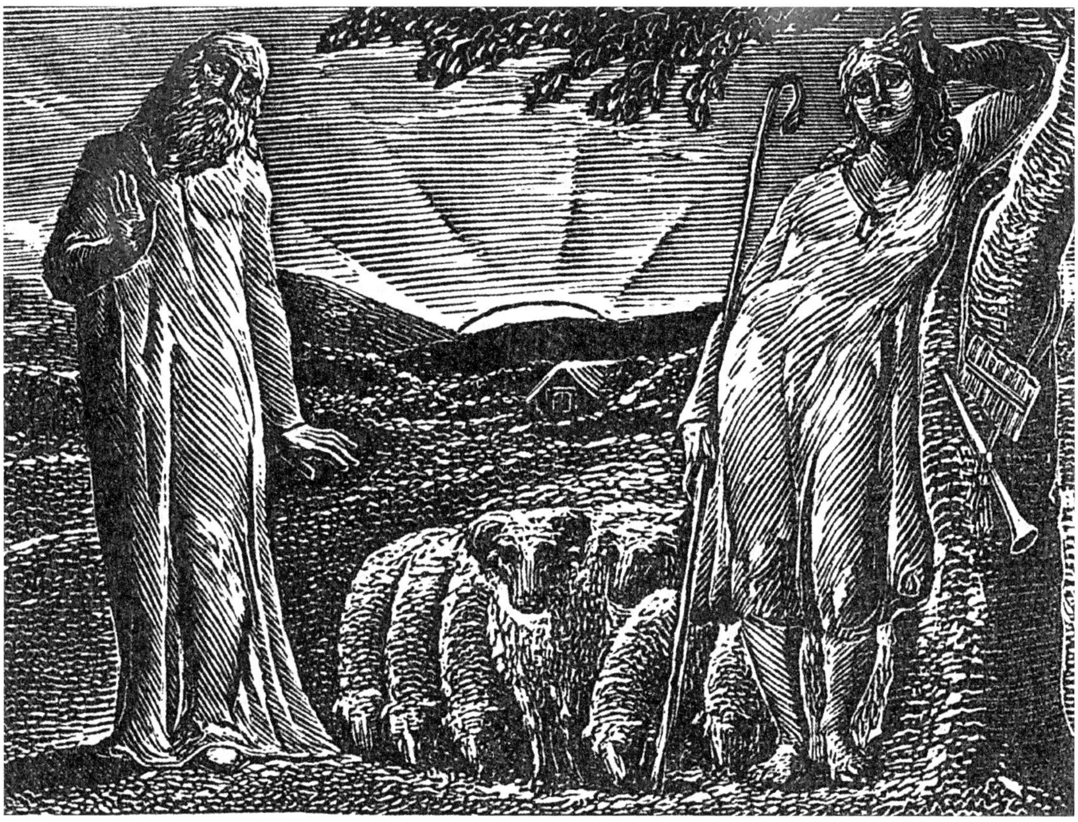

3. William Blake (1757-1827)
Illustrations to Thornton's *The Pastorals of Virgil*, 1820-21
Frontispiece 62 x 84 mm
Southampton City Art Gallery, David Brown Bequest

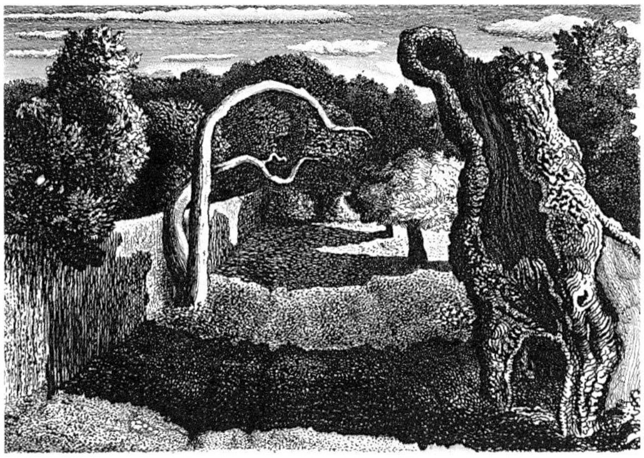

1. Graham Vivien Sutherland (1903-1980)
Pastoral (1930)
etching and engraving, 128 x 191 mm
private collection, Stuart M. Southall

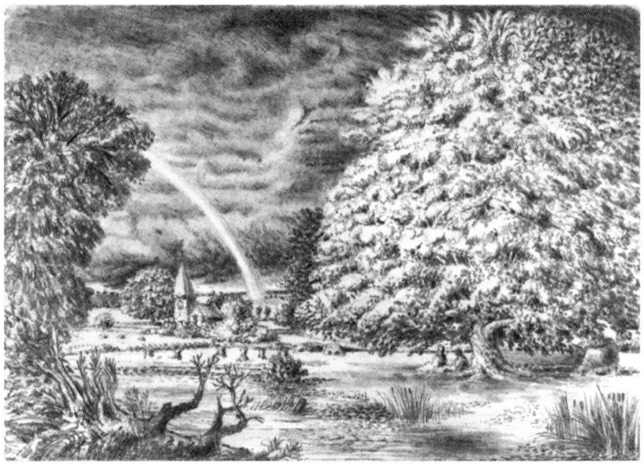

2. Alf Stockham (1933-)
To Dave and his search for England, 1970
pencil, 89 x 121 mm
David Inshaw

1

The forty etchings that Sutherland produced between 1922 and 1940 demonstrate his progression from talented student to mature artist. These works represent the first phase in a career that saw Sutherland become one of the great artists of the 20th century.

Sutherland came from a comfortable middle-class background, as did Nash and Piper. After an abortive engineering apprenticeship, Sutherland enrolled at Goldsmiths' College, staying until 1926, where he discovered his talent for etching. F.L. Griggs (1876-1938) offered Sutherland friendship and technical advice, which reinforced his enthusiasm for Palmer. There followed a series of Palmeresque works: *Cudham, Kent* (1924); *Barrow Hedges Farm* (1924); *Number Forty-nine* (1924); a tumbled down thatched cottage, *Crayfields* (1925); *The Village* (1925); *Pecken Wood* (1925); *St Mary's Hatch* (1926); *Lammas* (1926); *May Green* (1927); *Michaelmas* (1928) and *Meadow Chapel* (1928). Described as 'pious landscapes of the mind', appropriating from Blake, Palmer and Griggs symbolic motifs such as white doves, single huge stars, praying or working figures, churches, sheep, apple trees and corn sheaves, all subsumed in the encroaching shadows of twilight, these works are in a borrowed style.[27]

But 1929 saw a marked change in Sutherland's mood, seen in *Pastoral*. Here, although still densely textured and dark in tone, Palmer's vision has been replaced by something more ominous; two thin tree trunks undulate like sinuous snakes, whipping over like tentacles to menace a gnarled, suggestively animalistic, stump. Having befriended Paul Nash, Sutherland seems to have adopted his 'monsters' and 'presences' lurking in trees. Roberto Tassi has described *Pastoral* as a 'tragic landscape'; the leafy trees cannot dispel the sense of decay and despair. This change in mood may have been caused by the death of the Sutherland's three-month-old son; following this anguish they decided to remain childless. [28] Moreover, after a period of success, Sutherland was facing problems, as the Wall Street Crash of October 1929 decimated the lucrative American market for prints. Sutherland diversified into glassware, ceramics, tapestries and posters for Shell-Mex and London Transport. The later etchings are 'no longer Christian in feel and neither are they optimistic. It is as though Palmer's sun had finally set and a chill had crept into Arcadia'.[29] *Pastoral* looks forward to Sutherland's Pembrokeshire landscapes, *Entrance to a Lane* and *Green Lane*, in which his individual style emerges.

Pastoral seems to have fallen victim to the collapse of the print market following the Wall Street Crash; only five or six proofs were printed in 1930. It was not printed as an edition until 1973: 'It is perhaps significant that it remained unpublished for over forty years, for its implications were unpalatable'.[30]

2

David Inshaw met Alf Stockham at the School of Art in Bristol, where they were both teaching. Ten years older than Inshaw, Stockham initially joined the Navy; his father having spent thirty years at sea. But then he decided to 'throw himself into art', first by attending the Camberwell School of Art and then the RCA. Starting his full-time art education in 1960, he enrolled at the RCA just before he was thirty. He then applied for and won the Rome Scholarship, during which time he was offered a Fellowship at York. Bristol School of Art

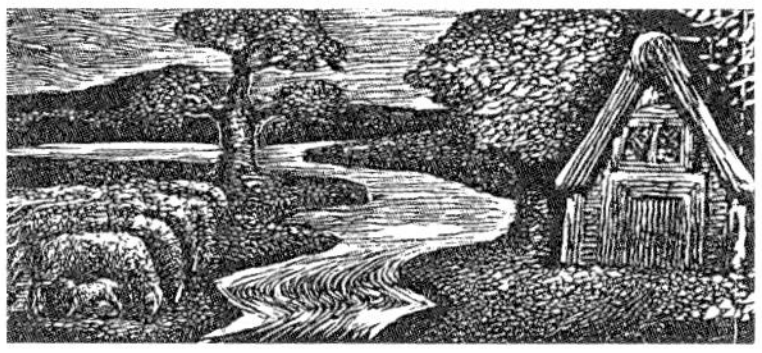

3.5

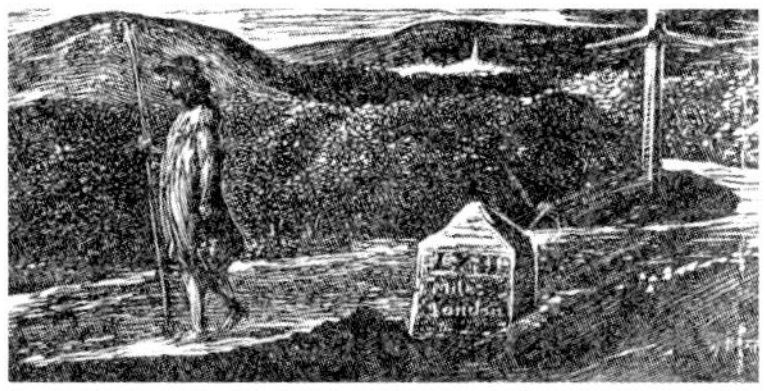

3.6

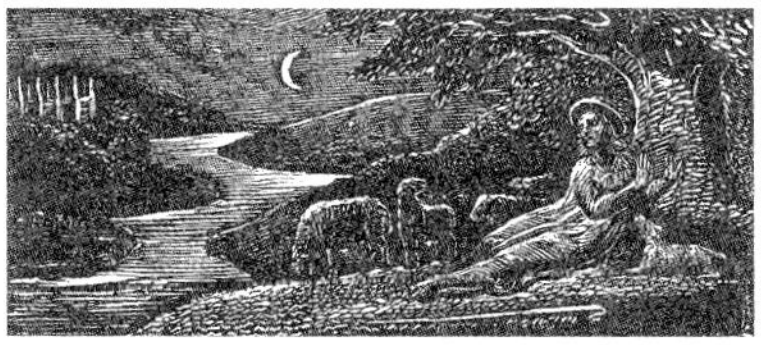

3.8

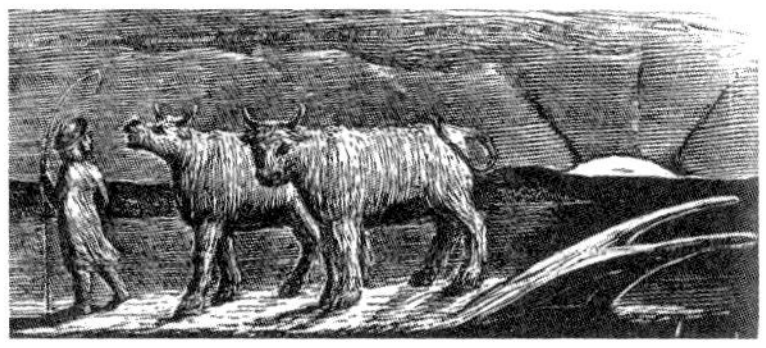

3.12

3. William Blake (1757-1827)
Illustrations to Thornton's *The Pastorals of Virgil*, 1820-21
Thirteen wood engravings on paper
each approximately 25 x 75 mm, frontispiece 62 x 84 mm
Southampton City Art Gallery, David Brown Bequest

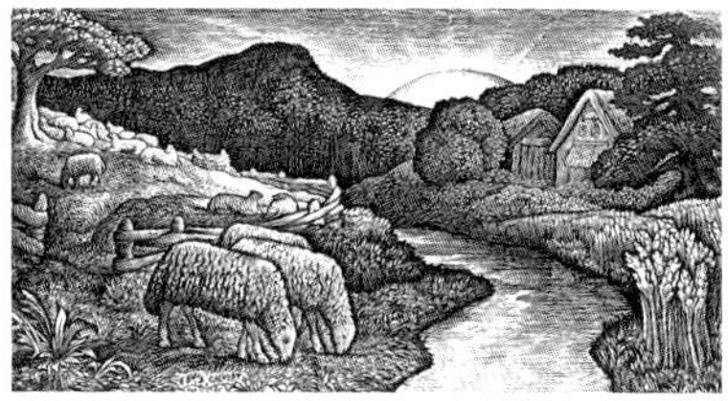

4. Edward Calvert (1799-1883)
The Sheep of His Pasture, 1828
copper engraving on paper, 41 x 79 mm
Pallant House Gallery
Chichester Hussey Bequest

offered him some part-time teaching, which turned into a full-time position teaching Fine Art. Stockham had no real intention of staying in Bristol; he planned to return to his London studio but upon discovering that his grandfather had come from the Bristol area he acquired an affinity for the city. Stockham recalls that he and Inshaw were producing 'sub-standard Pop art' when he suggested their 'Search for England'. They then set out to discover Dorset, finding Burton Bradstock, West Bay, and Little Bredy, where Inshaw's well-known *Cricket Match* is set.

3

3.1 Thenot remonstrates with Colinet, Frontispiece.
3.2 Thenot remonstrates with Colinet, Lightfoot in the distance.
3.3 Thenot with Colinet wearing his arms in sorrow.
3.4 The Good Shepherd chases away the Wolf.
3.5 Sabrina's Silvery Flood.
3.6 Colinet's Fond Desire Strange Lands to know.
3.7 A Rolling Stone is Ever Bare of Moss.
3.8 Colinet resting at Cambridge by Night.
3.9 Colinet Mocked by two boys.
3.10 Menalcas, Yearly Wake.
3.11 Thenot and Colinet sup together.
3.12 Unyoked Heifers, Loitering Homeward.
3.13 With Songs the Jovial Hinds Return from Plow.

Illustrations to Ambrose Phillips, *Imitation of Virgil's First Eclogue*, a pastiche of the classical pastoral.

In 1820 Dr Robert John Thornton, a noted physician and botanist, needing illustrations for his edition of *The Pastorals of Virgil...Adapted for Schools*, commissioned Blake to make seventeen woodcuts. Following ridicule from the publisher, Thornton had doubts but Thomas Lawrence, James Ward and John Linnell convinced him to retain Blake's work. Blake's 'gems' carried a disclaimer: 'they display less art than genius, and are much admired by some eminent painters'. They certainly exerted a profound influence on Sutherland:

> '...we see Blake at the height of his powers, and achieving complete unity of expression...we see a mysterious grandeur and a flaring ecstasy. What strange and exciting vistas they open up for us! This tree, so like yet so unlike the trees of our visual knowledge, so universal yet so intimate, obeys no laws except those of its creator... What power they have to move us!' [31]

4

Calvert, the son of a soldier, entered the Royal Academy Schools in 1824, meeting Blake and the Ancients through Palmer's cousin, John Giles. This plate, with its pastoral motifs of sheep in their fold, rural cottages and meandering stream, parallels Blake's 'Sabrina's Silvery Flood' from Thornton's *Pastorals*.

Calvert subscribed to the intense mystical vision of an ideal pastoral world cultivated by Palmer during the Shoreham years (1825-35) but the mood is often sensual rather than religious, as seen in *The Cyder Press* (1828). He would adopt neo-paganism, worshipping the Greek gods, and was said to make sacrifices to Pan on an altar in his London garden. This paganism worried his colleagues and was to lead to the rather 'feeble classicism' of his later works. [32]

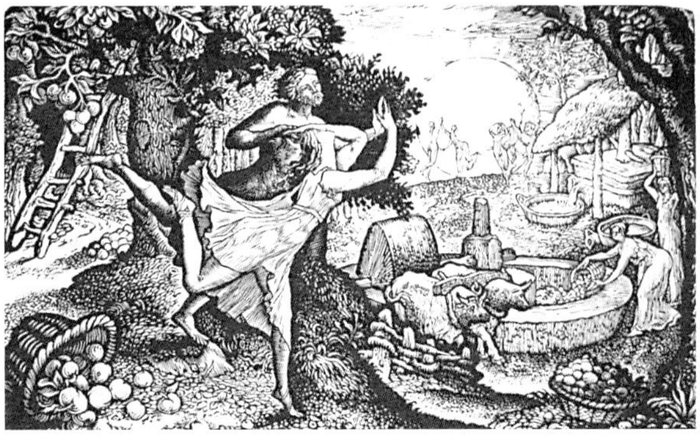

5. Edward Calvert (1799-1883)
The Cyder Feast, 1828
Wood engraving, 76 x 127 mm
Victoria Art Gallery, Bath (Bath only)

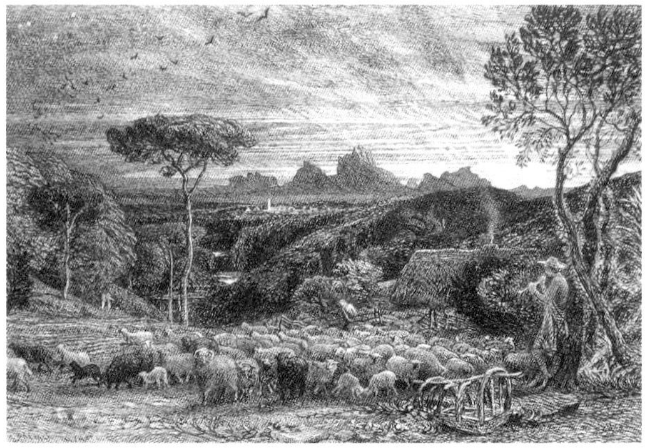

6. Samuel Palmer (1805-1881)
Opening the Fold or Early Mooring, 1880
etching on paper, 162 x 230 mm
Stuart M. Southall

5

In Calvert's works the mood is sensual rather than religious, even though *The Cyder Feast* originally bore a religious inscription; 'By the Gift of God in Christ'. The image exudes the paganism that was a central component in Calvert's life. The cavorting couple appear to be about to join a bacchanalian revel; we are closer to Virgil's arcadia than a Christian paradise. The motif of the apple tree, as a symbol of nature's fecundity, will be much used by the Ruralists, as will the giant harvest moon.

6

Opening the Fold was the only etching completed by Palmer for his translation of Virgil's *Eclogues* before he died in 1881. Framed by a landscape that recalls the Roman Campagna, the shepherd Damon leans against an olive tree piping a lament for his lost love Nysa, while his companion unfolds his sheep by an English thatched cottage; classical Arcadia merges with the bucolic English idyll. It illustrates Eclogue VIII, lines 23-8:

'Scarce with her rosy fingers had the dawn
From glimmering heaven the vale of night withdrawn,
Or folded flocks were loose to browse anew
O'er mountain thyme or trefoil wet with dew,
When leaning sad an olive tree beside,
There, his last numbers, hapless Damon plied.' [33]

7

Griggs antedated and to a certain extent influenced all the Palmerites, who saw his work at the Twenty One Gallery, the leading dealers during the 1920s etching boom. In the early 1890s Griggs discovered, in the Hitchen Mechanical Institute, a copy of *The Eclogues of Virgil*, translated and illustrated by Palmer, which had a profound influence on his development as an artist: 'My love for the things Samuel Palmer loved is my first and last love, and I know no other artist who loved them so well, and whose love so showed forth in his work'.[34] Grigg's love of Palmer informed the way he printed; he wiped a plate to leave just enough tone to enrich the lines without blurring them. A mesh of luminous lines, Palmer's 'intricate beauty', enabled Griggs to suffuse his ecclesiastical buildings with a spiritual atmosphere; the artist converted to Roman Catholicism in 1912. This depiction of an country church, bears a dedication to Grigg's closest friend, the writer and painter Russell George Alexander (1877-1951), followed by a quotation from Milton's *Lycidas* (1638), a pastoral elegy to his drowned friend Edward King:

'For we were nurst upon the self-same Hill,
Fed the same flock, by fountain, shade, and rill.
Together both, ere the high Lawns appear'd
Under the opening eyelids of the morn,
We drove a field, and both together heard
What time the Gray-fly winds her sultry horn,
Batt'ning our flocks with the fresh dews of night,
Oft till the Star that rose, at Ev'n-ing, bright
Toward Heav'ns descent had slop'd his westering wheel.' [35]

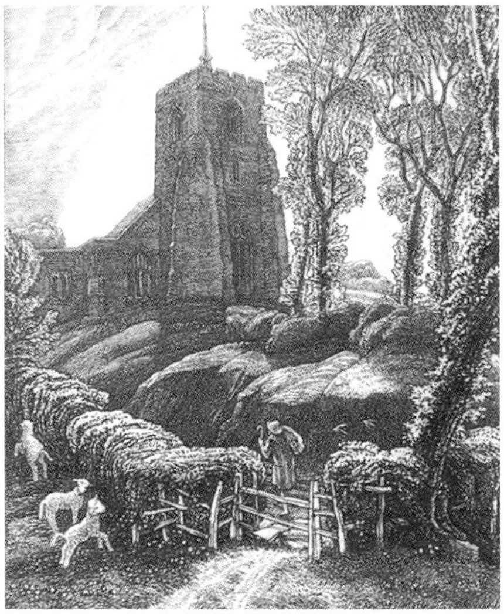

7. Frederick Landseer Maur Griggs
(1876-1938)
St Ippolyts, 1927
etching on paper, Comstock 36
140-120 mm
Stuart M. Southall

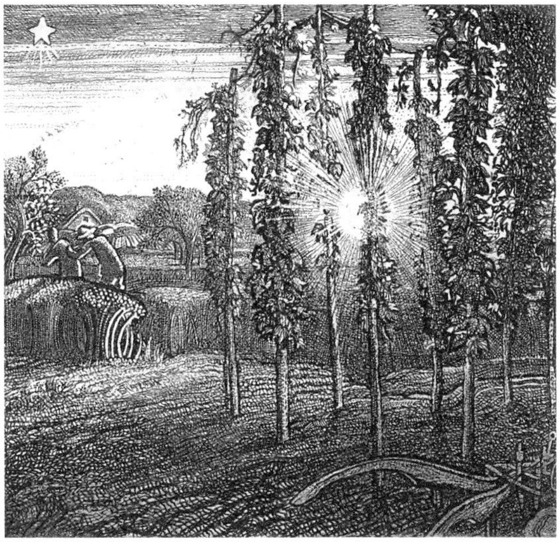

8. Graham Vivien Sutherland
(1903-1980)
Cray Fields, 1925
etching on paper
State 7 of 7, 117 x 124 mm
Pallant House Gallery, Hussey Bequest

St Ippolyts, based on the parish church a few miles from Hitchen, Herts, where Griggs was born, was to cast 'a sort of gentle solemnity over the radiance of a May morning':

'For me it's in the heart of that lost country-Oh God, how lovely it was! There was a wonderful road, difficult to find, – it seemed to have no beginning, and I, for one, never knew the end…it ran by woods and meadows with untrimmed hedges, rich in flowers and birds…I've often wondered if I dare seek it again'.[36] In the etching, a man, carrying a crook, walks this lane, the burden on his back suggesting a pilgrim.

Dedicated to Alexander, the work commemorated their imitate friendship: 'The thing that stuck me most was the way we had fallen into the same paths together almost at once, and had travelled together in the same paths ever since. And it would be difficult for me to overestimate the value of that companionship'. [37]

Comstock succinctly sums up the charms of the print:

> 'It suggests a meditation, full of the sweetness of nature, upon a well-loved place, remembered as in the light of spring. The lambs in the meadow, the swallows in the lane, the lark in the sky, the rook's nests seen amid the 'glad light green' of the elms, the grass and leaves sparkling in the sunlight and shadows with dew and raindrops from a departing shadow, all help to recall a May morning, casting its radiance over a scene of ancient country beauty and pastoral innocence.' [38]

The three lambs privately symbolised Griggs and Alexander's three children.

In 1903 Griggs settled in Chipping Campden, where he founded the Dover's House Press. Here he forged links with the Cotswold Craftsmen, collaborating with Ernest Gimson of the Sapperton group. His best known etchings include *Owlpen Manor* (1930), dedicated to his friend, the architect Norman Jewson, *Maur's Farm*, *St Botolph's, Boston*, *The Almonry* and *Memory of Clavering*. He illustrated thirteen of Macmillan's *Highways and Byways* county guidebooks, which inspired the young Sutherland and Piper. Sutherland recalled, having been tutored by Griggs: 'He thought real England had been damned, as one of his titles, *Ex Anglia Perdita*, suggests. But he taught me a great deal about printing. Everything I know about printing I owe to him; how thick the ink should be, how many rags one had to use, and what stages'. [39]

8

Sutherland and Drury took trips to Shoreham, Palmer's 'Valley of Vision', in 1925 in search of Palmeresque subjects. Sutherland would move to nearby St Mary Cray, near Farningham, Kent, in 1927. The motif of the radiating sun, setting behind hop-poles, is derived from Palmer's *The Herdsman's Cottage* (1850), the print discovered by William Larkins and introduced to the Class of 21. The overly large rising evening star 'creates the suggestion of a passing moment of poetic intensity'. [40]

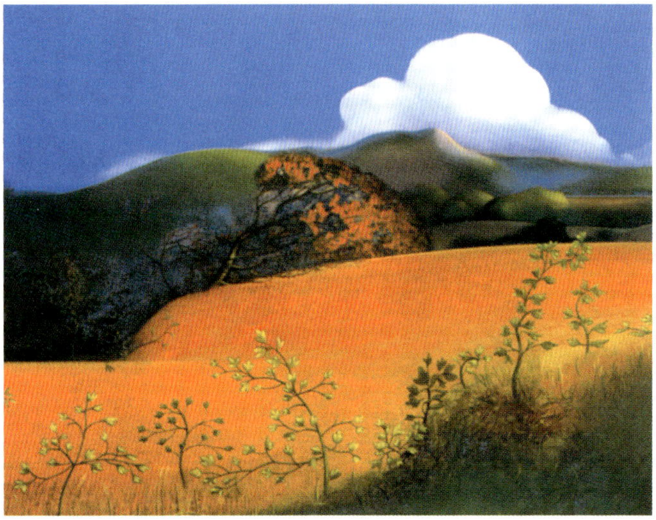

9. Graham Ovenden (1943-)
The Evening Cornfield 1976
oil over pastel, 222 x 305 mm
Fred Olsen.

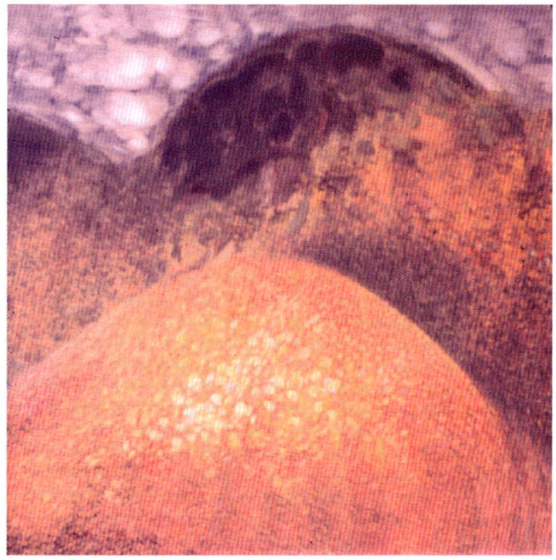

9a. Graham Ovenden (1943-)
Burning Bush, Cathedral Rock, 1964
oil, private collection

9

Graham Ovenden, born in Alresford in 1943, grew up in Southampton and studied at the College of Art between 1960-64, where his tutor and mentor was James Sellars (1927-2000), 'Artist-Writer-Teacher'. [41] He then progressed to the RCA, where Peter Blake taught him, from 1965-68. In 1975 he was one of seven artists who formed the 'Brotherhood of Ruralists'.

This work was begun at Southampton College of Art in pastel. When the college moved to the East Park Terrace campus in 1973 this work was found in a cupboard at Marsh Lane. It was reworked as an oil painting in 1976. This work is very 'Palmeresque', showing the influence of *The Valley with* a *Bright Cloud* (1825, Ashmolean) and the *Bright Cloud* (1833-34, Manchester Art Gallery). It would have been based on the countryside between Southampton and Alresford. Ovenden would have been about the same age as Palmer at Shoreham; and the work shares a youthful intensity, with the light falling on the corn.

10

Painted for Brian Bearne, *The Red Field* uses motifs taken from Palmer's *Valley with a Bright Cloud* (1825), subsequently much used by Palmer himself; the peaceful valley and the billowing cumulus, which were for Palmer further manifestations of the divine in nature; Palmer inscribed the work with lines from Shakespeare's *As You Like It:*

> 'This our life, exempt from public haunt,
> Finds tongues in trees, books in ye running brooks,
> Sermons in stones, and good in everything.' [42]

The 'secret valley' is the rural retreat, with the soaring cloud introducing the sublime or sense of awe This is Palmer's 'image of a higher reality beyond the vale of comfortable rural peace, or "Beulah" as it was referred to by Blake'.

The soft folds of the countryside lead the eye to voluminous clouds on the horizon; this is an imaginary 'secret valley' comparable to Palmer's Shoreham. Ovenden's 'secret valleys' can be found around Alresford, where he was born, Coombe, Morwenstow, and Barley Splatt, where, with his wife Annie, he created a remarkable home. Ovenden's landscapes are not 'portraits' of a place but a compilation of his preferred elements. Here the rounded forms of the clouds are echoed in the smooth curves of the land, creating an interplay of line and form, a pattern reminiscent of Robert Louis Stevenson's *Land of Counterpane.* This is nature as a safe haven; Ovenden's Eden may lack Adam and Eve but the spirit of Pan seems to infuse his personal paradise. Ovenden's interest in photography can be seen in the use of varying focal lengthens, with the foreground less highly worked. The use of a red ground creates a pink bloom around the tree on the far left, reminiscent of a halo.

Ovenden discovered Blake and Palmer through James (Jim) Sellars (1927-2000), his teacher and mentor at the Southampton College of Art. Sellars took his willing pupil to the Ashmolean, Oxford to see Palmer's famous sepias; these influenced his black and white work at the Royal College of Art. At the Ashmolean he also encountered Pre-Raphaelite works; the famous Thomas Coombe collection includes early works by John Everett Millais, William Holman Hunt

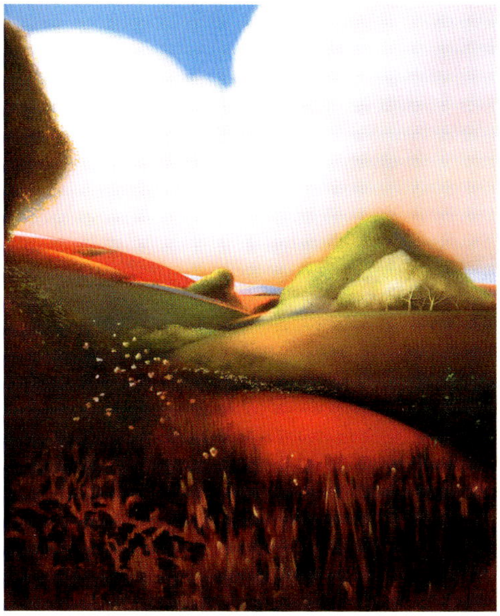

10. Graham Ovenden (1943-)
The Red Field
oil on panel, 490 x 420 mm
Diana Wilkinson

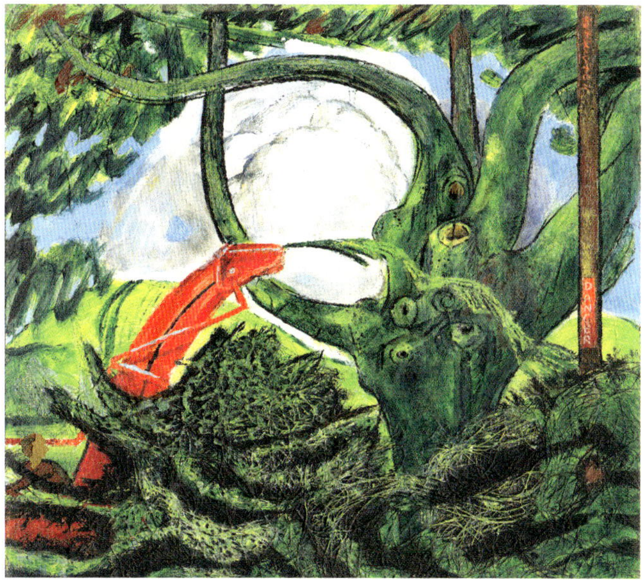

11. John Lefevre (-)
The Great White Cloud, c. 1960
oil and mixed media, 318 x 347 mm
Graham Ovenden

and Dante Gabriel Rossetti. In contrast to Palmer's sepias these offered jewel-like colours and a radiant luminosity. Their literary subjects, drawn from Dante and Shakespeare, inevitably appealed to Ovenden's Romantic inclinations. Despite his admiration for Palmer, Graham's RCA dissertation was on J.W.M. Turner, from whom he absorbed the techniques of rendering light and colour. Ovenden developed his distinctive technique in his youth; he flattens the painted surface, thereby creating the highest colour values and luminosity.

Stuart Durant, later an authority on C.F.A. Voysey and Dr Christopher Dresser, then living in Richmond, acquired some of Ovenden's early works; meeting in the mid- 1960s Durant and Ovenden shared a passion for High Victorian Design, at that time still unfashionable. Barley Splatt, the Ovenden's extraordinary Cornish home, is filled with Victorian treasures; great cabinets in the style of A.W. Pugin and tiles by Dresser. Ovenden has formed a remarkable collection of 19th century illustrated books; from design manuals such as Owen Jones's lavish *Grammer of Ornament* to classic fairy stories. Arthur Hughes is probably his favourite Victorian illustrator, but he is also passionate about the Moxon edition of Tennyson's poems (1857) illustrated by Millais and Rossetti, and the etchings of F.L. Griggs.

11

John Lefevre was headmaster of Barrow-in-Furness School of Art in the 1950s, an extremely erudite man, brilliant teacher and exceptional artist. Lefevre and Jim Sellars developed a rapport which was rewarding for both parties. He gave up the headmastership in order to paint full time and moved south to Verwood, which was then a small village on the edge of the New Forest. He lived on his own, he and his wife having separated when he decided to give up teaching. He stayed with the Sellars until he found a suitable property, spending many evenings talking about and discussing painting and art history. He lived in Menton in the South of France for a time; the works from this phase of his life being especially colourful. The title references Palmer's *Bright Cloud* but the colour owes something to Matisse.

12

In 1973, largely due to ill-health, Graham Arnold resigned all his teaching posts and moved to Devizes the following year to paint full-time. In 1975 Arnold became a founder member of the Brotherhood of Ruralists and his paintings still embody Ruralist thought. According to his wife, Ann Arnold, 'He creates whole worlds from contrasting dualities. Time itself is implied in a fading surface. The past and future are contained in the present of his paintings'. [43] Arnold derives this negation of time from the visionary naturalist writer Richard Jefferies, who has been of supreme importance to him since the late 1940s. It was Arnold's father, who worked for the Lutterworth Press, who introduced his son to Jefferies's intense vision of nature, his philosophy, his humanity, his love of solitude and his ability to be 'in the moment' have all shaped the artist's development:

> 'I cannot understand time. It is eternity now. I am in the midst of it. It is about me in the sunshine; I am in it, as the butterfly floats in the light-laden air. Nothing has to come; it is

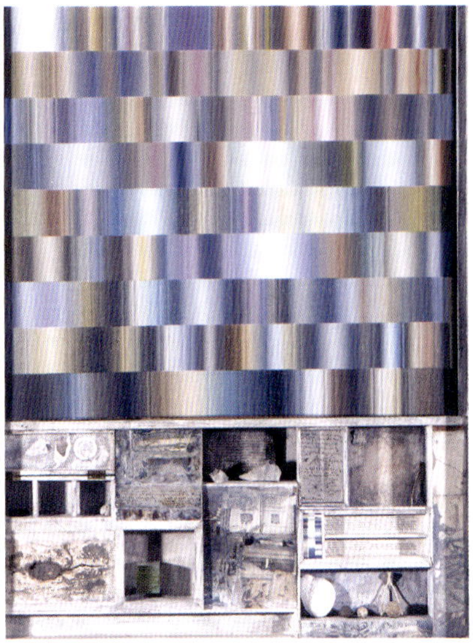

12. Graham Arnold (1932-)
Harmonies Poetiques et Religieuses III - Richard Jefferies, 1976; mixed media construction, 940 x 711 x 76 mm
Peter Nahum at the Leicester Galleries

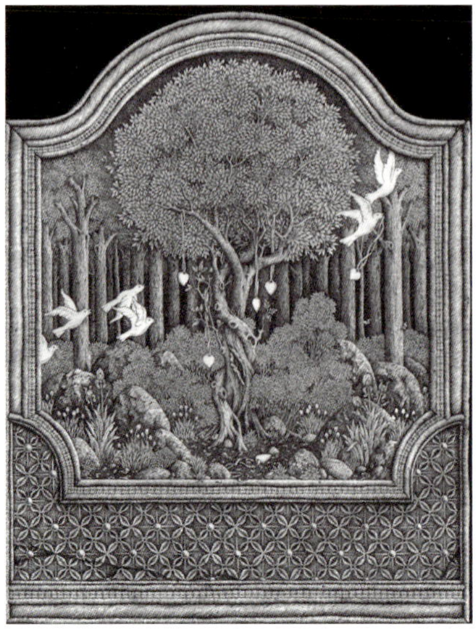

13. Brian Partridge (1953-)
Chanson de Matin, 1984
pen and ink, 340 x 275 mm
Graham Ovenden

> now. Now is eternity; now is the immortal life. Here this moment, by this tumulus, on earth, now; I exist in it. The years, the centuries, the cycles are absolutely nothing; it is only a moment since this tumulus was raised; in a thousand years more it will still be only a moment. To the soul there is no past and no future; all is and will be ever in now...Time has never existed, and never will; it is a purely artificial arrangement. It is eternity now, it always was eternity and always will be...There is no separation-no past; eternity, the Now is continuous. When all the stars have revolved they only produce Now again. The continuity of Now is forever'.[44]

Jefferies's musings take place at the foot of a 'grass-grown tumuli' (Jerfferies loved Liddington Hill, an Iron Age hill fort, that now looks down on Swindon; the Ruralists were naturally attracted to Silbury Hill, Wiltshire); he feels at that moment, enjoying the 'glory of the day', like the spirit of the man interred in the tumulus: 'I could understand and feel his existence the same as my own. He was as real to me two thousand years after interment as those I have seen in the body. The abstract personality of the dead seemed as existent as thought'.[45] In effect memory collapses time and the soul lives beyond time. Arnold, like Jefferies, understands the eternal, spiritual presence associated with the timeworn monument. One needs to look for signs and forms that communicate physical transience in Arnold's painted collages. Here we are faced 'with multiple infinites... unified into a greater whole'.[46] Arnold's love and technical understanding of music provides his point of departure, in both poetic and structural terms. He may enclose specific pictures, literary fragments and objects within a constructed framework to add a third dimension; the chalk-bleached landscape of Wiltshire lies behind this work, the countryside that possesses the spirit of Jefferies.

These chosen remains are deeply personal, only revealing their mysteries after intense perusal. His 'cabinet of secrets' locks away memories while simultaneously reliving them. Still-life paintings seem to hold more than the objects depicted; 'they are in fact deeply mysterious works fraught with emotive values. The same book, vase, crystal appears in numerous Arnold paintings... "Obsession in all things" (William Blake)'.[47] Arnold, who was taught by his father, was set to draw the same objects over and over again. The artist rediscovered this 'box of objects' after his father's death in 1971 and has subsequently used them as 'icons' and 'totems'; now Arnold arranges them in his own boxes.

As originally conceived *Harmonies Poetiques et Religieuses*, the name given by Liszt to ten piano pieces, was going to be a series of ten works, each one expressing a pattern of experience but at the same time dominated by a particular theme. Each work was to pay homage to a hero or heroine; only four were completed – Franz Liszt (I), John Ruskin (II), T.S. Eliot (IV) and Richard Jefferies. Arnold's grand plan was to hang all ten works as a 'glorious Garden of Remembrance, to the glory of the human spirit'.[48]

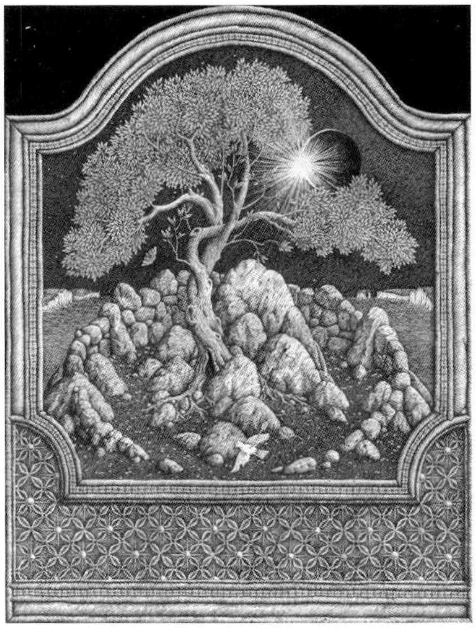

14. Brian Partridge (1953-)
Chanson de Nuit, 1984
pen and ink, 340 x 275 mm
Graham Ovenden

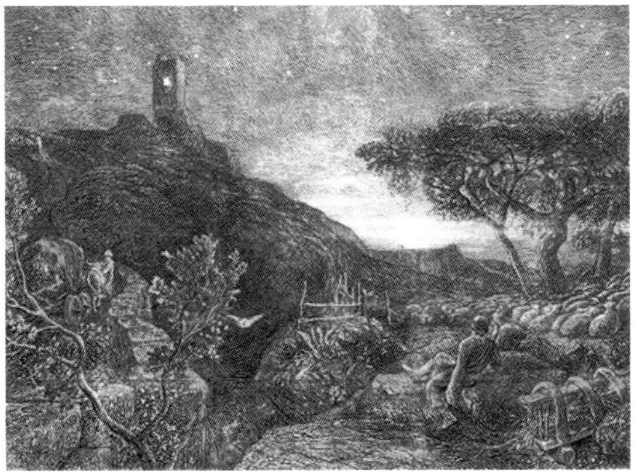

15. Samuel Palmer (1805-81)
The Lonely Tower, 1879
etching on paper, sixth and final state Edgar Holloway impression, 190 x 253 mm
Stuart M. Southall

13 - 14

Partridge began drawing in pen and ink in 1976 and has worked full-time as an artist/illustrator since 1988. He has exhibited extensively, at the Fine Art Society, Glasgow, Wraxall Gallery, London and Bath City Art Gallery. His work is associated with the Ruralists and there have been several collaborations with Graham Ovenden, *Alice in Wonderland*, a book of Acrostic Poems and a series of poetry broadsheets. Both these pieces were created for the 50th anniversary of the death of Elgar in 1984. (Brotherhood of Ruralists, *Salute to Elgar*, at the David Paul Gallery, Chichester).

15

Like its pendant *The Bellman*, this etching relates to one of the watercolours, for Leonard Valpy, illustrating Milton's *Il Penseroso* (lines 85-88):

> 'Or let my lamp at midnight hour,
> Be seen in some high lonely Tower,
> Where I may oft out-watch the Bear,
> With thrice-great Hermes...'

With the constellations of the Great Bear and the Heavenly Twins twinkling in the night-sky, two shepherds gaze across a chasm to a hilltop tower, illuminated by a light shining from an upper window. As Palmer explained:

> 'Here poetic loneliness has been attempted; not the loneliness of a desert but a secluded spot in a genial, pastoral country, enriched also by ancient relics, such as those so-called Druidic stones upon the distant hill. The constellation of the 'Bear' may help to explain that the building is the tower of *Il Penseroso*. Two shepherds, watching their flocks, speak together of the mysterious light above them.' [49]

Although A.H. Palmer declared his father was 'no antiquary', *The Lonely Tower* captures the 'pastoral antiquity' that pleased him. The tower may be based on the one at Leith Hill, Surrey that Palmer could see from his studio window, which lay close to the spot where the artist's son Thomas Moore Palmer had died; perhaps Palmer identified with Milton's lonely melancholic philosopher in his tower.

Edgar Holloway printed this edition of *The Lonely Tower* from the repaired cancelled plate by order of David Gould in 1973. Holloway, recognised as a fine etcher and master printer, spent much time and effort on the project, producing a few excellent prints.

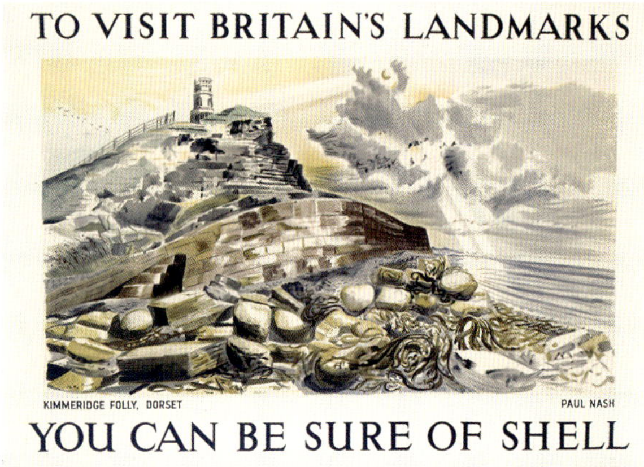

16. Paul Nash (1889-1946)
Kimmeridge Folly, Dorset, 1937, *Visit Britain's Landmarks*
Shell advertising campaign, colour lithograph
framed dimensions 795 x 1175 mm
Shell Art Collection

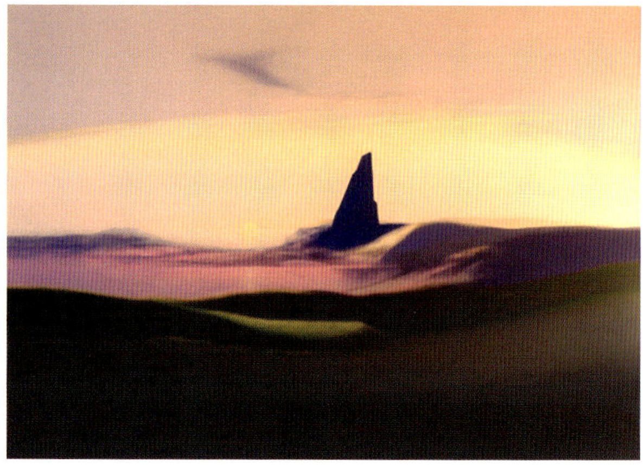

17. Graham Ovenden (1943-)
The Tower of Babel (The Sea Tower), 1984/5
oil on panel, 610 x 915 mm
Fred Olsen

16

In 1935, at the invitation of John Betjeman, Nash compiled the *Dorset Shell Guide*, writing its text, taking photographs and making watercolours. He visited Corfe Castle, Maiden Castle, Badbury Rings, the Cerne Abbas giant, the petrified forest at Lulworth and Kimmeridge Bay; all 'ancient lanscapes'. The design of *Kimmeridge Folly* echoes Palmer's *The Lonely Tower*, with the terrain falling away sharply on the right; one can imagine Milton's philosopher looking out over the sea. The theme of the tower was potent in Romantic literature from Robert Browning's *Childe Rowland to the Dark Tower Came* (1855) to *Jane Eyre's* (1847) 'mad woman in the tower'. In Rowland's case it is more important to travel than to arrive; a fitting assocation for a travel poster.

During the 1930s, the Shell oil company took the whole of the British Isles as inspiration for one of its most effective advertising campaigns, 'Visit Britain'. Innovative young artists were commissioned to produce eye-catching posters of the unusual landmarks, historic sights and inspiring landscapes of England, Wales, Scotland and Northern Ireland.

17

This striking image of a stark, angular shape in the smooth folds of nature has an explicit biblical meaning, the fragmentation of the human race caused by 'speaking in many tongues':

> 'And they said, Go to, let us build us a city and a tower, whose top may reach unto heaven; let us make us a name, lest we be scattered abroad upon the face of the earth' (Genesis, Chapter XI).

It was painted for *The Continuing Tradition: an Exhibition of Biblical Subjects* in 1985. Ovenden would return to this symbol of 'over-reaching confusion' several times; 'blank, windowless monoliths rising on green but barren coasts'.[50] Northrop Moore sees these 'unholy erections', 'faceless monuments' as Ovenden's attempt to integrate the sea into his landscapes. But Wainwright perceives the true purpose to be that 'exquisite melancholy prompted by the contemplation of ruins'.[51] Ovenden is referencing the Claudian motif of the classical ruins in Arcadia, the abandoned and forgotten buildings of a lost civilisation, the Ozymandian cliché that the mightiest works of man decay:

> 'My name is Ozymandias, King of Kings:
> Look upon my works, ye Mighty, and despair!"
> Nothing beside remains. Round the decay
> Of that colossal wreck, boundless and bare
> The lone and level sands stretch far away.' (Shelley)

Nature encroaches and will eventually reclaim man's efforts; Griggs's *Launds* (1928, Cat. 87) also explores this theme. While Griggs evoked 'some sadness for beauty departed', Sutherland and Piper's images of war-ruined churches were to remind the British people what they were defending. The tower is also reminiscent of *The Obelisk* (1979), the eye-catcher on the horizon, a common 17th and 18th century ploy in the landscaped garden. These works hark back to Palmer's *Lonely Tower* and Milton's *Il Peneroso*. Ovenden's 'conception of Babel is both mystical and primeval and though undoubtedly rooted in the dis-

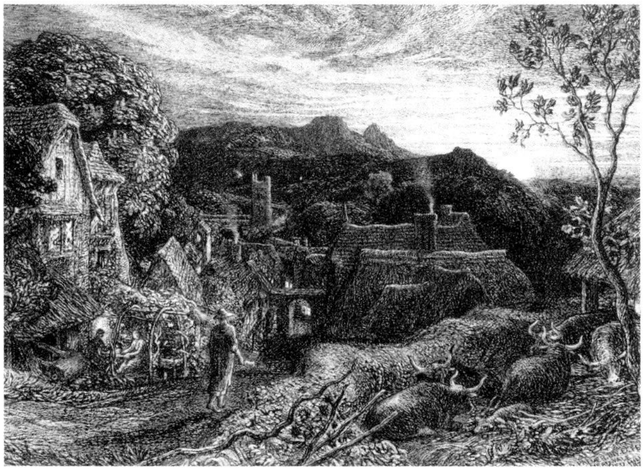

18. Samuel Palmer (1805-1881)
The Bellman from Il Penseroso, 1879
etching on paper, 167 x 233 mm
Stuart M. Southall

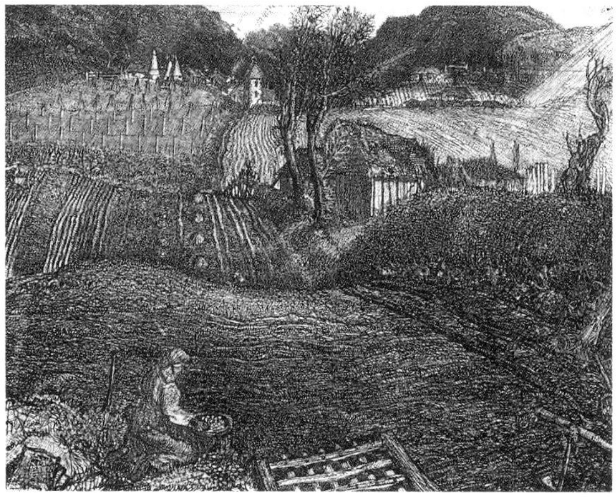

19. Graham Vivien Sutherland (1903-80)
Village, 1925
etching on paper, second state, 175 x 225 mm
Stuart M. Southall

tant past, also has a singularly modern aspect'.[52] Ovenden explored the associations of the monolith in *Spring Morning Wiltshire* (1984, Cat. 108) and *Sentinels of Silbury* (1982, Cat. 100) is similar in character.

The Pastoral Idyll

18

Following a commission from Leonard Valpy, Palmer began a series of watercolours depicting subjects from Milton's *L'Allegro* and *Il Pensieroso*. *The Bellman* relates compositionally to one of these watercolours, illustrating a passage from *Il Penseroso* (lines 83-4):

> 'The bellman's drowsy charm,
> To bless the door from nightly harm'.

In 1878, three years before his death, Palmer conceived two new plates from Milton, *The Bellman* and its companion *The Lonely Tower*. He hoped to leave 'a set making a book, a compact block of work, which I might fain hope might live when I am with the fallen leaves'.[53] Palmer was 're-approaching etching not from the line-engraving side, but wholly from the racy and picturesque'.[54] Clearly Palmer was trying to rekindle the ecstatic vision of his Shoreham days:

> 'It is breaking out of village-fever long after contact – a dream of that genuine village where I mused away some of my best years, designing what nobody would care for... There were the rumbling mill, and haunted mansion in a shadowy paddock...the vicarage with its learned traditions; and Wordsworth brought to memory every three hours, by 'the crazy old church clock, And the bewilder'd chimes'. [55]

Heading towards a village nestling in a valley, passing figures cocooned under an arbour and 'picturesque cattle', the bellman tolls his bell as the setting sun disappears behind the distant hills. Palmer was aiming for:

> 'Seclusion without desolation is aimed at here, and darkness without horror. While light enough is left to show that a village is completely sheltered, and that the ground heaves well, and is richly wooded, increasing gloom sometimes enforces the sentiment of exuberance by giving more play to the imagination. If, as Dr Johnson says, "there is always some melancholy in his mirth", there is certainly no wretchedness in Milton's melancholy.' [56]

19

Village is the first in a series of six intensely pastoral works that Sutherland produced between 1925 and 1927. The densely worked and reworked plate clearly shows Sutherland's debt to Palmer, who broke all the technical rules imposed on the students at Goldsmiths'. The plate is covered, edge-to-edge, and 'overbitten', which Sutherland's teachers considered to be sins. The village set in a valley recalls *The Bellman*, while the girl with a basket of potatoes echoes Palmer's sepia drawing *Girl in a Ploughed Field* (*c.*1826, Tate Britain), which had astonished Sutherland 'with its total disregard for conventional composition'.[57] The land undulates, accentuated by the sharp

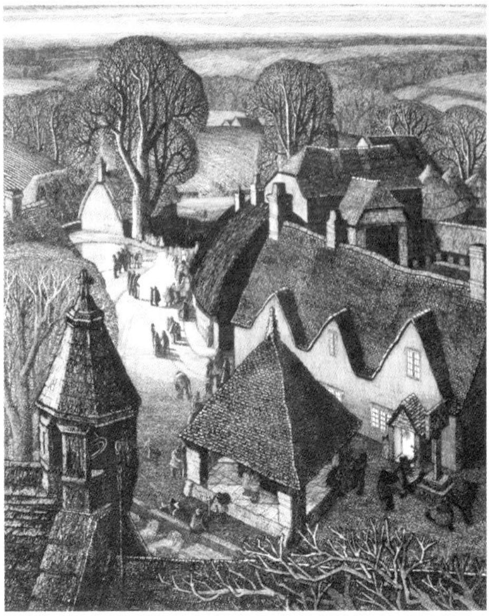

20. Robin Tanner (1904-1988)
Christmas, 1929
etching on paper, 335 x 280 mm
Stuart M. Southall

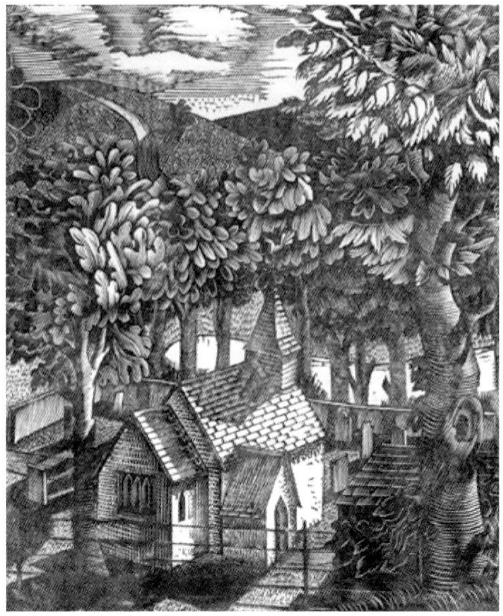

21. Eric Ravilious (1903-1942)
Church under a Hill, 1926/27
wood engraving, 165 x 140 mm
Stuart M. Southall

perspective and resembles a closely woven pattern. The sentiment, of spiritual peace, echoes Jean-Francois Millet's *Angelus* (1857-59, Musee d'Orsay, Paris), an artist much admired by Sutherland.

Village was based on the scenery around Cudham, Kent, but with elements from Warning Camp in Sussex.

20

Although clearly influenced by Palmer's vision, Tanner claimed that he was 'bowled over' and 'permanently damaged' by Griggs's 'marvellous realisation of stone and water, foliage and sky, and the intense feeling for Cotswold England'.[58] A native of northwest Wiltshire, Tanner 'craved for my small enclosed landscape, ancient, deep and sheltered, and rich with foliage and ferns...Always my sights were fixed on the hedgerows of home, the great cruciform barns and the conical topped ricks standing on saddlestones, and the old footpaths over fields of flowers'.[59] The Class of 21 adopted Tanner when he joined Goldsmiths' as a teacher-trainer in 1924; he obtained his art education from evening classes whilst teaching at local schools to support himself.

An idyllic vision of life in the English village, *Christmas* was based on studies made from the church tower of Castle Combe in Wiltshire, while the bell-turret, pond and thatched cottage were taken from Biddestone, near Chippenham. Tanner, surrounded by the sleeping villagers, remembered 'it was an eerie feeling working through the small hours in that empty village'.[60]

21

Ravilious made his reputation as a wood engraver before he became well known as a painter. This traditional printing method, revived by the Arts and Crafts movement, was fashionable in the 1920s, alongside the etching revival; Ravilious became the acknowledged master of the medium. Wood engraving facilitated the accurate reproduction of an artist's work in large quantities without loss of quality. Pioneered by Thomas Bewick (1753-1828), whose authority was long lasting, Ravilious also responded to the visionary spirit of Blake and Palmer; Blake's illustrations to Thornton's *The Pastorals of Virgil* were wood engravings. *Church under a Hill* is especially Palmeresque. The church framed by trees both embodies the belief in nature as God's creation and recognises the sacred grove of trees as the origins of Gothic architecture. The subject is a mystery, though the setting and building suggests Lullington Church, south of Wilmington, East Sussex. Equally Palmeresque are Ravilious's 42 wood engravings for the *Kynoch Press Notebook* of 1933. These delightful vignettes of rural life stand among the best of his engraved work.

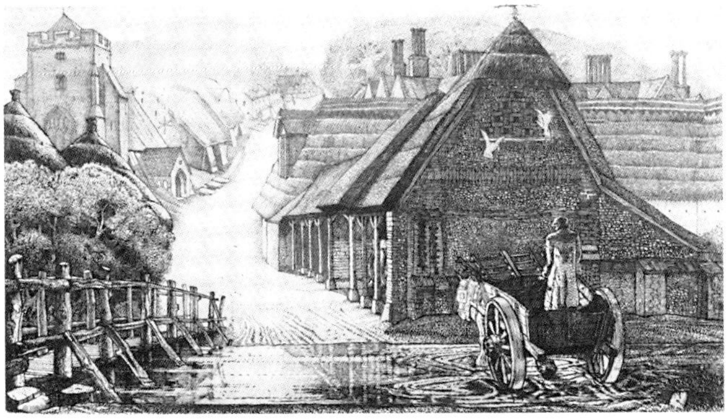

22. Joseph Webb (1908-1962)
Streamend, 1936
etching on paper, 175 x 307 mm
Stuart M. Southall

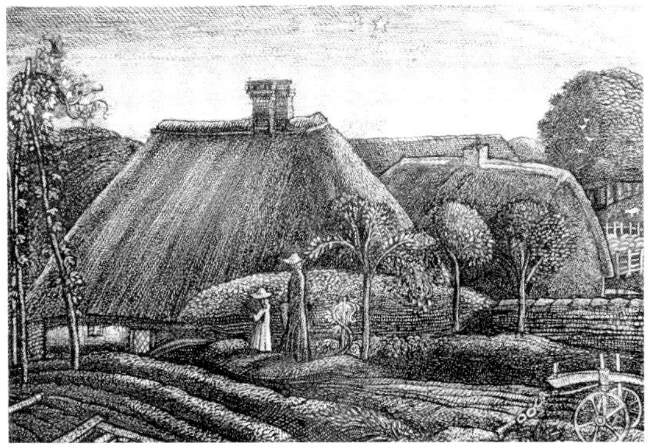

23. Graham Vivien Sutherland (1903-80)
Lammas, 1926
etching on paper, 110 x 162 mm
Stuart M. Southall

22

Although a contemporary of Drury, Sutherland and Tanner, Webb was not a Goldsmiths' student. After attending the Chiswick School of Art in 1922-23, he spent four years at the Hospitalfield Academy, Arbroath. The market for etchings, which peaked 1925-27, was already in decline when Webb came to the scene. The market declined sharply following the Wall Street Crash of 1929. In 1930, the year Webb was elected Associate of the Royal Society of Painter-Etchers and Engravers, he established himself at Bent Tree Studio at Harrow-on-the-Hill. Here he conceived many 'visionary-mystical' subjects: *Stoke Poges* (1931, Cat. 126). Despite solo exhibitions at Colnaghi's (1933) and Ryman's Galleries, Oxford (1934), commissions were scarce and print sales diminished. *Streamend* marks Webb's return to printmaking after a gap of three years. A romantic interpretation of the ford at Water End, a small village on the banks of the River Lea between Wheathampstead and Welwyn Garden City, Webb improved the composition by importing both the farm and the church. The serenity of this image, with its hovering doves, belies the growing uncertainty, with war in Europe looming. [61]

23

Lammas Day is the 1st August, when loaves made from the first ripe grain were consecrated. The print repeats motifs found in *St Mary's Hatch* and *Cray Fields*; the evening star, ascending doves and the rounded forms of thatched cottages. The sentiment is overtly Christian: Sutherland was to convert to Catholicism in the same year. There is a pervading sense of contentment in these works, of well-earned rest at the end of a fruitful day. They convey the unchanging experience of life in the countryside, the generations that have worked the land and the way in which the seasons govern such a way of life. These images were popular; by 1925 Sutherland had been elected associate of the Royal Society of Painter-Etchers and Engravers and was making about £700 a year from the sale of prints and drawings.

Griggs invited Sutherland and Drury to Chipping Campden in November 1926, where *Lammas* was printed at Dover's House Press. Sutherland admitted: 'It was Griggs as an enthusiast and technician from whom perhaps we gained most. A master printer of the copper plate, with infinite knowledge and patience, he had a palm as delicate as gossamer'.[62]

24

Badmin was not directly associated with the Class of 21 but he did benefit from the etching revival, being introduced in 1928 to the Twenty One Gallery, the leading dealers in the vibrant print market. The Twenty One Gallery published the work of Sutherland, Drury and Griggs. Badmin had his first one man show in 1930, by which time he had produced seventeen etchings, his preferred method. The years 1930 and 1931 produced his finest work, 'his craftsmanship coming closest to the idyllic and poetic vision of the English pastoral tradition'. [63] Badmin was clearly influenced by the 'Palmerists', combining 'design, craftsmanship and romance':

> 'Some of the most satisfying English engravings, particularly etch-

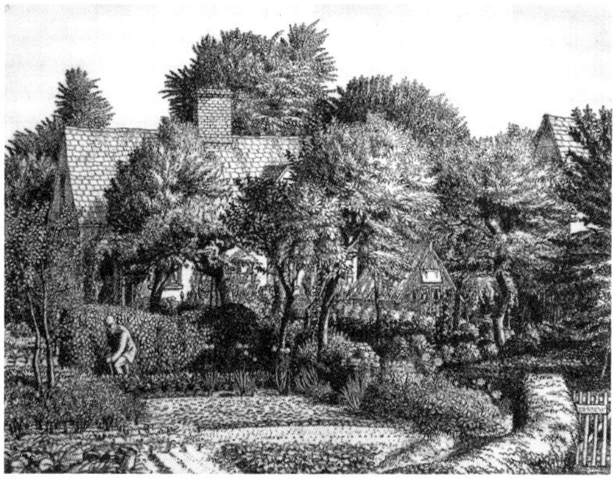

24. Stanley Roy Badmin (1906-1989)
Darby and Joan Cottage
etching on paper, 124 x 165 mm
Stuart M. Southall

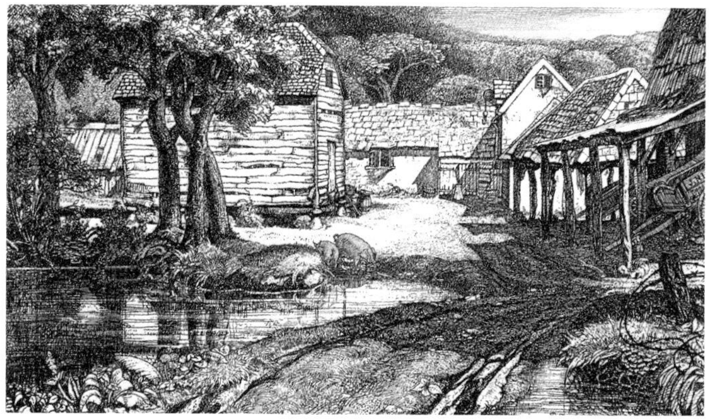

25. Paul Drury (1903-1987)
Nicol's Farm, 1925
etching on paper, 111 x 192 mm
Stuart M. Southall

ings, fall into the class of romantic illustrations, as if his interest in craftsmanship caused the artist to brood upon the subject with a desire to get out of it all that it contains of poetical suggestion. One might almost say that Samuel Palmer invented the type of the best English etching. The most accomplished contemporary artist in the kind is Mr F.L. Griggs RA...'Potato Clamps, Kent' by Mr S.R. Badmin is a characteristic example'. [64]

Beetles considers Badmin 'closer to the primitive vision of Samuel Palmer, since his etchings are more deeply rooted in the earthy humanity of the countryside...Badmin's peopled drawings give life to village green and country seats alike'. [65] This 'human touch' can be seen in *Darby and Joan Cottage*. This was Badmin's last but one etching and it was not published as a full edition in 1935. With the collapse of the market, Badmin forsook etching for illustration; 'he had only eight productive years, but they had produced a distinctive *oeuvre* full of interest and small-scale fascinations'.[66]

25

Paul Drury, whose father was the eminent Victorian sculptor, Alfred Drury, was one of the leading figures in the 1920s etching revival and later the Principal of Goldsmiths' College and President of the Royal Society of Painter-Etchers and Engravers. As students Drury and Sutherland paid a number of visits to Drury's grandmother's house at Hayling Island. Adjacent to this property was Nicol's Farm, depicted by Drury as picturesquely ramshackle. The etching was printed during his stay, in the company of Sutherland, with Griggs, who wanted to use their work for demonstrating his printing techniques: 'I hope you will bring all your recent plates and tell Sutherland I hope to see all his since *Village*'. [67]

26

Although John Elwyn chose to live in Hampshire for over forty years, Wales remained his spiritual 'home'. But it was not the mountains of Snowdonia or the romantic coastal scenery of his native land that fired his imagination, rather it was the isolated farming communities of south Cardiganshire. His paintings reflect his Welsh heritage, his sense of identity and his love of narrative:

> '...for centuries these elements have traditionally been the raw material of the poet in the Welsh bardic tradition. He has always drawn from his own observations, experiences and memories – inspired by a love of the landscape, a love of painting and an empathy with the Welsh people, their language and long-established social traditions, religious and secular. The Welsh have a word to convey this affection for a community, the love of a locality and regional character, "Brogarwch"'. [68]

In 1938 Elwyn was awarded a Royal Exhibition Scholarship to study for three years at the Royal College of Art; Sydney Morse Brown, the Principal of Carmarthen School of School, where Elwyn had begun his education, looked forward to his protégé initiating a Welsh 'school' of painters. With his education disrupted by the war, Elwyn faced a tribunal for objection and was committed to land work and food production. 1941 found him in Cardiff,

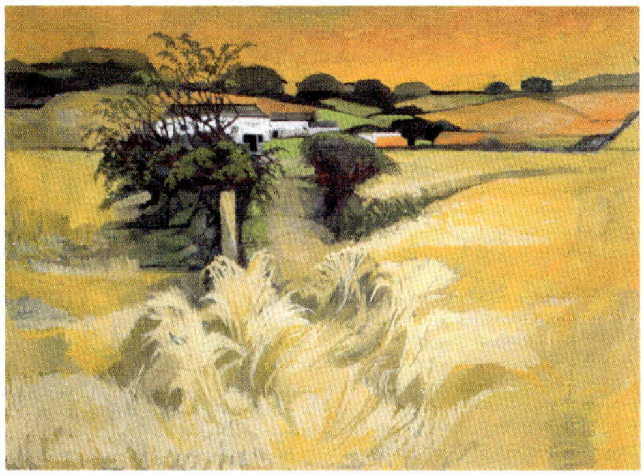

26. John Elwyn (1916-1997)
Entrance to a Farm
oil on canvas, 390 x 540 mm
Robert Meyrick

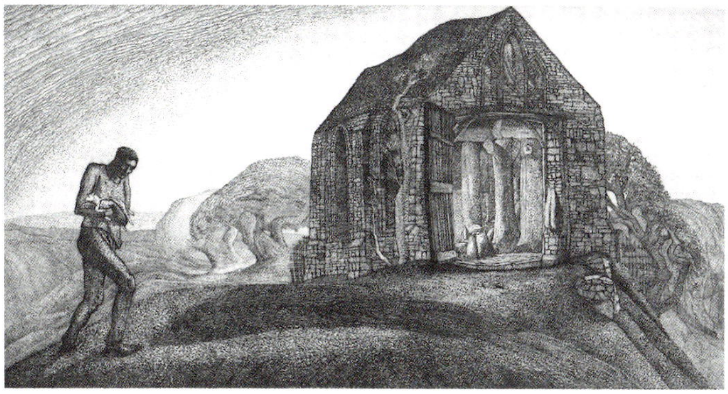

27. Joseph Webb (1908-1962)
The Shepherd's Haven, 1929
etching on paper, 264 x 136 mm
The School of Art, University of Wales, Aberystwyth

where he was able to sign up for evening life classes at Cardiff College of Art under Ceri Richards, who was Head of Painting from 1940 to 1944. By 1946 he was able to resume his studies at the RCA but he was now a very different person. He kept abreast of the latest developments in English art, as well as studying works by his favourite French artists, Bonnard, Cezanne and Vuillard but 'current styles and fashions for its own sake did not appeal to me. I wanted to discover an area that would preoccupy me in a visual and possibly literary sense, of my own choice – in other words I was searching for a reason for painting'.[69] He secured his financial position by accepting a post at Portsmouth College of Art in 1948, moving to Winchester College of Art in 1953.

Elwyn's landscapes of the meadows, dairy farms and barns of the Teifi and Ceri valleys and upland rural areas of Cardiganshire record the daily activities of rural life, as they vary from season to season and at different times of the day. These 'farmyard' paintings occupied him for much of the 1950s; 'labour is seen as pure and dignified, the real hardship of working the land is overlooked. The commonly perceived view of the exposed, cold and wet Welsh countryside is rarely depicted; their bright colours and almost Mediterranean light evoke a continental landscape similar to the paintings of Corsica by John Minton in the late 1940s'.[70] By the late 1950s Elwyn was concentrating on pure landscape, enriched by strong colour and the impression of bright sunlight, while the countryside, organised and divided into fields by hedgerows and stone walls, appealed to his sense of design. Titles betray his fascination with symbolic colour: *Harvest Yellow* (1953), *Yellow Silence* (1957), *Carmarthenshire Green* (1957) and *The Red Evening* (1960).

27

Influenced by Griggs, Webb frequently etched ecclesiastical buildings in landscapes, conveying an atmosphere of spirituality and rest. Webb was drawn to Eastern religions, astrology, mysticism and the occult. Edgar Holloway recalled his interest in Theosophy, which has its origins in 'Ancient Wisdom' religions. *Shepherd's Haven* is an idealistic view of man's place in nature, resonating with the pastoral poetry of Blake and Palmer. A shepherd cradling a lamb approaches an ecclesiastical looking barn, its welcoming interior glowing with a positively religious light. The Christian symbolism, the Good Shepherd and Lamb of God, is explicit, God as guardian of his people, rescuing strayed sheep. But its earlier title, *The Infinite Compassion*, also alludes to Buddhist teachings of warmth, mercy and inner peace, beliefs also shared with Theosophy.[71]

28

Minton was a leading figure in the second generation of Neo-Romantics as much for his life-style as his art. His background was tragic, with his eldest brother institutionalised and his younger brother killed in the D-Day landings. Minton arrived at the St John's Wood School of Art in 1935 aged 18, where the Principal, Patrick Millard, passed on his enthusiasm for Palmer's prints and drawings. The young Minton was encouraged to emulate 'his mazey linear style'.[72] The following year Michael Ayrton enrolled as a fellow student and the two became firm friends. A trip to the 1936 Surrealist Exhibition confirmed that the way forward was 'through the depiction of

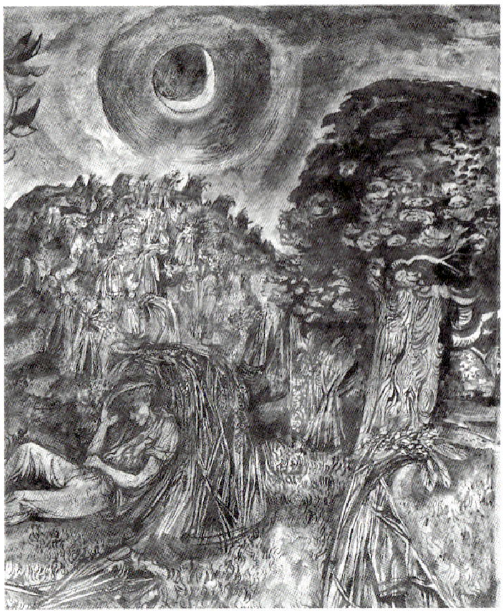

28. John Minton (1917-1957)
Landscape with Harvester Resting, c. 1944
ink and wash with body colour on paper,
480-410 mm; Pallant House Gallery, on long term loan from Dr John Birch

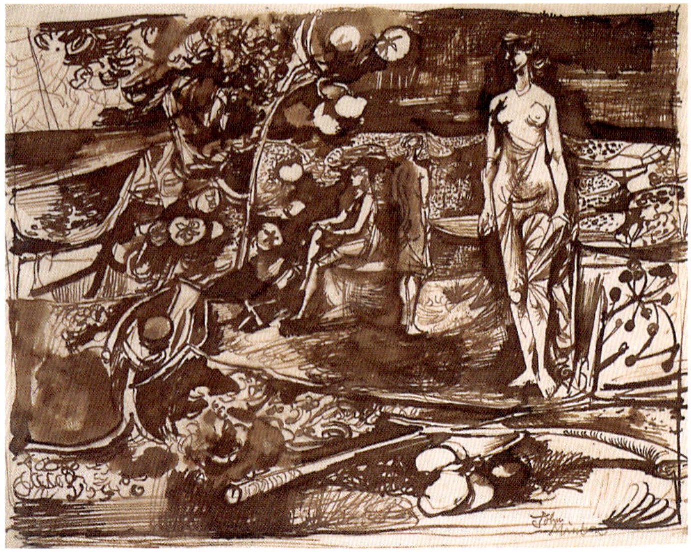

29. John Minton (1917-1957)
Figures in a Landscape, c. 1945
pen and ink and sepia wash on paper
255 x 330 mm
Peter Nahum at the Leicester Galleries

human emotions and people in strange and dramatic settings'.[73] 1938 saw them both in Paris, seeking direction; they fell under the sway of the Parisian Neo-Romantic movement, which numbered Christian Berard (1902-49), Eugene Berman (1899-1972) and Pavel Tchelitchew (1898-1957):

> 'Scampering back to London as the war broke out these young men had packed in their mental luggage the tilted perspectives and dramatic lighting of de Chirico, the nostalgic and sweet harmonies of Picasso's Blue and Pink periods, and the stagy Tableaux of the Parisian Neo-Romantics'. [74]

Minton only served briefly in the Pioneer Corps, until 'discharged for homosexuality'. By 1943 Minton was sharing digs with Robert Colquhoun and Robert MacBryde, protégés of Peter Watson, who financed the avant-garde journal *Horizon*. It was at this point that Minton rediscovered Palmer; Rothenstein observed:

> 'For Minton the example of Palmer was particularly inspiring. Without it one of his finest works, *Surrey Landscape* (in Indian ink and wash, of 1944...) would hardly be imaginable. It is remote from a slavish imitation: more precise, muscular and altogether crisper than a Palmer, yet it is imbued with much of Palmer's spirit. It could hang without discredit in a collection of Palmer's; indeed in my opinion it is superior to most of his work except that of the sublime 'Visionary Years' of Shoreham.' [75]

Ayrton declared that 'Minton is English and Palmer shines through him but his work is personal none the less'.[76] *Landscape with Harvester Resting* may be Minton's most 'Palmeresque' work, featuring a crescent moon, of which he joked 'Moons are in! Half-moons are really selling this year'.[77] Other works in ink and wash show the same artistic debt: *The Orchard* (1945); *Road to the Sea* (1943); *English Landscape* (1944?); *Recollections of Wales* (1944); *Harvest Moon* (1944) and *Summer Landscape* (1945). These works relate more closely to Palmer's early drawings than to his later prints. *Early Morning* (1825) and *The Valley Thick with Corn* (1825) were reproduced in *Horizon*. But as Martin observes, Minton's lyrical landscapes peopled with young males speak of his homoerotic urges. Minton is closer to Calvert than Palmer in his frank paganism; there is also a nervous energy agitating his drawings that is totally absent from Palmer's hushed valleys. But he was not seeking the sinister in nature, like Sutherland and Nash; his vision was elegiac:

> 'The physical aspect of things has always been of great importance to me and with it the touching and melancholic impermanence of all physical beauty – a sort of hopeless aching nostalgia.' [78]

29

Minton was clearly influenced by Sutherland, acquiring a taste for spiky forms and battered roots but he used these motifs in a more decorative way. His figures are effortlessly drawn. The drooping branch that dominates the foreground reappears in *Withered Plants and Landscape* (1947); its theme of tomato plants was taken from Picasso and Colquhoun but the mood of disconsolation is typically Minton. Minton might

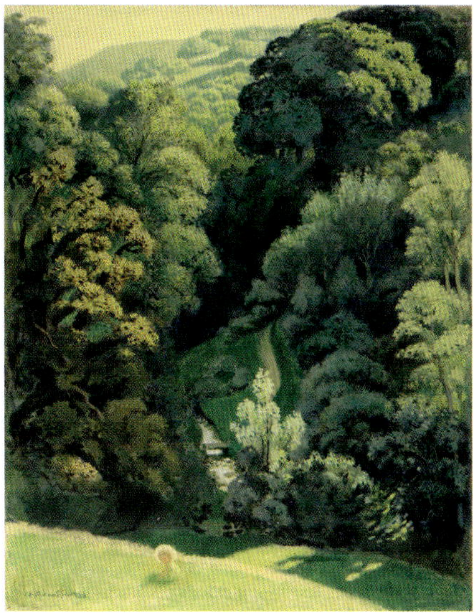

31. Walford Graham Robertson
(1866-1948)
Under Hindhead (in Fairyland)
oil on canvas, 1275 x 1017 mm
Southampton City Art Gallery,
presented by Mrs Ernest Milton (1953)

have been no more than a facile pasticheur, 'passing from one borrowed style to the next…but he managed to assimilate each new discovery into his own sweet-sad vision: softening the roughness of Sutherland and Picasso and diluting the spiritual fervour of Palmer and Blake; filtering them through his formidable charm so that all his works, from whatever period, are recognisably his own'.[79] Sadly Minton was to commit suicide in 1957.

30

Alf Stockham (1933-)
Hop Garden, 1984
etching on paper, 124 x 210 mm
David Inshaw

Stockham learned a variety of printing techniques at Camberwell School of Art; this etching harks back to his childhood in Surrey. Stockham recalls hop picking in the Wey Valley, around Farnham, Surrey, as a child during the war (he would have been 9 or 10 at the time) and in his late teens he worked in the hop fields. This work is highly nostalgic; both in subject and technique it is reminiscent of Palmer's Shoreham period works.

31

Graham Robertson is best remembered as the author of *Time Was* (1931) and as the effete young man, aged 26, in a long black coat immortalised by John Singer Sargent in 1894. M.H. Spielman summed him up in the *Magazine of Art*, December 1899: 'Of great natural ability, he is a man of high-cultivation… Oil painting, watercolour, decoration, theatrical designing, black and white, posterwork…portraiture, figure painting, landscape, flowers- he has practised all and is at ease with all, and invests every work of his with a charm so personal and infectious'. Of his illustrative work, the best known is Robertson's frontispiece for *Wind in the Willows* by Kenneth Graham published in 1908.

Robertson's weekends were spent at 'Sandhills', Witley, a rather charming Queen Anne house that had been the haven of William and Helen Allingham until 1888. The Surrey village of Witney has long been associated with artists, notably Myles Birket Foster; such was its charm that Robertson made 'Sandhills' his permanent home in 1896. His London friends readily paid him visits; Robert Melville, an associate of the Glasgow Boys, was so enchanted by the place that when Robertson bought a nearby farmhouse, 'Redland', Melville and his wife rented it. The two artists worked side by side, forming a deep friendship cut short by Melville's untimely death in 1903 having contracted typhoid. Deeply affected, Robertson lost the motivation to paint but to entertain Melville's young daughter, Binkie, Robertson invented stories of elves and fairies that inhabited the nearby fields and woods. His imagination fuelled, Robertson began to write verses and plays for children, his graceful, boldly coloured, illustrations appealing to all ages. Robertson conjured up an imaginative land for Binkie's fourth birthday; treated to an elfin party in the woods at dusk, in a glade lit by coloured lights and exotic fruits and flowers. The child was entranced and convinced of the existence of the 'little folk'. This was the genesis of *Pinkie and the Fairies*, a Christmas play that also drew on local legends and folklore. In 1908 his fantasy was transformed into a full-length play, under the encouragement of the great impresario Herbert Beerbohm Tree, with Ellen Terry taking a leading role. With an unrivalled cast the production

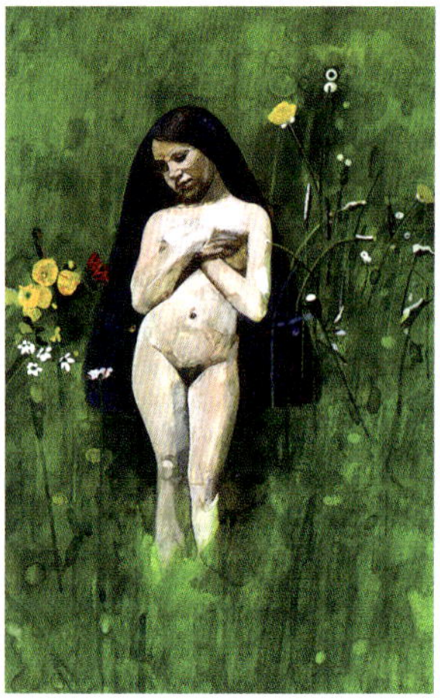

32. Peter Blake (1932-)
Fairy, 1972-76
watercolour on paper
209 x 133 mm
Graham Ovenden

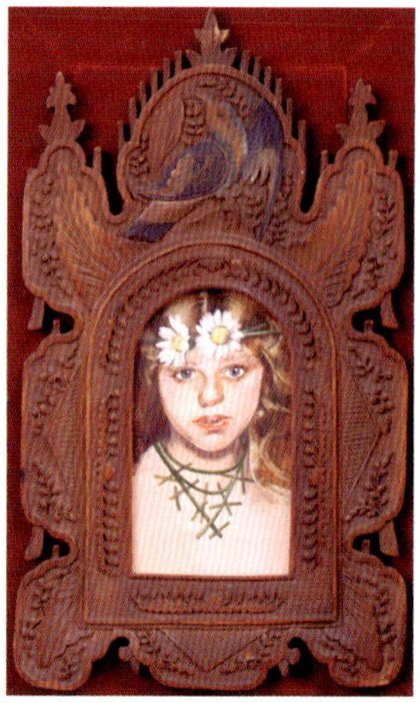

33. Peter Blake (1932-)
Daisy Fairy, 1981-2
oil on board, 117 x 65 mm
Victorian Gallery, Bath
purchased 2007 with the aid of the Art Fund
the MLA/V&A Purchase Grant Fund
and the Friends of the Victoria Art Gallery
(Shown Bath only)

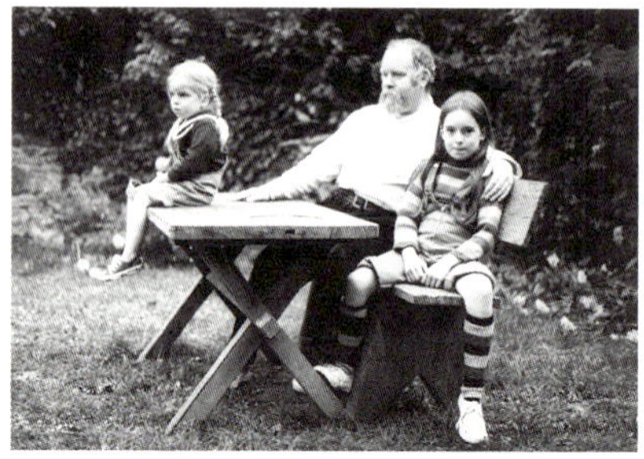

33a. Peter Blake and daughters, Juliet Liberty and Daisy

was a resounding success; it was rerun the following Christmas and in subsequent years *Pinkie and the Fairies* toured the country.

Robertson returned to painting, *Under Hindhead* being typical, with his juvenile model posed in a heavily wooded landscape, the small child overwhelmed by nature. Evidently the idea was to convey the massive, ageless dignity of the great woods and the insignificance of the 'human interest'. Hindhead, near Witney, the famous 'top of the hill' near the Devil's Punch Bowl, an area of outstanding natural beauty, provides the setting. The First World War shattered Robertson's idyllic world; but he lived on at 'Sandhills', in his 'safe haven', until his death aged 82.

32

This fairy belongs to the 'full-blooded', fleshly type that Blake produced in the early 1980s.

33

Blake produced a series of 'bread and butter' fairies but although designed to be money making he painted them with his usual care, affection and imagination. They are exquisite and jewel-like, with each work featuring the head of a single fairy in an elaborate frame. Blake was consciously attempting to revive the appreciation of picture frames, which he collected (the Pre-Raphaelites had designed their own). *Flora-Fairy Child* (1977, private collection) typifies the type, which was derived from a magazine picture of a model coincidentally called Florence; she is encased in an Italianate frame to reflect her supposed Roman lineage. The effect is reminiscent of an icon. *Daisy Fairy* (Blake's second daughter was named Daisy) is also based on a magazine picture. She has the doe eyes and luscious 'bee-stung' lips that Blake favoured, his sexy girl-woman, painted with realism reminiscent of Hans Holbein or John Everett Millais. The carved frame is Asiatic in style; the necklace of daisy stalks or grasses being more homely.

34

Nicholas Usherwood encapsulates Anne Arnold's work:

> 'Ann Arnold is an intuitive painter who works in the tradition of artists inspired by the poetry of the English landscape. The spirituality of places is always present in her work. She paints about her feelings towards people and places with an intensity which recalls William Blake's illustrations to Thornton's *Virgil* or Samuel Palmer's paintings of the Shoreham period. There is also a sense, often present in her work, of fragile balance between individual existence and the outside world.' [80]

This work is based on a real hill that rose up behind the Arnold's home, 'Pentre', in Shropshire; they allowed it to become a sanctuary for wild animals. Two amiable donkeys lived on the hill. The central motif of this work, a white donkey, is often mistaken for a unicorn, symbolic of chastity and purity. The unicorn can be found in medieval art as a guardian of the Tree of Life or alongside

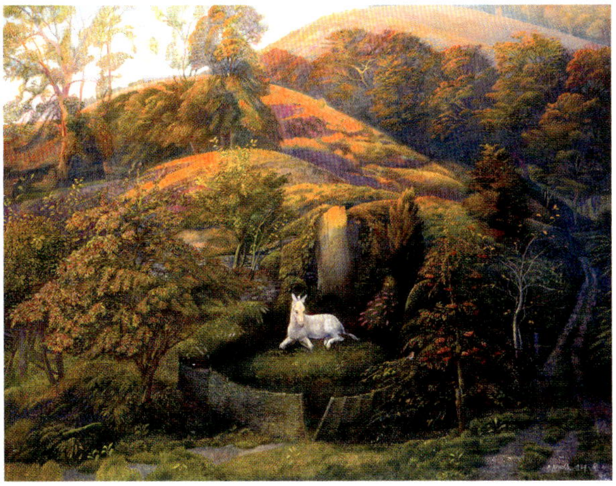

34. Anne Arnold (1936-)
The Sanctuary, 1989
oil on canvas, 720 x 915 mm
Peter Nahum at the Leicester Galleries

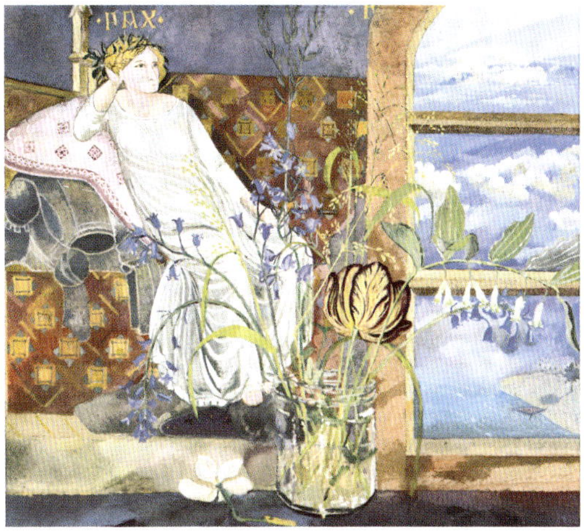

35. Diana Howard [Morley] (1947-)
Peace; Flowers for Ambrogio Lorenzetti oil on board, 330 x 407 mm
Diana Morley

the Virgin Mary in the *hortus conclusus* or enclosed garden. This legendary magical animal is easily associated with the fragility of nature and human existence; although in a safe haven Ann's white donkey has a tense pose, with its legs tucked underneath its body. Usherwood would see this as adding a 'pervading sense of fatalism'.

35

Diana Howard studied at Sutton and Epsom Schools of Art and the Royal Academy Schools under Peter Greenham until 1971. Howard was a founder member of the Broadheath Brotherhood, seen as a precursor of the Brotherhood of Ruralists and has exhibited with them. Her paintings of the 1970s have a dark intensity and mystery, with a preference for medieval subjects. This work is a tribute to the early Renaissance Sienese artist Lorenzetti (*c*.1290-c.1348) and is therefore in effect a Pre-Raphaelite work. An early interest in the poems of Dante and later with Celtic Mythology and the theme of the Holy Grail, has led more recently to an interest in Eastern Mysticism: 'These are some of the ingredients that make her vision such a personal and informed one and give her work its quiet but intense spiritual charge'.[81] The peaceful sentiment expressed in this work again suggests nature as respite or haven from the rigours of daily life.

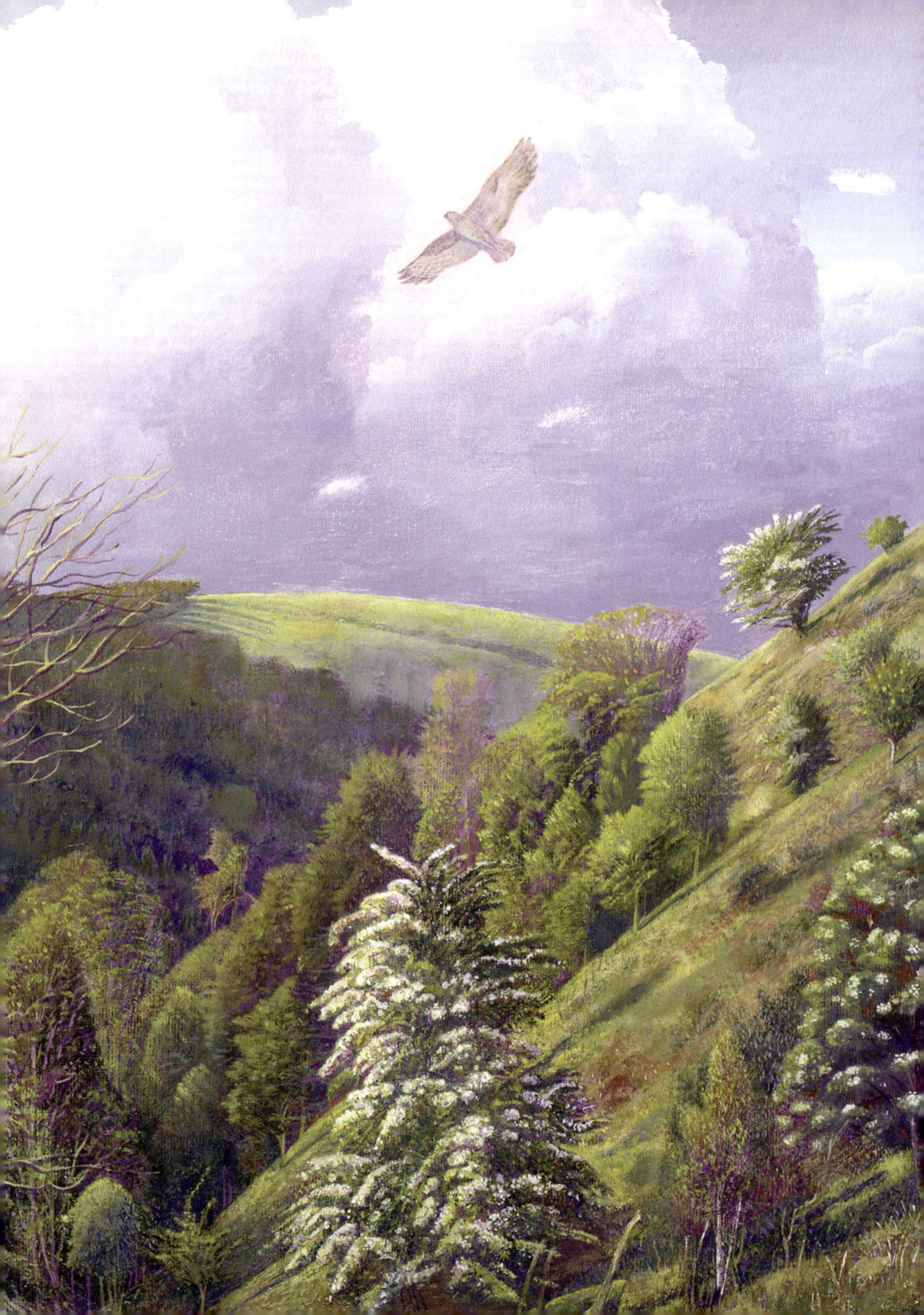

In Search of England

We all have a vision of 'England'; the village, the pub, the thatched cottage with the roses round the door and the village green which on Sundays hosts the cricket match. It is a cliché exploited by the media, from BBC Radio Four's *The Archers* to *Midsommer Murders*. Yet it is still highly persuasive; at the weekends David Inshaw and his friend Alf Stockham would leave their flat in Clifton, Bristol, to go in 'Search of England'. It was often to be found in Dorset, especially at Burton Bradstock, which constantly wins the prettiest village award; Burton Bradstock is everything you imagine an English village should be, though the idyll is somewhat marred by the nearby caravan park. Real life is ever encroaching on Arcadia. This 'Shell-Guide to Britain' affection for England is essentially Ruralist; the urban dweller looking out of his 'concrete jungle' in search of the 'greensward'. Paul Nash both wrote and illustrated the *Shell Guide to Dorset* (1935), concentrating on the county's castles, forts and tumuli. Betjeman and Piper teamed up for 'church crawling', enthusiastically recording on their antiquarian rambles both rood screens and branch-line railways. This was Little Britain; its nooks and crannies revealed to as many people as possible. Their search soon became a campaign against post-war planning and the wholesale destruction of our Victorian cities; the Victorian Society was founded fifty years ago in 1958. Betjaman wished to protect all that was well made, of whatever period, standing up for St Pancras in the face of historical and architectural snobbery. Poet and painter sought a sympathetic picture of all that was British and best in our 'enchanted isle', from the middle class suburb, with its trim lawns to the great country houses of England and Wales.

The Shell campaign to 'Visit Britain's Landmarks You Can Be Sure of Shell' had us all taking to the roads for a Sunday 'leisure' drive; in the 1950s one could still head off down the open road, like Toad of Toad Hall. Even today, despite all the antagonism towards the car, there are tourist routes designed for those of us who enjoy 'the getting there' as much as arriving. The very act of travelling engages our imaginations; what will we discover at our final destination? This of course evolves into bigger questions; what exactly are we doing here? What do we want out of life? We need to discover who we are and ultimately where we belong. Faith transforms the tourist and traveller into a pilgrim or seeker of the truth. The journey becomes a quest, the road the 'path of life', each junction offering us personal choices, the path of fame and worldly riches or the path of personal satisfaction and integrity. Although clichés, worked to death by succeeding generations looking for meaning and purpose in both life and art, these commonplace themes still mean something to us. In Ovenden's vision the 'View to Paradise' becomes an incessant quotation.

The Ovendens have created their Paradise in a 'hidden' Cornish Valley near Bodmin; Barley Splatt was literally created with Graham's own hands, a product of the arts and crafts imagination, lovingly fashioned with blocks of granite cut and laid by the master builder himself. It has been described as Neo-Gothic; it certainly enshrines many of Graham's enthusiasms, his passion for William Burges, the architect of Cardiff Castle and Castel Coch and A.W.N. Pugin. But despite its High Victorian antecedents it is pure Graham, quirky, strange and romantic. In front of the house the Ovendens have created a large pool, 'which under a leaden skies can look like some haunted mere from *Morte d'Arthur*. Around lie thirty acres of pure ruralism; a gurgling river, woods, overgrown meadows and a glimpse of the moors above. This is Ur-Rurlist country; the scene of many a convivial get-together, the dripping woodlands the location for many famous artistic endeavours like the series of '"Ophelias", once a Ruralist theme'.[1] Graham

Ovenden's England is essentially still Victorian, a combination of Pre-Raphaelite and Palmeresque motifs, flower strewn glades and enfolding valleys; here he can live and paint as he chooses, ignoring the hype of the YBAs, Young British Artists, in the 1990s. Graham has little time for the cult of the celebrity artist; he still sees art as a craft and artists as master-craftsmen-Shakespeare, Milton, Stanley Spencer. In effect Barley Splatt 'shields him in the woods'; cocooned by the melodies of Bach, Schubert and Elgar, Graham creates 'his works of ecstasy, rejoicing in the presence of nature, celebrations of a glorious relationship' between man and the Creator.[2] England as Aracdia springs out of the romantic imagination; it is a place in the mind but that does not stop us from searching for it or imposing our vision on nature itself; since the eighteenth century the English have been trying to fashion nature 'like a picture'.[3] The landscape garden (Stourhead and Stowe may be the best) was an attempt to redesign England as Arcadia; the vision itself transposed from Italy via the idealized classical landscapes of Claude Lorraine (1600-1682) and Nicolas Poussin (1594-1665). Salvator Rosa (1615-1673) injected a more rugged, mountainous terrain; most English Arcadias have a Wilderness to provide a foil, the pastoral offset by the primitive. This taste for landscape developed out of the cultural aspirations of the landed elites; the Claudian prospect was familiar to them from the Grand Tour; it could be memorialized in paintings and engravings. Returning tourists, like Lord Burlington, built their Arcadia in Chiswick, Wiltshire or Buckinghamshire. Tourists sought comparable prospects in the British countryside, to recreate the experience or substitute for a continental trip; an emerging middle class might possess the wealth to travel but they did not have the extended leisure of the landed elites. With the outbreak of war in Europe, following the French Revolution of 1789, the English Grand Tour assumed a new importance; Britain's insularity sparked an interest in our native history and archaeological sites; 'Englishness' was vested in our unique countryside. While fashionable society flocked to the spa towns, Bath, Buxton, Tunbridge Wells, Cheltenham and Harrogate offering the tourist an abundance of 'delights', including medicinal waters and gaming tables, keen antiquarians, such as John Aubrey (1626–1697) and William Stukeley (1687-1765), travelled to see and record ancient sites. Medieval buildings and ruins, a 'sequestered spot', were increasingly visited, along with country houses and landscape gardens, as part of tours to 'picturesque' regions, such as the Derbyshire Peak district, the Lake District and the Wye Valley.

The Age of Reason attempted to codify our response to Nature; 'Landscapes of association' were born out of the late 18th century concept of Sentiment, as expressed by the 'sentimental tear', linking experience or the senses with feeling. Landscape should stimulate the mind; it was a function of the imagination, offering mental variety; it could engender different emotional responses- thoughts, feelings and memories. This response had been encouraged by the formulation of the Beautiful, the Sublime and the Picturesque, which encouraged the associative qualities of experience, especially through the observation of nature; 'ways of seeing' inducing 'ways of feeling'. Edmund Burke categorised these landscapes of association in his *Philosophical Enquiry into the Origin of Our Ideas of the Sublime and the Beautiful* (1757). The Beautiful was embodied in a classicising 'Claudian' landscape, named after and conceived by the artist Claude Lorraine, a realisation of the 'Virgilian' pastoral idyll of the Roman poet. Such harmonious and balanced landscapes evoked peace, calm and Arcadian bliss, recalling an archaic Golden Age.

The Sublime was 'pleasurable terror', a cathartic release, largely induced by the grandeur of nature and seen in awe inspiring mountains, precipices, torrents and caverns. While the Beautiful was light, the Sublime was dark. It was the Vast, the Infinite and the Abyss, the limitless oceans, the mountainous chasm and the terrifying primordial Alps; Snowdonia became a substitute for the French and Swiss Alps. As Thomas Gray wrote in 1765 of the Scottish Highlands 'The mountains are ecstatic... None but God knows how to join so much beauty with so much horror.' It was nature untamed and untameable, in the face of which man was powerless. This response to nature was to reach a climax in the work of J.R. Cozens (1752-99) and J.W.M. Turner (1775-1851); both epitomise the Sublime.

In contrast, the Picturesque, initially meaning 'like a picture', was pleasurably reflective and emotive, inspired by rolling hills, woodland glades, and bubbling brooks: roughness, variety and irregularity were sought, but not the extreme. The Picturesque mediated between the Beautiful and the Sublime. Essentially the picturesque was eye-catching, defined in Johnson's *Dictionary* (1801) as 'what was pleasing to the eye, what strikes the viewer as singular or appeals to him with the force of a painting, what would afford a good subject for a painting or help in conceiving one'. The Great Oak tree, the 'Heart of England', was a key picturesque motif, embodying national identity.[4] The venerable antiquity of trees, how they have watched over British history and even contributed to it, was captured in Wordsworth *Yew Trees* of 1803, written at a time when we were at war with France:

'There is a Yew-tree, pride of Lorton Vale,
Which to this day stands single, in the midst
Of its own darkness, as it stood of yore:
Not loathe to furnish weapons for the Bands[5]
Of Umfraville or Percy ere they marched
To Scotland's heaths; or those that crossed the sea
And drew their sounding bows at Azincour,
Perhaps at earlier Crecy, or Poictiers.
Of vast circumference and gloom profound
This solitary Tree! – a living thing
Produced too slowly ever to decay;
Of form and aspect too magnificent
To be destroyed. But worthier still of note
Are those fraternal Four of Borrowdale,
Joined in one solemn and capacious grove;
Huge trunks! – and each particular trunk a growth
Of intertwisted fibres serpentine
Up-coiling, and inveterately convolved…' [6]

Trees, like ruins, could embody history; admiring the 'ruins of a noble tree', the Revd William Gilpin (1724-1804) felt that 'these splendid remnants of decaying grandeur speak to the imagination in a stile of eloquence, which the stripling cannot reach: they record the history of some storm, some blast of lightening, or other great event, which transfers its grand ideas to the landscape'.[7] Decay suggested not only the past but the passage of time, the 'accretion of experience'; above all ruins implied evanescence and transience- 'A life spent without contemplation of death is a denial of life, since death is the logical and inevitable end for us all'.[8]

The Picturesque would evolve into an artistic movement, emerging in 1794 with the publication of Richard Payne-Knight's *Didactic Essay on the Picturesque* (1794) and Sir Uvedale Price's *An Essay on the Picturesque, as Compared with the Sublime and the Beautiful; and on the Use of Studying Pictures, for the Purpose of Improving Real Landscape* (1794). Gilpin gave the Picturesque firm principles; composition was his main interest and evidently nature often needed help. Artist and traveller were encouraged to reassemble the various features of a scene, be it lake, mountain, rocks or ruin, into a more pleasing whole: 'let us hasten to the chief object of our pursuit, the wild scenes of nature – the *wood* – the *copse* – the *glen* – and *open-grove*'.In Gilpin's view, rotten and withered trees were 'capital sources of picturesque beauty', hollow trunks made invaluable foregrounds, withered tops lent artistic diversity, and when 'ideas of wildness and desolation are required, what more suitable accompaniment can be imagined than the blasted oak, ragged, scathed and leafless?'[9]

Gilpin, variously headmaster of Cheam and Vicar of Boldre in the New Forest, was one of the new generation of 'scholars', rather than aristocrats, who explored ideas of sensibility and aesthetics, not on the European Grand Tour but in the wilder and rougher scenery of his native land. He was particularly fond of the Lake District and mountainous scenery; his picturesque verges on the sublime. Gilpin had a particular love for antiquities in the landscape and summed up his views in 1792:

> '...among all the objects of art, the picturesque eye is perhaps most inquisitive after the elegant relics of ancient architecture; the ruined tower, the Gothic arch, the remains of castles, and abbeys. These are the richest legacies of art. They are consecrated by time; and almost deserve the veneration we pay to the works of nature itself.' [10]

The Picturesque brought the Gothic to the fore, as the British countryside was littered with ecclesiastical and secular ruins, which were visually stimulating and loaded with associations. Antiquarian remains were perceived as constituent parts of the landscape, and given increased status through their association with ruins seen in idealized painted landscapes. Artists, engravers and publishers responded to a rising demand for visual images and information relating to British history. The sense of loss felt after the dissolution of the monasteries in the 1530s and the ravages of the Civil War had originally stimulated this antiquarian impulse in the 1640s. Religious and social dislocation prompted many scholars, including William Dugdale (1605-86) and John Aubrey to seek out and record the nation's antique and medieval remains; Stukeley made his name with accounts of Stonehenge and Avebury. This resulted in a burgeoning demand for topographical drawings and for prints of monasteries, castles and other sites. By the mid-18th century, many influential patricians were avidly studying the architecture and literature of British antiquity, including Richard Gough (1735-1809). On a tour of East Anglia in 1756, the medieval buildings captivated Gough. His *Anecdotes of British Topography* (1768) was the result of twelve years of original research and reading. He summed up his early aspirations in the Preface:

> 'Curiosity to visit as much of my native country as I had opportunity, excited a desire to know all that related to its topographical antiquities...These *Anecdotes* have informed and amused the collector:- if they only amuse the readers I shall not be absolutely condemned:- if they inform them, my passion for British antiquities becomes a zeal to serve the public.'

Gough saw the pernicious effects of the Continental Grand Tour:

> 'We penetrate the wilds of Europe, and the desarts [*sic*] of Asia and Africa, for the remains of Grecian, Roman and earlier architecture, while no artist offers himself a candidate for fame in preserving those of our forefathers in their own country...Temples and palaces of the polite nations of antiquity engross our attention, while the works and memorials of our own priests and heroes have no effect on our curiosity.'

The 'barbarous' ruins of Fountains Abbey and Tintern soon quickened the curiosity of the English traveller; nobody was quite sure how old they were, as scholars had not yet dissected the various phases of the Gothic but there was no doubting that they were the legacy of our forefathers. Authors stressed the independence of the Gothic style and dwelt on its ability to engender feelings of religious awe. In 1751 William Warburton praised Gothic as a 'new species of architecture, unknown to Greece and Rome; [founded] upon original principles and ideas much nobler than what had given birth even to classical magnificence'. Seven years later, the architect John Gwynn contrasted the 'magnificence...of true, pure, and antient Gothick' found in Westminster Abbey, with the 'cold rules' of 'antient Rome and Greece'; he lauded the ability of Gothic buildings to give 'religious impressions…of the Deity'. Such research and writing, together with pictorial recording, like Thomas Hearne (1744-1817) and William Byrne's *Antiquities of Great* Britain (1786), demonstrate the unprecedented desire to collect, study and promote everything pertaining to the national past.

The 18th century mind located the Gothic in the visual repertoire of the Picturesque; it was primarily seen as an ornamental style that enhanced the tourist experience or suggested the notion of an ancient Britain. Romanticism would develop the Gothic as an architectural language associated with individual and national identity rooted in northern culture; moreover it was seen to represent a code of moral conduct based on medieval chivalry and courtly love. Walter Scott's 'Waverley Novels', paticularly *Ivanhoe* (1819), best represent these developments. As the Industrial Revolution encroached on society, undermining the class structure and traditional values, the Gothic offered the promise of a perfect feudal past, where everybody understood their place and what was expected of them. Simultaneously Germany, France and England claimed the Gothic as their own; the new Palace of Westminster, begun at the moment Queen Victoria ascended the throne, embodied this new national sentiment. The picturesquely playful Gothic was transformed into the Romantically earnest and symbolic. The Gothic was still largely seen as a stylistic vocabulary of crockets, cusps and pinnacles, but one that signalled Faith, pre-Reformation 'Catholic wholeness', and Christian moral virtues. The Gothic Revival, spear-headed by Augustus Welby Northmore Pugin (1812-1852), a Catholic convert, created a national style, one with a clear Christian message, expounding duty, hard work and family values. Simultaneously Nature was sanctified as God's creation; England became Blake's Jerusalem. Ruskin advised young artists to 'go to nature', not just because it was a subject worthy of art but because of its moral value; being God's handiwork it revealed His purpose. One hundred and fifty years on the Ruralists still see Nature bathed in a divine light; it is still the handiwork of the Creator, whoever he may be:

> 'In their more exalted moods they feel at one with their great and much invoked mentors William Blake and Samuel Palmer, seeing every hill, wood, blade of grass, blade of corn as invested with a spiritual presence; with, in the words of another of their heroes, William Wordsworth,
>
> "A sense of something far more deeply interfused
> Whose dwelling is the light of setting suns
> And the round ocean, and the living air,
> And the blue sky and in the mind of man"'.[11]

Catholic antecedents may have worried the non-conformists, whose chapels resolutely clung to the classical tradition as a matter of principle, but Gothic's mysterious, barbarous past, its dark connotations, fuelled the Gothic novel. The Gothic, like nature itself, was of two kinds, the beneficent and the horrific. The Gothic allowed ghosts, goblins and witches, who in turn legitimised paganism and pantheism; the menacing witchwood and the primordial forest conjure up the satanic. A tree can symbolise Christ's suffering on the cross, promise immortality and resurrection or speak of decay, death and even damnation. They would become Nash's 'monsters' and Sutherland's 'personalities' or 'personages':

> 'It is not a question so much of a "tree like a figure" or a "root like a figure" – it is a question of bringing out the anonymous personality of these things: at the same time they must bear the mould of their ancestry. There is a duality; they can be themselves and something else at the same time. They are formal metaphors.' [12]

As Yorke notes, the personalities that were emerging were far from benign; verging on the melodramatic, they are more expressionistic than Nash's 'monsters';*Gorse on a Sea Wall* (1939), *Green Tree Form: Interior of Woods* (1940) and *Horned Forms* (1944). The sense of decay is unpleasant, the lurid colours violent. Like Dylan Thomas, Sutherland concluded that Nature works 'implacably and simultaneously to create and destroy':

'The force that through the green fuse drives the flower
Drives my green age; that blasts the roots of trees
Is my destroyer.
And I am dumb to tell the crooked rose
My youth is bent by the same wintry fever.' [13]

Sutherland stored nature in his mind; back in the studio nature was paraphrased, the subconscious 'shedding irrelevances and accreting powerful emotional associations'.[14] Sutherland declared, 'For me it was always a question of starting with the concrete and re-creating something more concrete'; he found he 'could express what I felt only by paraphrasing what I saw…I felt just as much part of the earth as my features were part of me. I did not feel that my imagination was in conflict with the real, but that reality was a dispersed and disintegrated form of imagination'.[15] Yorke calls this Sutherland's 'inward territory', although he could always tell you where he found a motif, the bend in the lane or spray of leaves, which sent him down this inward path. Sutherland referred to 'poetic truth', where 'the artist is merged completely into the subject and ceases to express a romantic reaction to the subject'.[16] Martin observes that whereas in the 1920s Sutherland, Drury and Tanner had turned their back on modernity, the romantic art of the 1940s and 1950s was informed by continental artistic developments, Abstraction and particularly Surrealism; in the case of Sutherland it was Picasso who injected modernity into his vision; for Keith Vaughan, writing in 1943, 'What Picasso did to the human figure Graham Sutherland is doing to the English Landscape. I think he is the first painter to relocate the full discoveries of the twentieth-century in France to the English Romantic tradition'.[17] Likening painting to poetry, Sutherland wanted his connotations to be ambiguous: 'Coleridge said that poetry gives most pleasure when generally and not perfectly understood…So in painting it might be argued that its very obscurity preserves a magical and mystical purpose'.[18] However, the contradictory sense of enveloping protection or menacing constriction, felt in '*Entrance to a Lane* (1939), may be his subconscious intimations of the impending war.

Like Sutherland, Nash was creating 'personalities', 'personages' and 'equivalents', based on a constellation of favourite motifs: the hill, the copse, the bird, the stone, the gate, the moon and the sun, the clouds and the sea. These became Nash's 'visible signs': Graham Ovenden has similarly developed his own language: trees, apple trees, three trees, the monolith, the owl, the cloud and the moon. Nash's vision was shaped 'by a poetic attachment to the hidden qualities of natural things',[19] but in his case this was allied to the aesthetic possibilities of Abstraction and Surrealism. Nash was drawn to certain places, to 'the spirit of place' or *genius loci* and he mediated on them over long periods; there may be no humans present but Nash's landscapes are soaked with humanity, in fact the very landscape can take on human form. For Nash Wittenham Clumps, which he revisited time after time, took on the form of breasts. The rounded hills had symbolic meaning but also formal and aesthetic qualities that attracted him, the 'curiously symmetrical sculptural form'.[20] Nash balanced 'formal features' against 'associative force' but in Nash's case 'form' almost always carries associative resonance. Nash's search for England went deeper; it became a search for self, his landscapes revealing his private sensibility, 'a special sort of autobiography wherein introspective preoccupations achieve expression within a code of symbolic forms'.[21] Nash's work shows a commitment to Nature, an attempt to reveal its latent meaning that tracks the course of his life, ending with a confrontation with death and even desolation (Cat. 133).

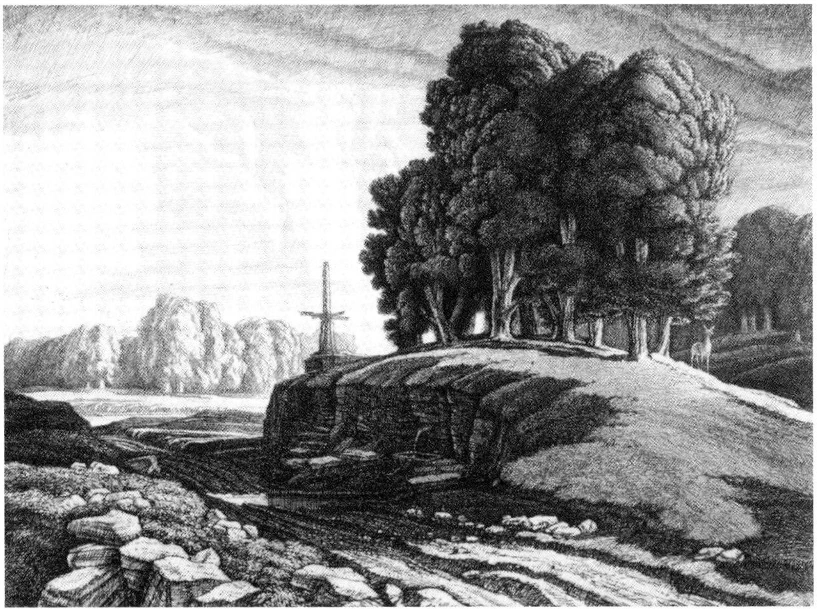

36. Frederick Landseer Maur Griggs (1876-1938)
Cross Hands, 1935
etching on paper, Second State (one of six) Comstock No. 52, 181 x 240 mm
Stuart M. Southall

36

Griggs dedicated this work to Thomas Pegram, a long time friend, who came to his aid in the early 1930s, when the ongoing building of Dover's House resulted in financial difficulties. In August 1933 he purchased Grigg's complete set of Turner's *Liber Studiorum*, followed by his collection of Samuel Palmer etchings and drawings in 1935; it must have been very hard for Griggs to part with these treasures.

The origins of this etching may be traced back to a pencil drawing of 1912, relating to an illustration in the *Highways and Byways of Lincolnshire*. However, a pencil drawing of *Sybil's Cross* (1932), inscribed with a quotation from Sir Walter Scott's *Marmion*, also helped to shape Grigg's conception: 'Drink weary Pilgrim, drink and praye for the kinde soule of Sybille Greye, who built the cross and well'. In the final image the cross and well were transformed into a signpost, with four hands pointing to the different directions, and a spring. Jerrold Northrop Moore also notes that there is a cross hands on the London road above Campden; a crossroads with macabre associations, where criminals were hung and people took their own lives. Grigg's *Cross Hands* does not carry such sinister undercurrents; the signpost rises like a sword or cross, illuminated by shafts of sunlight. Rough steps descend to a rutted lane or pilgrim's way, where a spring trickles and forms a pool. On the far side of the trees, stands a young hind or hart, alert to catch the slightest threat; we intrude on its privacy. Moore speculates that it may be a white hart; Norman Jewson recalled seeing one: 'So beautiful did it look as I glimpsed it between the tree trunks...that it was easy to understand what a hold the white hart had on the imagination of the men of the middle ages'.[22] Comstock notes:

> 'The plate is...perhaps the best of the pure landscapes so dear to the artist; it is uniquely his, the product of his creative imagination. There is an atmosphere of other days in the deserted scene: the rutted road, the broken cross, even the hind. There now remain few such scenes of this vanished heritage of England: its beauty evokes thoughts of sadness and regret over the despoliation of her countryside.' [23]

37

Pembrokeshire cured Sutherland of any desire to paint 'scenic' pictures in the manner of Claude: 'From the moment I set foot in Wales I was obsessed'.[24] Sutherland forsook the obvious appeal of Snowdonia for the small intricate valleys and twisty lanes of the countryside encircling St Bride's Bay. The preference for an 'intimately enfolding view' can be seen in *Entrance to a Lane* (1939) and *Green Lane* (1945):

> 'These valleys possess a bud-like intricacy of form...the roads form strong and mysterious arabesques as they rise in terraces, in sight, hidden, turning and splitting as they finally disappear into the sky. To see a solitary human figure descending such a road at the solemn moment of sunset is to realise the enveloping quality of the earth, which can create, as it does here, a mysterious space limit – a womb-like enclosure.' [25]

Sutherland's 'womb-like enclosures' verge on the claustrophobic; he creates a sense of 'burrowing into the land'. *Green*

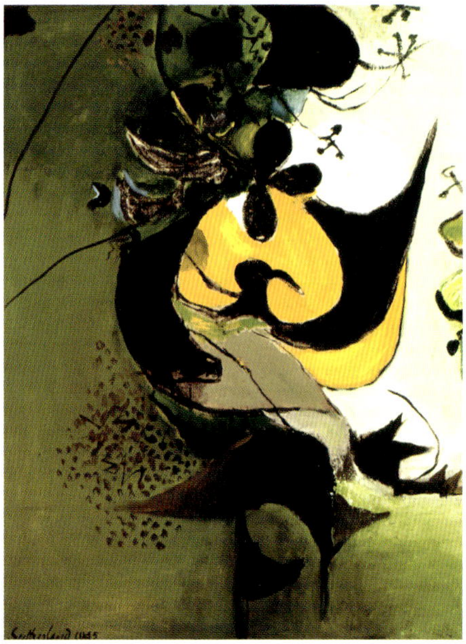

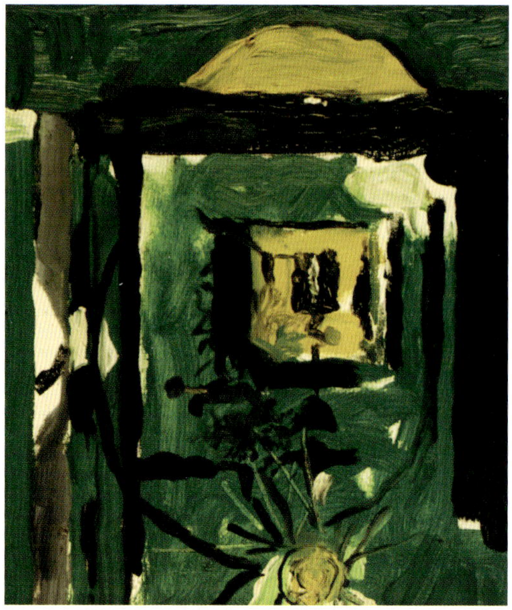

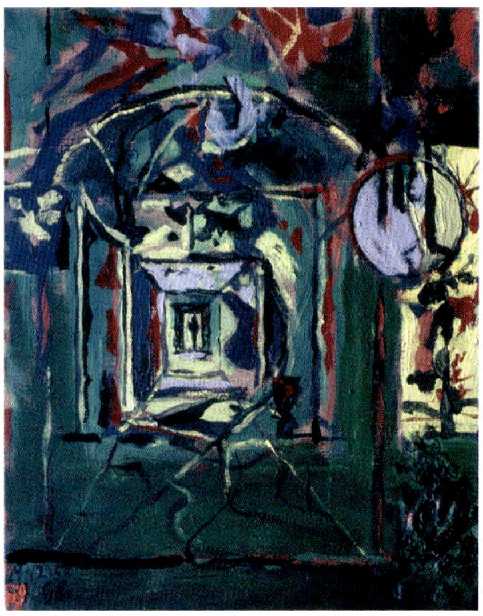

37. Graham Vivien Sutherland (1903-1980)
Green Lane, 1945
oil on canvas, 660 x 507 mm
Southampton City Art Gallery
Chipperfield Bequest

37a. Graham Vivien Sutherland (1903-1980)
Path Through Woods
oil, Southampton City Art Gallery

37b. Graham Vivien Sutherland (1903-1980)
Path Through Wood, 1958
oil, Southampton City Art Gallery

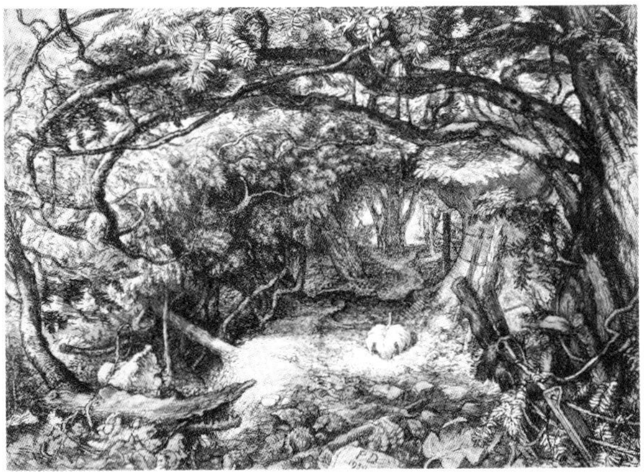

38. Paul Drury (1903-1987)
Michelham Yews, III, 1950
etching, 162 x 226 mm
Stuart M. Southall

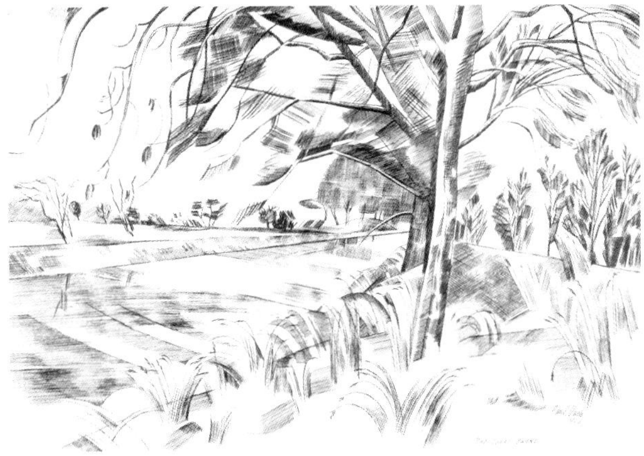

39. Paul Nash (1889-1946)
Canal Banks, 1923
pen and ink, 383 x 566 mm
Southampton City Art Gallery
Chipperfield Bequest

Lane is tunnel-like, making us feel 'the enveloping quality of the earth' but there is also a sinister element creeping in; the impenetrable damp green gloom, the sense of disquiet. Coming close to his subject matter, he began to paraphrase nature, producing 'personages', a term he probably borrowed from Nash.

Green Lane reworks the motif seen in *Entrance to a Lane*, including 'the scratching black foliage which might also be winged creatures swarming in from the top'[26]; the leafy forms are distinctly prickly. One critic asked: 'What is that lurking in the shadow? Is it a man's head, an insect? A broken implement or the mere illusion of light on leaves?' *Path through Woods* (SCAG) and *Path through Wood* (1958, SCAG) takes the theme even further, the verticals and horizontals creating a clear tunnel; we are now entering a mine. Sutherland experienced the Cornish tin-mines during his time as a war artist; here he encountered the same tubular enfolding forms he had found in the overgrown lanes of Pembrokeshire, the same dividing byways, which offered a world of 'such beauty and such mystery'.[27] All these images share a sense of foreboding and trepidation; dare we enter, will we get out? Neither *Entrance to a Lane* nor *Green Lane*, both framed by the war, offers pleasure or safety round the corner; Sutherland had 'destroyed perspective' to enhance this disquiet. However, Sutherland's connotations remain ambiguous; nature as haven or nature as hell.

38

After the war Drury continued to develop his pastoral etching, 'evolving the form with the feeling of the age'.[28] Drury's series *Mickleham Yews* develops a form of Pastoral Expressionism, with the sinuous sculptural tree forms presaged in Sutherland's *Wood Interior* and *Pastoral*. Palmer's *The Morning of Life* inspired *Michelham Yews III*:

> 'How the eye is tossed from one form to another, from blinding light to luminous depth; how one gasps – in the clean joyous experience of what? Of the Morning, and of Life. Much has been said of his (Palmer's) debt to Blake, but not enough of his debt to Claude Lorraine.' [29]

Jolyon Drury considers this print to be a 'true bridge from his pre-War pastoral work, now exploring bold forms such as the inverted leaf, out of proportion and startlingly illuminated in the otherwise sombre pathway'. The split log, resembling the open jaws of a crocodile, is threatening. The nightmarish menace of these woods brings to mind the trials of Snow White, fighting off branches that have assumed animalistic qualities. Drury would develop the theme as *Forms in a Wood*, which displays 'a strange element of lyrical surrealism'. [30]

39

Paul Nash's work often combines the English landscape tradition with European Modernism. Here, the simplified natural forms, geometric elements and crosshatching show the influence of Cézanne.

The scene is thought to be the Royal Military Canal on Romney Marsh. It was built in 1804-06 as defence against Napoleon and to control smuggling. In the early 1920s, Nash lived at Dymchurch on the Romney Marsh. He formed a strong attachment to the area and found it: 'a delightful place with

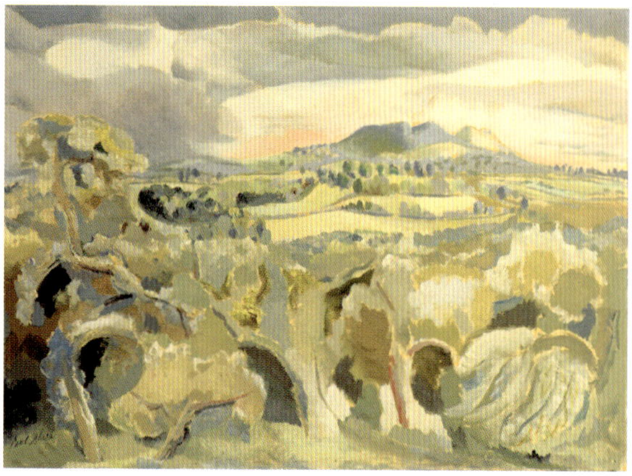

40. Paul Nash (1889-1946)
Landscape of the Malvern Distance, 1943
oil on cardboard, 535 x 742
Southampton Art Gallery
Chipperfield Bequest

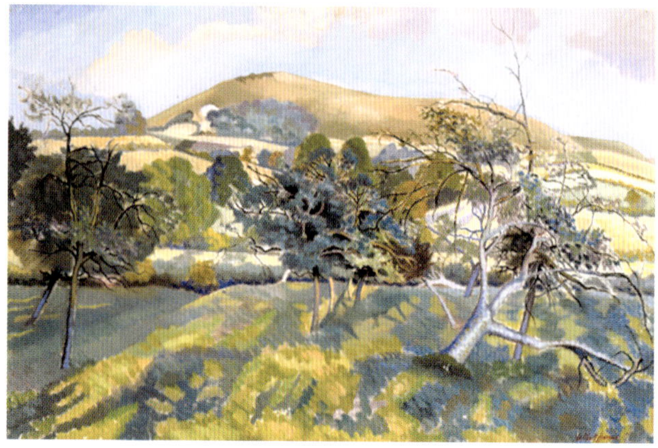

41. Gilbert Spencer (1892-1978)
Melbury Beacon
oil on canvas, 610 x 915 mm
Southampton City Art Gallery, presented
by the Dean of York, the very Rev. E.
Milner-White in memory of his father

much inspiring material for work'. The attraction of Romney was that it allowed Nash to meditate on the inter-changeability of land and sea; at one time Romney Marsh had literally been the sea floor.

40

Nash was drawn to particular places that he felt had a certain mystical or magical quality, which he called *genius loci*, the spirit of a place. In the case of the Malvern Hills the resonances are deep, not just for Nash, but for all the Ruralists as this is Elgar country. Sir Edward Elgar (1857-1934) was born at Broadheath, Worcestershire, the name chosen by the Arnolds, David Inshaw and John and Diana Morley for their Brotherhood.

For 55 of his 76 years, Elgar lived within sight of the Malvern Hills, a range of hills that run south from Great Malvern for about 9 miles. Their very names conjure up the English Idyll, Hollybush Hill, Swinyard Hill, and Midsummer Hill. A favourite haunt of Elgar's, he was often to be found walking, cycling or exercising his dogs on the Hills. He once declared 'If ever after I'm dead you hear a little tune amongst the bracken on these Hills, don't be frightened as it will only be me humming the opening bars of my *Cello Concerto*'. While living at Malvern he composed many of his most famous works – The *Enigma* Variations, *The Dream of Gerontius* and the *Pomp and Circumstance March No 1.*, better known as *Land of Hope and Glory*, our 'second national anthem'. No other piece of music encapsulates England more fully except perhaps *Jerusalem*.

The view painted by Nash is north from 'Madams', in Gloucestershire, the home of Charles and Clare Neilson, friends of the Nashes, to the Malvern Hills. It was while staying at 'Madams', in 1939, that Nash discovered his 'Monster Field' (see Cat. 64).

41

Although an accomplished painter of portraits, Gilbert regarded his landscapes as 'my happiest painting'.

This work, in a style close to that of his brother, Stanley, shows Melbury Beacon a popular beauty spot near Shaftsbury in North Dorset. It was painted out of doors possibly in the early 1930s when Spencer and his young wife Ursula were living in a cottage that looked out across to Melbury Beacon. In *Memoirs of a Painter* he recalled: 'Waking in the morning to the freshness of these little valleys with Melbury across the meadows, was... a heartening experience [...] How many times I tired to master Melbury Beacon it would be difficult to say...But I regarded it as a challenge, not a defeat, and certainly not a halt sign'.

42

In 1989 this image of Pound Field, where the stray animals were rounded up, was used to spearhead a successful campaign to save the 15-acre grazing meadow from developers. Cookham, Berkshire, is best known as the birthplace of Stanley and Gilbert Spencer. Stanley lived and worked in the village for most of his life, it was his *genius loci*, being at the centre of his art and personal theology. For Spencer, Cookham was a sacred place imbued with spiritual significance, 'a kind of earthly paradise'. Spencer's lush, detailed landscape recalls Pre-Raphaelite painting and suggests a communion with nature; the village nestles in the countryside. Looking in, from the edge of the village, evokes home as a safe haven, creating a sense of well-being. A Ruralist hero, back

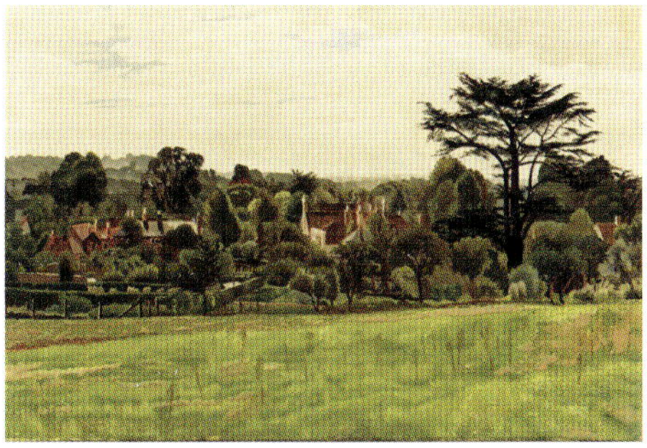

42. Stanley Spencer (1891-1959)
Pound Field, Cookham, 1935
oil on canvas, 508 x 761 mm
Southampton City Art Gallery
Smith Bequest

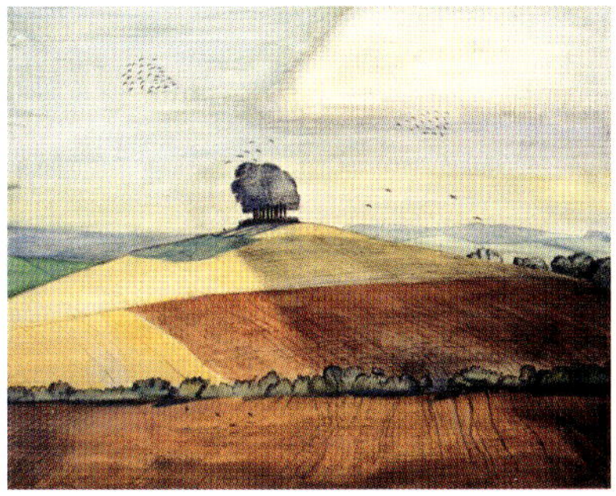

43a. Paul Nash (1889-1946)
Under the Hill
(*Wittenham Clumps*) 1912
Tullie House, Carlisle

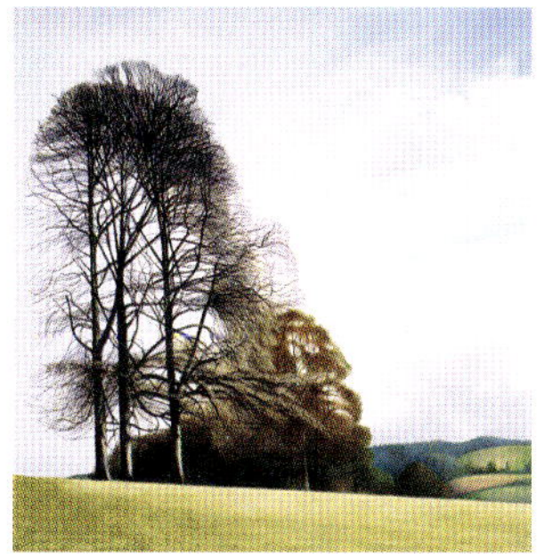

44. Annie Ovenden (1945-)
February Morning
in Lanhydrock Park
oil on canvas
590 x 580 mm, 2001
John and Julia Dixon

in the 1970s Graham Ovenden bemoaned Spencer's banishment to the Tate Gallery's basement, a casualty of the modernist scorn for figurative and landscape painting. Thirty years on Spencer's reputation and position in British art has been fully recuperated.

43

Paul Nash (1889-1946)
Landscape with Rooks, 1913-14
chalk and watercolour on paper
259 x 284 mm
Syndics of the Fitzwilliam, Cambs

This work straddles the themes of this exhibition; it would sit just as well with the notion of Ancient Landscapes, as the clumps are the site of a long barrow and an Iron Age fortification. Wittenham Clumps, a 'potent and enigmatic site' was Nash's most favoured spot, a *genius loci* or 'Spirit of Place'. The clumps were a landmark to be approach with respect and reverence. *Wood on the Hill* (1912 private collection) shows the clumps from a distance, the crown of protective trees offering shelter or sanctuary. In *Under the Hill* the trees still offer protection but the rooks coming home to roost have a menacing air; traditionally the rook is seen as a harbinger of death. They also suggest nightfall. This gives the clumps a more sinister character, reminding us that for centuries this was a place where death was commemorated. The Clumps were redolent with such mysteries; it was for Nash a locus worthy of prolonged meditation. The Clumps also take up the theme of repossession, as the works of man will in time be absorbed back into Nature. But Cardinal notes that this notion seems 'consoling rather than disturbing'.[31]

44

All of Annie's paintings, the landscapes and portraits of her children, derive from her practical day-to-day involvement with country life. She is very much the 'mother' of the Ruralists, looking after the garden, the land, the animals and the inmates of Barley Splatt. While doing these more mundane chores, ideas come to her for paintings:

> 'Usually I'll be working outside when suddenly I'll see something in the landscape and then respond to it inside. It is this quality which I've seen the light create, and the feeling I've received from it which I try to put into my painting.' [32].

Lanhydrock Park, the famous National Trust house, lies close to the Ovendens' home near Bodmin. This was one of a series of landscapes of the Park for the 2001 Ruralist show, held at Barley Splatt. Annie is a painter of trees, either soaring heavenward or plunging down into their tangled roots. Here majestic leafless trees are framed by a cold winter sky. In the distance we can see the folds of the surrounding agricultural farmland, contrasting the contrived 'wild idyll' of the park and with the productive land. One also is reminded of Graham Ovenden's poem *The Great Beech Tree*:

> 'He stands with girt girth
> that grappling grudging earth
> bears greener hope.
> Whose sightless root-bones press, slope
> outwards: wrest, so there to knot
> in air as gnarled hands grasp and grope.' [33]

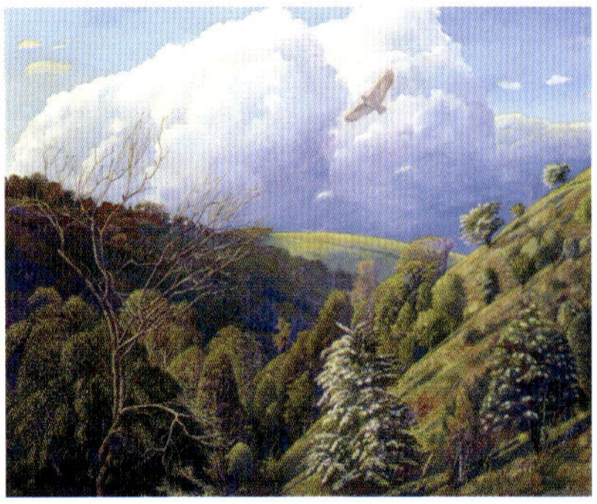

45. ANN ARNOLD (1936-)
The Hill in Spring, 1987
oil on canvas, 508 x 610 mm
Peter Nahum at the Leicester Galleries

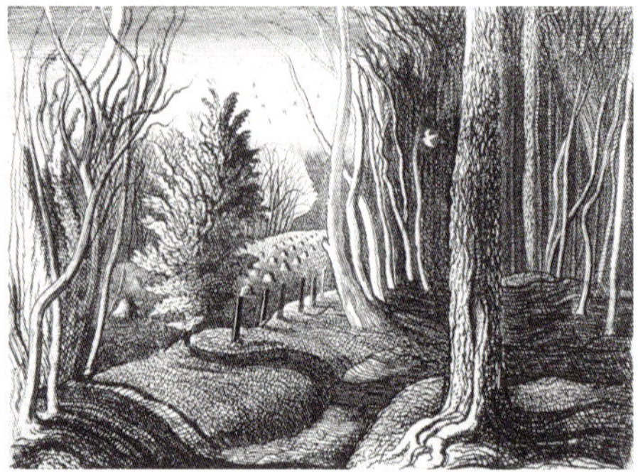

46. GRAHAM VIVIEN (1903-1980)
Wood Interior, 1929
etching on paper, 119 x 162 mm
Stuart M. Southall

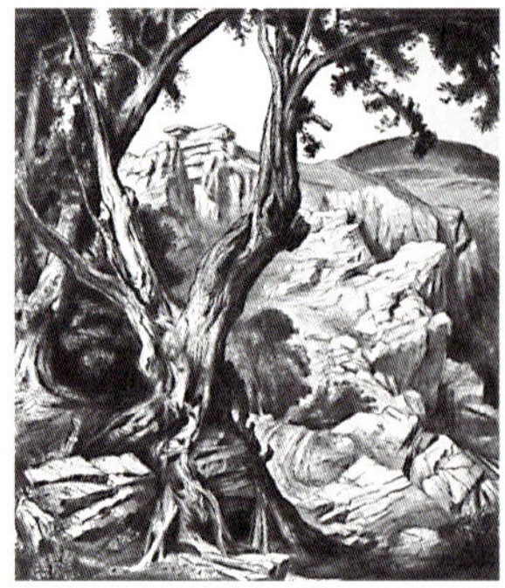

47. EDWARD BOUVERIE HOYTON (1900-1988)
A Devon Tor, 1930s?
etching on paper, 274 x 231 mm
Stuart M. Southall

45

The Arnolds moved from Devizes to Shropshire, to an old farmhouse called Pentre:

> '...as the evening light fades on the hills and orchards, Pentre can seem more like Shoreham than Shoreham and one can believe that here, if anywhere, the Ruralist quest might be achieved'.[34]

The wilder and mysterious countryside of the Welsh borders, the land where the hills are crossed by Offa'a Dyke and 'melt into Wales are a Ruralist dream': 'All around them are strangely shaped hills, rivers, and forests but the Arnolds seem content to paint the valley that surrounds their home. It is A.E. Houseman Country, "the land of lost content"'.[35]

This is a view of the hill behind Pentre, which the Arnold's once owned; they planted many Oaks there. The spiralling flight of the buzzard that nested nearby and was often seen circling overhead, evoked for Ann a great sense of freedom.

Usherwood describes how 'she paints scenes that are very much part of her daily life, but seen at a particular and intense moment'.[36] A member of the Brotherhood of Ruralists, the spirituality of the English landscape is perhaps the most important element within Ann Arnold's work.

46

The *Village* and *Pecken Wood* completely express the pastoral ideal; Sutherland had taken his chosen imagery to the limit. It is easy to see that a young artist in his twenties would feel the need for a change. By 1927 Sutherland had already begun to consider his idyllic imagery a 'total cul de sac', the death of his son in July 1929 souring his view of nature still further.[37] With the collapse of the Etching Boom, the need for change was now vital. Sutherland's unease found expression in a series of powerful etchings, the idyll being replaced by a disquieting air. *Wood Interior* reflects this new mood. The unspecific title conveys something universal about nature; there is no connection with a specific landscape, Nash's 'Spirit of Place'. The leaf-less trees suggest winter, the only sign of growth being the abundant ivy that clings to the tree on the left. The bird seems forlorn and trapped. The overall effect is ominous, the wood is threatening and sinister; Sutherland expresses the 'dark side' of nature.

47

Edward Bouverie Hoyton was one of the Class of 21, a group of talented etchers, which included Graham Sutherland, Robin Tanner and Paul Drury, who sought inspiration in William Blake, Samuel Palmer and the densely etched plates of F. L. Griggs. In 1941 he was appointed Principal of Penzance School of Art. He remained a close friend of Graham Sutherland who stayed with him when, as a war artist, he was sent to draw the Cornish tin miners. Hoyton introduced Sutherland to Ben Nicholson (1894-1992) and Naum Gabo (1890-1977), who were committed to Abstraction and Constructivism.

Hoyton was a meticulous craftsman and either printed his etchings himself or supervised their printings. He rarely numbered his etchings, but all appeared in small editions, usually seventy or less.

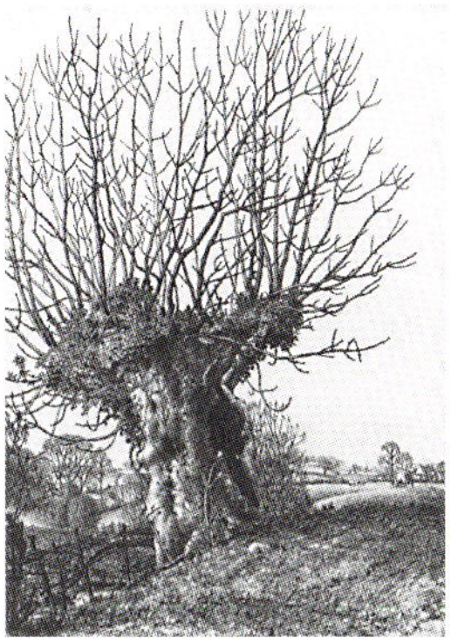

48. Stanley R. Badmin (1906-1989)
The Old Ash, 1929
etching on paper
140 x 100 mm
Stuart M. Southall

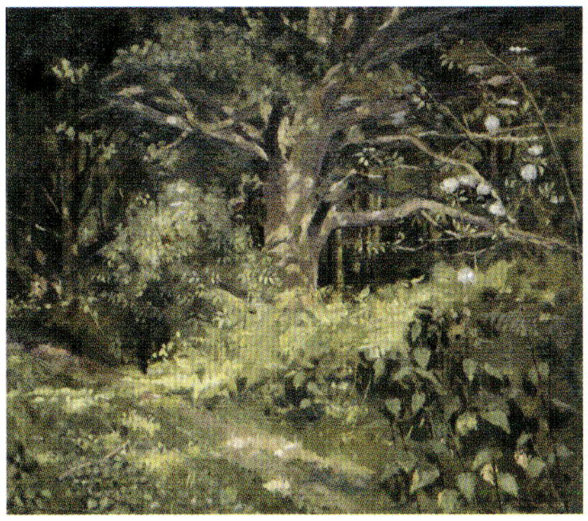

49. John Morley (1942-)
Eastern Wood, Benacre, 1995
oil, 330x 381 mm
John Morley

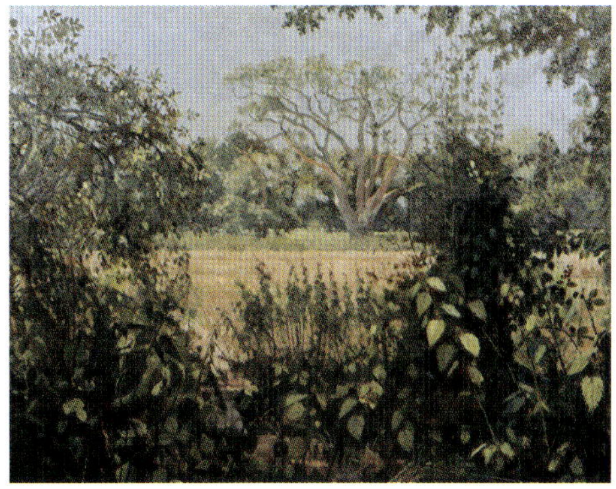

50. John Morley (1942-)
Old Oak Tree, Sotterley, 1995
oil, 349 x 451 mm
John Morley

48

Badmin's peculiar sensitivity to trees was noticeable by the late 1920s; in 1932 the *Sunday Times* considered his watercolour of Clapham Common to be 'distinguished by the delicate drawing of the bare trees'.[38] A review in *The Morning Post*, as early as 1930, noted 'the linear beauty and significance of trees in winter are revealed with eyes sensitive to the subtleties of form and a hand in sympathy with his sight and mind'.[39] Badmin found *The Old Ash* near Balcombe, Sussex; the Twenty One Gallery published an edition of forty.

Badmin illustrated many books, the first being *The Highways and Byways of Essex* in 1937; begun by Griggs the edition was finished by Badmin. The seventy-three illustrations are more or less equally divided between the two artists. He did three books for the Puffin Picture Book series for Penguin, including *Village and Town* (1942) and *Trees in Britain* (1943), both of which he wrote as well as illustrated. The latter, produced under difficult wartime conditions by Cowell's of Ipswich, with the illustrations drawn directly on the plate by the artist and costing just a few pence to buy, has been described as 'one of the most beautiful illustrated books of this century'. Later publications include *The Shell Guide to Trees and Shrubs* (1958) and *The Ladybird Book of Trees* (1963).

49 - 50

Born in Beckenham, Morley studied at the local School of Art from 1957-62 and the Royal Academy Schools until 1966. He met Graham Arnold as a schoolboy and they became friends during his time at Beckenham. Arnold and his pupil formed a Beckenham Scarlatti Society; at meetings they would drink Earl Grey tea while listening to the sonatas, which at that time were little known. Morley was actually 'thrown out' of the art school for being too traditional and a 'contaminating element'; but it was really his teacher who was leading a younger generation astray with lectures on Samuel Palmer. Arnold kept in touch with his former students, Morley and David Inshaw, via long and 'ecstatic' letters; together they formed the Broadheath Brotherhood, named in honour of Elgar's birthplace, in 1971. Due in part to the geographical distances involved, the Morley's in Suffolk and Inshaw and the Arnolds in Devizes, the Morleys were not present in 1975 at the Wellow dinner party at which the Brotherhood of Ruralists was born. But since then both John and Diana Morley have been thought of as 'friends and associates of the Ruralists', exhibiting with the Brotherhood on several occasions. Both these works show the Suffolk countryside around their home near Beccles. Here the Morleys have created a Ruralist haven rather like the Ovenden's Barley Splatt in Cornwall. John is a passionate gardener, with an enthusiasm for auriculas and snowdrops, continuing the traditions of fellow East Anglian painter-plantsmen Cedric Morris, John Nash and John Aldridge.

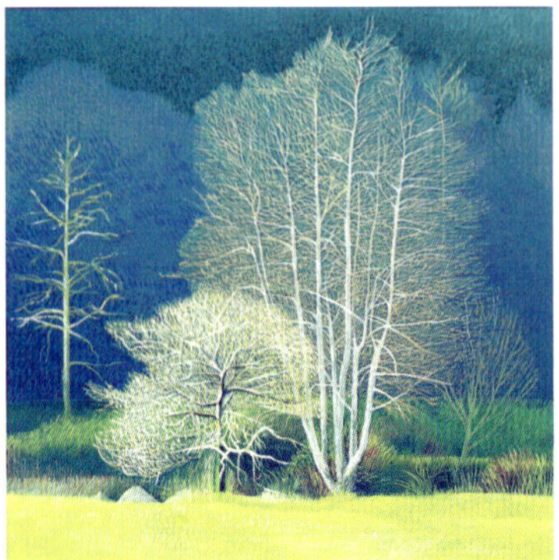

51. Annie Ovenden (1945-)
Barley Splatt Pond, 2003
oil on paper, 370 x 380 mm
John and Julia Dixon

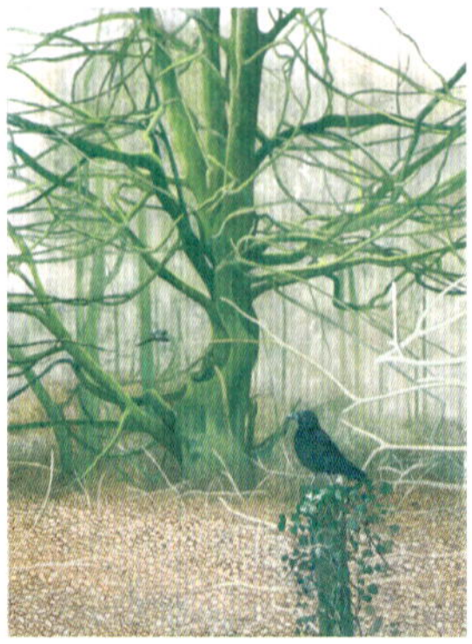

52. Annie Ovenden (1945-)
The Eye of the Bird
oil on canvas, 455 x 330 mm
Joanne Harris

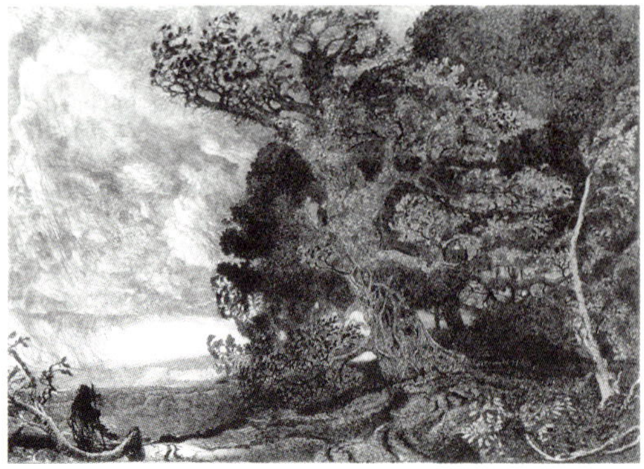

53. William Hyde (1858-1943)
The Poetical Works of John Milton. Etchings, Mezzotints, and Copper Engravings, Guildford:
The Astolat Press, 1904 (Book Case)

51

Living at Barley Splatt for 32 years the surrounding landscape has become very familiar, and yet Annie finds subjects and motifs that suddenly reveal themselves. She says 'you can pass something everyday of your life and feel that you know it and then suddenly one day the light catches it and it becomes transfigured'. Winter trees attract her the most, the patterning of the branches and light striking the limbs. The morning light gives the trees an unearthly glow, rather ghostly or haunting.

52

This work was directly inspired by a literary source, *The Underground Man* (1997) a novel by Mick Jackson, which was short-listed for the Booker Prize. It tells the story of an eccentric and reclusive aristocrat, based on the fifth Duke of Portland, who lived at Welbeck Abbey. Portland spent his days conceiving a network of carriage-wide tunnels to run beneath his sprawling Nottinghamshire estate. They take five years and hundreds of labourers to complete. The novel traces the Duke's descent into madness as, haunted by a childhood memory he even tunnels into his own head (trepanning). He takes to going into the park at night naked; coming out of a tunnel he sees the blackbird on a stump and believes the bird to have cast his evil eye on him. Eventually the Duke is shot and killed by a hunter mistaking him for a wild beast.

53

A truly beautiful edition of Milton, with text and decorative initials in the arts and crafts style, illustrated with a series of original plates by the noted illustrator and portrait painter, William Hyde. Born in New York, Hyde studied under Gustave Boulanger (1824-88), a French academic painter, at the Académie Julian, Paris and exhibited at the Royal Academy from 1889. Hyde was one of the principal illustrators for *Harper's Magazine* and also did some work for the famous *Yellow Book* (1894-97). He settled in England and eventually illustrated thirteen books. His engravings, often of landscape subjects, show great subtlety of tone, and striking effects of atmosphere.

54 - 55

Gertrude Hermes established herself as a leading wood engraver in the 1920s with work of great delicacy and complexity; 'All her work is elegant and concentrated, expressing the essential rhythms and detail of the natural world with economy'.[40]

In 1926 she married Blair Hughes-Stanton and collaborated with him in illustrations for *Pilgrim's Progress*, Cresset Press, 1926, and in murals for the World Fair, Paris, 1928. She subsequently received many commissions for wood engravings including work for Penguin's Illustrated Classics. From 1940-45 she worked in Canada and on her return to London began to make wood and lino block cuttings using colour. She exhibited regularly at the RA from 1934 becoming ARA in 1963 and RA in 1971.

Wood engraving did not become a common medium for book illustrations until Robert Gibbings took over the Golden Cockerel Press in 1924. Over the next fifteen years the Press commissioned work from many of the better-known wood engravers, including Paul and John Nash, Eric Ravilious and Eric Gill.

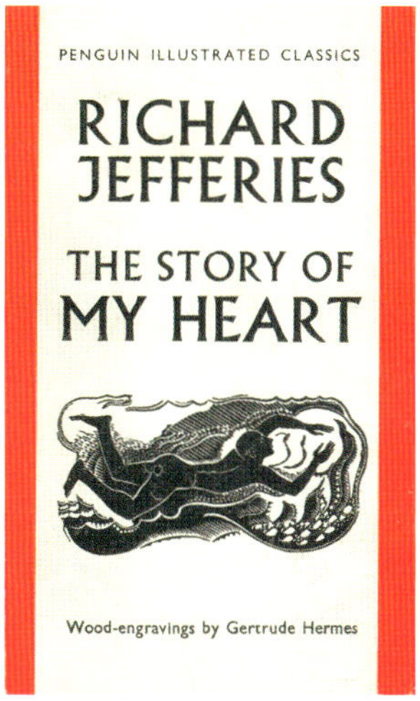

54. Gertrude Hermes (1901-1983)
cover, wood engraving, Richard Jefferies
The Story of My Heart
Harmondsworth: Penguin Classics
reprinted 1938, Anne Anderson
(Book Case)

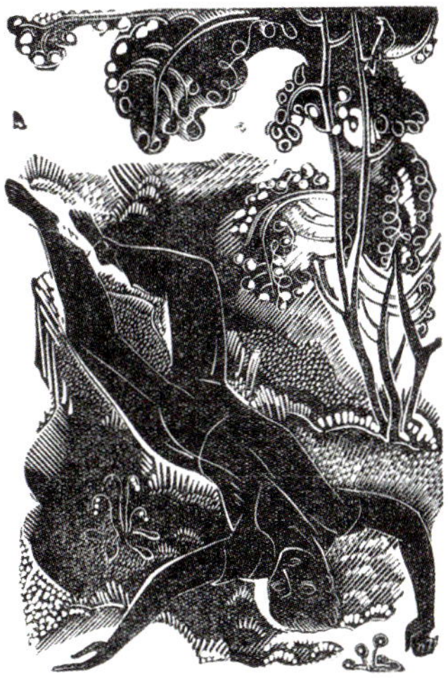

55. Gertrude Hermes (1901-1983)
illustration for Chapter I, wood engraving, Richard Jefferies
The Story of My Heart
Harmondsworth: Penguin Classics,
reprinted 1938, facing p. 17
Anne Anderson, (Book Case)

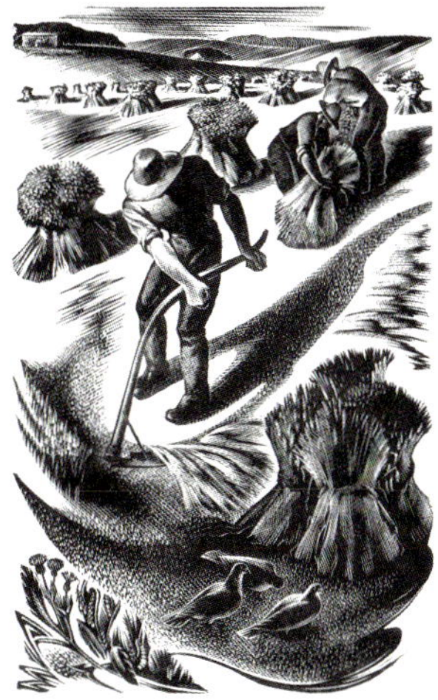

56. Agnes Miller Parker (1985-1980)
August Days
wood engraving, Samuel J. Looker (ed)
The Spring of the Year and other Nature Essays by Richard Jefferies. London:
Lutterworth Press 1946, facing p. 80
Anne Anderson, (Book Case)

Richard Jefferies (1848-1887) is best known for his prolific and sensitive writing on natural history, rural life and agriculture in late Victorian England, although a closer examination of his career reveals a many-sided author who was something of an enigma. To most people he is familiar as the author of the children's classic *Bevis* (1882). Since his death his books have enjoyed intermittent spells of popularity, but today he is unknown to the greater part of the reading public. Jefferies, however, has been an inspiration to a number of more prominent writers; W.H. Hudson, Edward Thomas, Henry Williamson and John Fowles are among those who have acknowledged their debt to him.

In late 1881 he contracted fistula, a painful disease of the bowels and during the remaining years of his life he was afflicted with a chain of illnesses. Yet it was during these years that Jefferies wrote some of his best and most original work, including his extraordinary autobiography *The Story of My Life* (1883). He had been planning this work for seventeen years and, in his words, it was 'absolutely and unflinchingly true'. It was not an autobiography of the events of his life, but an outpouring of his deepest thoughts and feelings, beginning with his first 'soul experiences' on Liddington Hill, expressed in prose poetry that is often impassioned, sensuous and evocative.

56

'Felise saw the beauty of the earth with tenfold quickened perceptions, and with that beauty she loved. She saw the clear definition of the trees, their colour, and the fineness of the extended branches-she was aware of the delicate leaves; she saw the hues of the wheat, shading from pale yellow to ruddy gold; her senses were alive to the minutest difference of tint or sound... She saw hitherto unknown glories in the light and beauty of the day, an art divine in these things. There came the low boom of distant thunder; but the hills slumbered, and the clouds were still. The reapers laboured in the corn.' (from 'August Days')[41]

Agnes Miller Parker was born in Irvine, Ayrshire, Scotland; she studied at Glasgow School of Art. She was one of the four engravers who in the early 1930s worked at the Gregynog Press, the brainchild of two wealthy sisters, Gwendoline and Margaret Davies: her husband William McChance, Gertrude Hermes and Blair Hughes-Stanton were the others. Between 1923 and 1940 forty-two handcrafted books were published by the Gregynog Press. The Gregynog *Fables of Esope* (1931) illustrated by Parker, has always been considered one of the Press' greatest books. Her wood engravings are distinctive with careful and delicate cross-hatching and stippling.

Agnes Miller Parker was also well served by Victor Gollancz, who published two of the most successful books of the period illustrated with engravings, H.E. Bates *Through the Woods: The English Woodland – April to April* (1934) and H.E. Bates *Down the River* (1937).

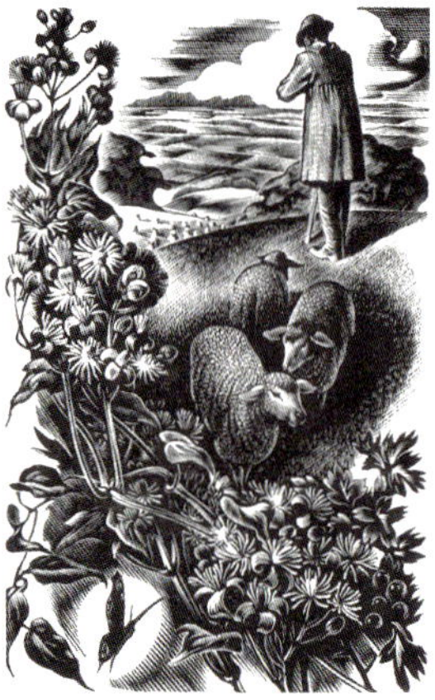

57. Agnes Miller Parker (1985-1980)
Clematis Lane
wood engraving, Samuel J. Looker (ed)
The Life of the Fields by Richard Jefferies
London: Lutterworth Press
first edition 1947
facing p. 98, Anne Anderson
(Book Case)

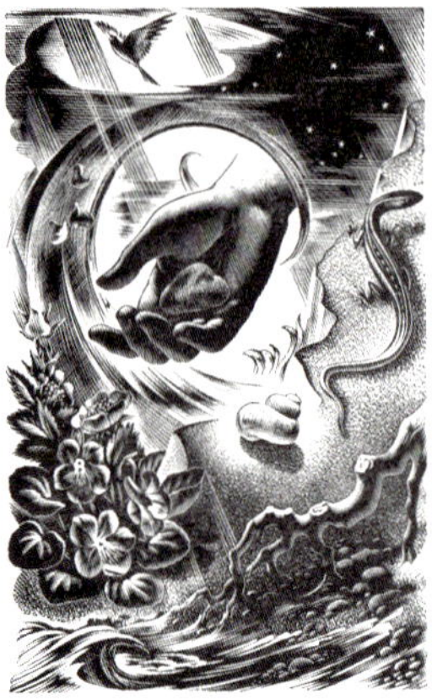

58. Agnes Miller Parker
(1985-1980) frontispiece,
wood engraving
Field and Hedgerow being the last essays of Richard Jefferies
London: Lutterworth Press
first edition 1948, Anne Anderson
(Book Case)

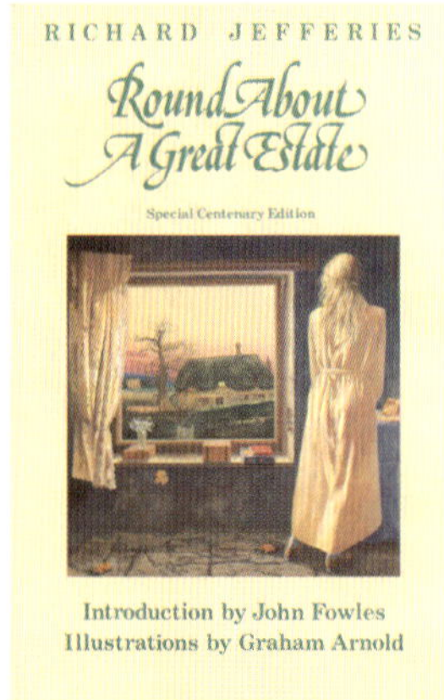

59. Graham Arnold (1932-)
cover, Richard Jefferies
Round About a Great Estate
Bradford on Avon
Ex Libris Press
reprinted 1987, Anne Anderson
(Book Case)

57

'While I have been thinking, a flock of sheep has stolen quietly into the space enclosed by the entrenchment. With the iron head of his crook placed against his breast, and the handle aslant to the ground, the shepherd leans against it, and looks down upon the reapers'. (From 'Clematis Lane') [42]

58

Much of Jefferies's best work in the years after 1880 was in the form of essays and articles published in magazines and journals including *Longman's Magazine*. A number of these were collected and reprinted in the books *Nature Near London* (1883), *The Life of the Fields* (1884) and *The Open Air* (1885). *Field and Hedgerow* appeared soon after his death, and in the 20th century Edward Thomas and Samuel J. Looker (especially the latter) brought out new books of previously unpublished or uncollected material covering all periods of his career.

59

'This is both the lightest and the richest, and easily the most attractive of Jefferies's output in what we may call his second period. It comes from the heart of his special landscape, in every sense: personally, historically, spiritually, aesthetically'.[43] *Round About a Great Estate* is the last of Jefferies's quartet of collected-article books which appeared between 1878 and 1880, the others being *The Gamekeeper at Home*, *Wild Life in a Southern County* and *The Amateur Poacher*. The 'great estate' is Burderop Park, south of Swindon, which bordered Jefferies' childhood home at Coate and was situated in the great wheat-growing plains below the Marlborough Downs. Jefferies' deep affection for the countryside of his youth, not merely its fields, woods and hamlets, but also the customs, traditions and outlook of its inhabitants, gives colour and life to his descriptions of even the most trivial matters.

60

'The first steep cornfield under the edge of the red moor lay all rough and warm with stubble in the evening light. The corns sheaves themselves were of a shining gold and leaned together in shocks that made long, low tents and invited the wayfarer to shelter and sleep. We had come over the moor for hours and this field was the beginning of a deep valley that stretched to the sea.' (from 'A Harvest Moon')[44]

Eric Fitch Daglish was born in London and studied science at university in London and Bonn. He served in the army in France during the First World War. He went on to become a professional naturalist lecturing on zoology at Toynbee Hall, the famous university settlement in the East End of London. He was a close friend of Paul Nash and learned wood engraving from him. Daglish was a fine draughtsman and engraver and illustrated many books on natural history and a series of books for children.

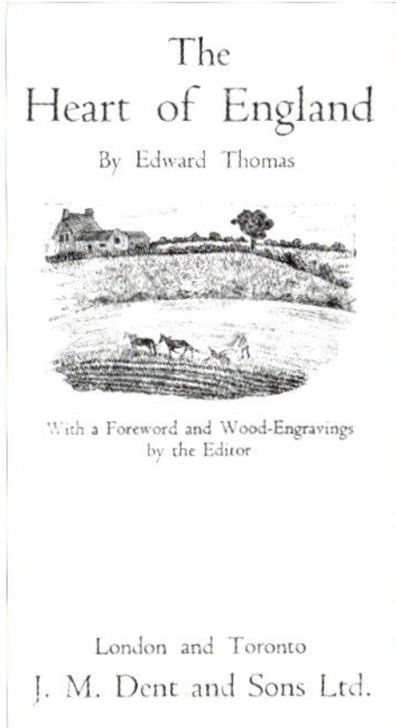

60. Eric Fitch Daglish
(1894-1966)
The Heart of England
by Edward Thomas
London: J.M. Dent, 1932
Anne Anderson
(Book Case)

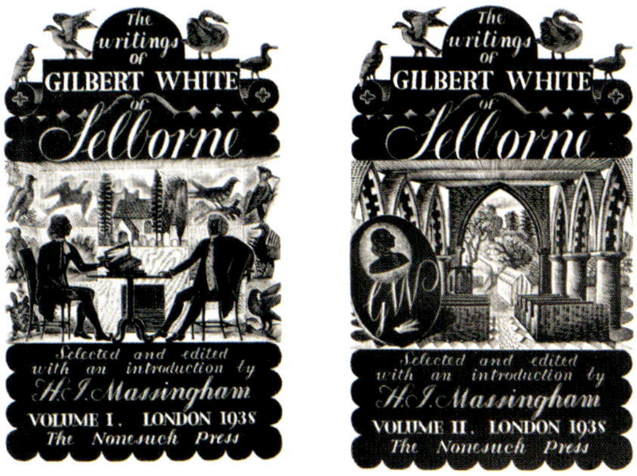

61. Eric Ravilious (1903-1942)
frontispieces, Gilbert White
The Writings of Gilbert White of Selbourne
Nonesuch Press, 2 Vols., 1938, Stuart M. Southall
(Book: Case)

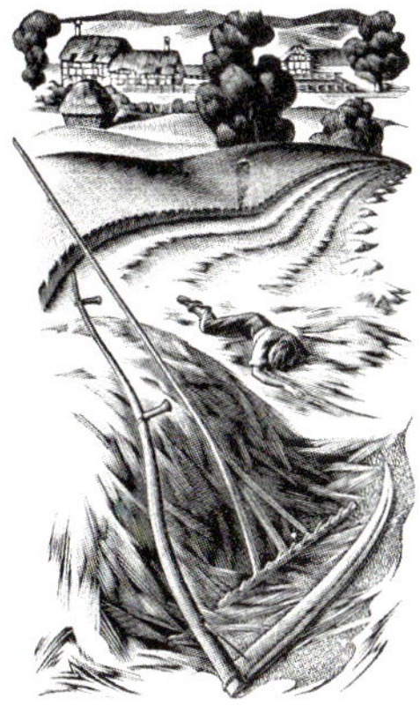

62. Agnes Miller Parker (1985-1980)
illustration for 'Farewell to barn
and stack and tree', Poem VIII
wood engraving
A.E. Houseman, *A Shropshire Lad*
London: Harrap, 1940
reprinted 1984, facing p. 18
Anne Anderson, (Book case)

> 'Mr. Daglish has quickly established himself as the Bewick of our times, with his exquisite woodcuts of birds and fishes and wildlife. He has done nothing more charming than his series of six animal books. Such delicate craftsman-ship, of both pen and the engraver's knife, is wholly delightful.' (*The Daily News*)

61

Tutored by Paul Nash, Ravilious understood how to design in sympathy with the book as a whole. Being well read his illustrations often extend the interpretation of a text. He considered the engravings for *The Writings of Gilbert White* of Selborne, (1938), edited by Harold John Massingham (1888-1952), an author he had loved since he was a student, to be among his best:

> 'In 1887, Richard Jefferies, a popular nature essayist, added his name to the list of several dozen individuals who had written either introductions or notes to Gilbert White's *The Natural History of Selborne* (1789). Jefferies, like many who chose to edit and introduce this text throughout the Victorian period, represents White as a model figure... Jefferies commends White and his *Natural History* as examples of simple, reflective engagement with a local, natural economy – an approach to nature that any inquisitive and observant person could emulate... All that is needed to become a student of natural history, Jefferies suggests, is curiosity and intelligence. He informs his reader that, "In the same manner [as White] any one who has a taste for out-of-door observations may study natural history without any previous scientific learning. There is not the smallest need to know the Latin names of the birds in order to watch them, or of the flowers in order to gather them."' (viii) .[45]

62

Farewell to barn and stack and tree,
Farewell to Severn shore,
Terrence, look your last at me,
For I come home no more.

The sun burns on the half-mown hill,
By now the blood is dried;
And Maurice amongst the hay lies still
And my knife is in his side.
My mother thinks us long away;
'Tis time the field were mown,
She had two sons at rising day
To-night she be alone.

And here's a bloody hand to shake,
And oh, man here's good-bye;
We'll sweat no more on scythe and rake,
My bloody hands and I...

Kingsley Amis wrote of Houseman that 'he put into words what for most of us is no more than a vague glimmering, perhaps intensified at dusk, a fleeting suspicion that there is more to nature than can ever meet the eye, something within or beyond it, and no illustrator yet born could ever do justice to such mysteries'.[46]

Alfred Edward Houseman (1859-1936), usually known as A.E. Houseman, is best remembered for his cycle of 63 poems *A Shropshire Lad*, first published at his own expense in 1896. At first selling slowly, it rapidly forged a lasting success, especially in America, and its appeal to English musicians helped to make it widely known before

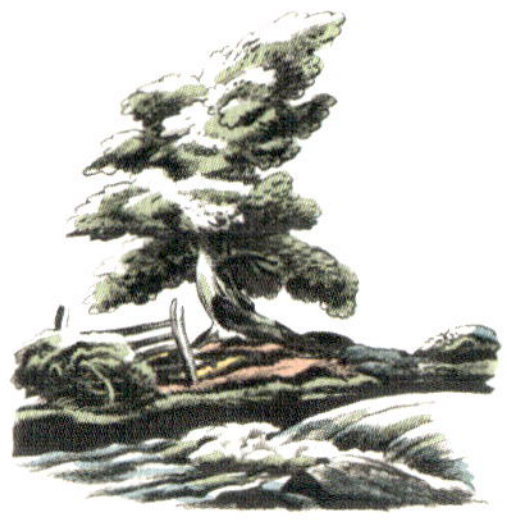

63. Edward Arthur Wilson (1886-1970, American)
Poem 54, coloured lithograph
A Shropshire Lad Poems by A.E. Houseman
New York: The Heritage Press, 1951, p. 117
Anne Anderson, (Book Case)

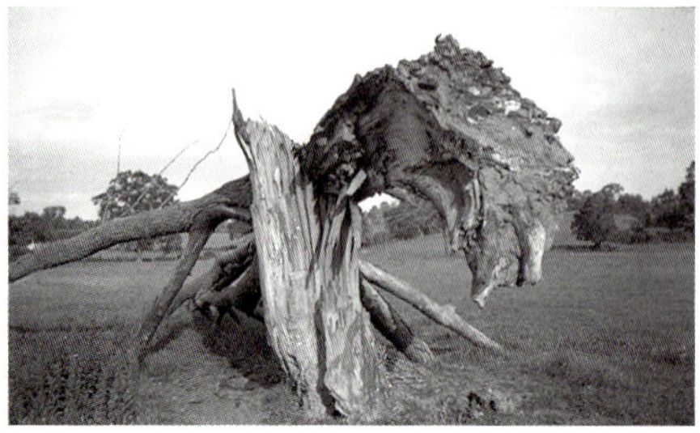

64. Paul Nash (1889-1946)
Monster Field: A Discovery Recorded by Paul Nash
collotypes, Oxford: Counterpoint Publications, 1946
756 of 1000 copies
Anne Anderson, (Book Case)

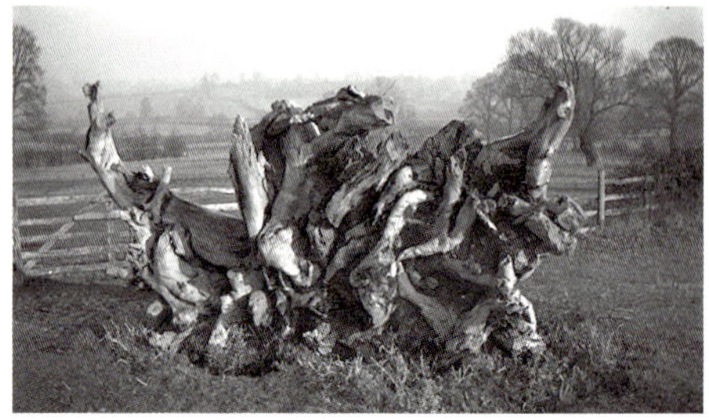

65. Paul Nash (1889-1946)
Laocoön 1941, Black and white photograph
From a Private World. Photographs by Paul Nash
Fischer Fine Art, 1978
Anne Anderson, (Book Case)

the First World War. A wistful evocation of 'doomed youth in the English countryside', *A Shropshire Lad* inevitably became associated with the generation that died in the trenches of Flanders. Almost epigrammatic in form, their spare language and distinctive imagery contrast with the exuberance of some late Victorian contemporaries (especially Jefferies). Pervaded by a deep pessimism and preoccupation with death, without religious consolation, Housman wrote most of the Poems before visiting the part of Shropshire (about thirty miles from his home) that he immortalised as his 'land of lost content'.

63

> With rue my heart is laden,
> For golden friends I had,
> For many a rose-lipt maiden
> And many a lightfoot lad.
>
> By brooks too broad for leaping
> The lightfoot boys are laid;
> The rose-lipt girls are sleeping
> In fields where roses fade.

Houseman's *Shropshire Lad* has achieved iconic status in the United States. This illustration by Wilson shows that even the Americans are susceptible to the motifs of the English elegiac pastoral.

64

Nash wrote *Monster Field* in 1939; the essay describes two fallen elms Nash discovered on Carswalls Farm, Newent, Upleadon, near Charles and Clare Neilsons' home Madams, in Gloucestershire, which Nash visited periodically between 1938 and 1944. These trees evoked for Nash the personality of a monster. In his essay Nash explains that they were not monsters in the animal sense but:

> 'monster objects outside the plan of natural phenomena. What reference they have to life should not be considered in relation to their past – therein they are dead – they now excite our interest on another plane; they have 'passed on' as people say. These now inanimate natural objects are alive in another world.' [47]

One reminded him of the cow in Picasso's *Guernica* (1937, Madrid). Another suggested itself as the 'equivalent' of Blake's horse in his interpretation of the 'sightless couriers of the air'.

The full potential of their power, came home to him, when a farmer's boy, on seeing Nash sketching the trees, pointed out that by crossing the fields he had probably contributed to the spread of foot and mouth disease. This led Nash to speculate on the effect foot and mouth would have on the monsters:

> 'Suddenly, a more disturbing thought occurred to me. Supposing the "monsters" became infected, how would they react? I did not know the nature of foot and mouth disease. It sounded highly dangerous, like rabies. Perhaps-milk fever! Madness? Stampeed [*sic*]; all sorts of words and images started going off like fireworks in my head.' [48]

Drawing on Surrealism, Nash isolated the 'monsters' from their natural setting as *objets trouvés*, enhancing their sinister personality:

> 'Nash was able to discern in their ruinous aspect a potential for poetic renewal, evinced in the sugges-

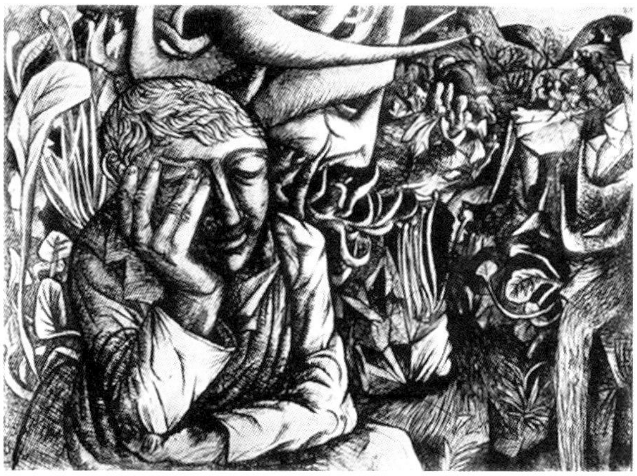

66. JOHN CRAXTON (1922-)
Dreamer in Landscape, 1941
pen and wash drawing, reproduced
in *Horizon*, March, Vol.V, No. 27, 1942
Anne Anderson, (Book Case)

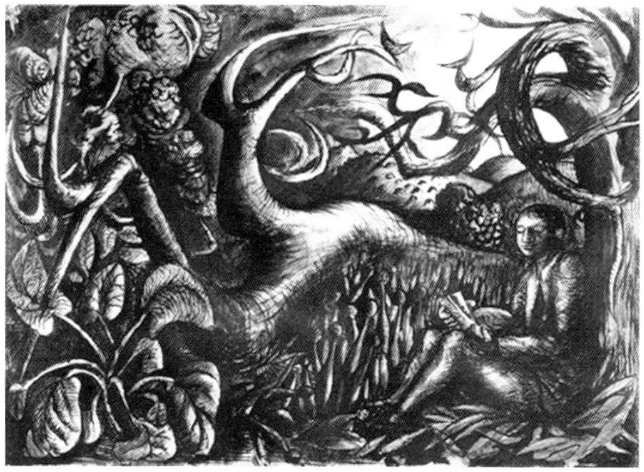

66a. JOHN CRAXTON (1922-)
Poet in Landscape, 1941
pen and wash drawing, reproduced
in *Horizon*, March, Vol.V, No. 27, 1942
John Craxton, (Book Case)

> tiveness of their monstrous, stricken shapes. Seen from the right angle, one site of devastation could be transformed into a new apparition of the *Stalking Horse* (1941), the negativeness of mere chaos being outweighed by the poetry-albeit the sinister poetry-of grotesque metamorphosis.' [49]

Nash's resourceful imagination transforms destruction and disaster into the 'poetic'; he achieved the same in *Totes Meer* (1940) his famous depiction of destroyed Second World War aircraft. The configuration of the monsters 'tugged at his sensibility for reasons of private association, poetic connotation, or aesthetic tension.' Above all Nash invested his feelings in these trees. Nash took a number of photographs of the fallen trees at Carswalls Farm, which, with the sketches he made, formed the basis for two major oil paintings, *Monster Field* and *Monster Shore*, both 1939. There are also two watercolours of the monsters.

65

Another of Nash's equivalents, this gnarled tree stump was photographed on Carswalls Farm in Gloucestershire. It was used for a watercolour (1941) now destroyed. The tree reminded Nash of the famous Classical sculpture the *Laocoön*, in the Vatican, a dramatic depiction of the death of the Trojan priest and his sons. Laocoön, who famously warned the Trojans to 'Beware of Greeks bearing gifts', was executed by serpents sent by Minerva from the sea; they strangled the priest and his sons.

66

Craxton was studying in Paris at the outbreak of the Second World War, completing his studies at Westminster School of Art and the Central School of Art. Having been rejected for military service, Peter Watson, tastemaker and patron, came forward to offer Craxton studio space; Watson's other beneficiary was Lucien Freud, Craxton's exact contemporary. All the doors opened for these two young men, few young artists have had so much support or direct access to the leading men of the day – Piper, Moore, Sutherland and Kenneth Clark all dropping into their studios to encourage them; Craxton toured the wilds of Pembrokeshire with Graham Sutherland in 1943. On Watson's walls were works by Miro, Picasso, de Chirico and Roger de la Fresnaye, alongside those of Christopher Wood, Piper, Sutherland, Minton and Frances Hodgkins. Watson provided an intellectual milieu where Craxton's ideas matured:

> 'Perhaps I am a romantic and romantic painters make pictures as extensions of themselves; they cannot be accused of being objective. I think nostalgia can be a motivating force.'[50]

In the autumn of 1941 Craxton produced two ink drawings, *Poet in Landscape* (the artist) and *Dreamer in Landscape* (Tate Britain), which Peter Watson reproduced in *Horizon* the following year. Craxton's poet and dreamer 'as projections of myself' were derived from Blake and Palmer. Watson had shown Craxton two of the sepia drawings of 1825 newly acquired by the Ashmolean, Oxford, via Geoffrey Grigson's article on Samuel Palmer in *Horizon*. Craxton comments 'I think you have to look at what I did, to see the influence: Palmer took the essence of something and paraphrased it so that one had a po-

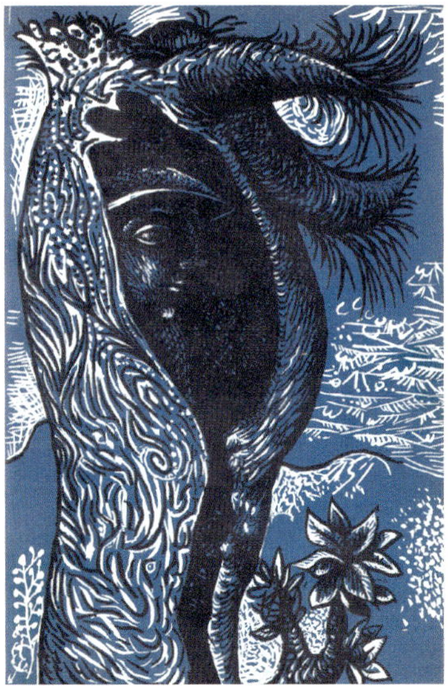

67. John Craxton (1922-)
The Poets Eye
anthology chosen by Geoffrey Grigson with 16 lithographs by John Craxton, 1944, Anne Anderson (Book Case)

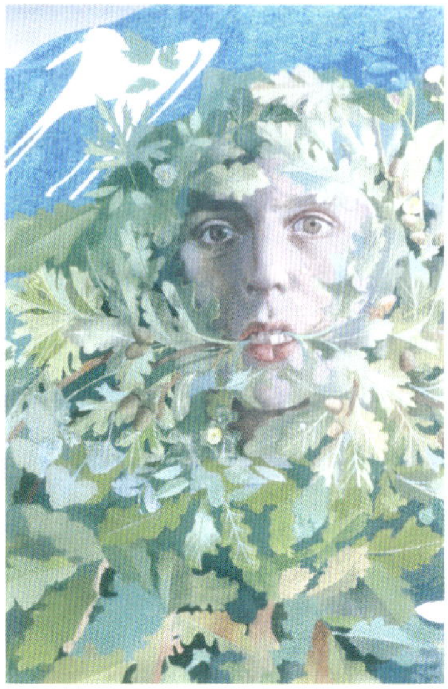

68. Jerrold Northrop Moore and the Ruralists with David Inshaw
Edward Elgar The Child of Dreams
Ruralist Fine Art, 2004, Graham Ovenden (Book Case)

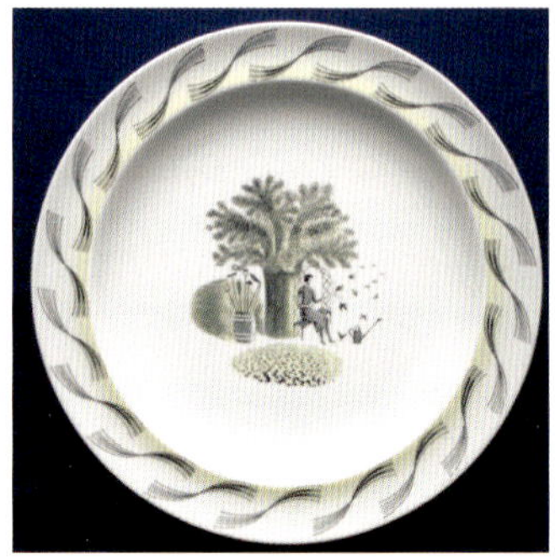

69.1. Eric Ravilious (1903-1942)
Garden Implements,
Garden Series
Travel Series, designed for Wedgwood, Staffordshire

etic image of it. It was a distillation of nature'. [51] His own 'distillation of nature' gave him 'clarity of purpose'. Craxton was 'simply obsessed' by Blake at this time, and had taken Blake's poems to his army medical examination, which he failed due to pleurisy. He later discussed these landscapes as 'my means of escape and a sort of self-protection. A shepherd is a lone figure, and so is the poet. I wanted to safeguard a world of private mystery, and I was drawn to the idea of bucolic calm as a kind of refuge'. [52]

Although Craxton adopted the solitary figure of the poet, calmly reading his poetry, the landscape around him rages and boils in a way Palmer would never have envisaged, while the *Dreamer* is submerged in jungle fecundity. Tree roots crash through the undergrowth, it is wild, stormy, full of fear and terror; Craxton tells us that it was a 'portrait of someone who has detached himself from a wild landscape. He is sitting there totally calm'.[53] Craxton had of course detached himself from the war: 'You might say my work is "escapist" art and, somehow, it became an antidote to the war in the same way that Palmer's was an antidote to his times'.[54]

67

'Essence' and 'distillation' became Craxton's watchwords as much as '*genius loci*' had been for Nash or 'paraphrase' for Sutherland. His plant forms develop conical branches or leaves like sickles; knife blades pierce the earth. This spikiness comes from Sutherland. He fell under Sutherland's tutelage during their trip to Pembrokeshire in 1943; he now learnt how to paraphrase entire landscapes in one intensely observed fragment. Nash's 'monsters' added a 'mild' Surrealism. Craxton also came into contact with Francis Bacon, just starting out as a painter but already gaining fame for his 'tortured psyche'. In his reviews of Craxton's work, Ayrton was rather disparaging – 'In that they cleverly combine the styles of Graham Sutherland and Picasso with a fairly original method, these minor works indicate that Craxton is gifted, but in that they lack a direct visual reaction to nature they are empty'. [55]

The Blake enthusiast, John Grigson, a poet and reviewer, commissioned Craxton to provide sixteen lithographs for his anthology *The Poet's Eye*. It was an inspired and daring choice, as Craxton was still only twenty-two. Byran Robertson considers, 'The later *Poet's Eye* drawings confirmed Craxton's gifts: I still think they are among the finest decorations made for any English book this century'. [56] The images are indeed impressive, the colours strong and the drawing bold and angular. There are attempts in the manner of Nash to make tree forms suggest human features. But Yorke concludes 'they are still clever pastiches of other men's styles'[57].

68

Jerrold Northrop Moore writes:

> 'A book conceived by the Ruralists and me one spring morning as we sat round the kitchen table at Barley Splatt. It seems to play, as we had hoped, about creative boarderland; 'that sweet boarderland', as Elgar once wrote, 'where I have made my home'.

From the 'Foreword':

> 'Many of its pictures were drawn and painted especially for it- and give my text a new dimension tran-

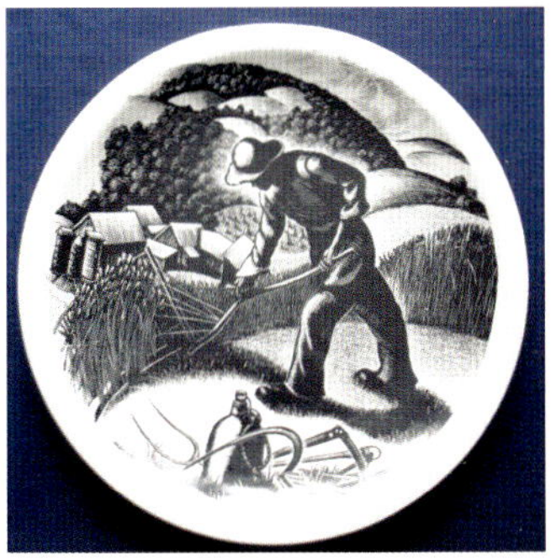

69.2. Clare Leighton (1898-1989)
New England Industries Series
for Wedgwood,
Staffordshire, issued in the 1950s
Mr and Mrs Taylor

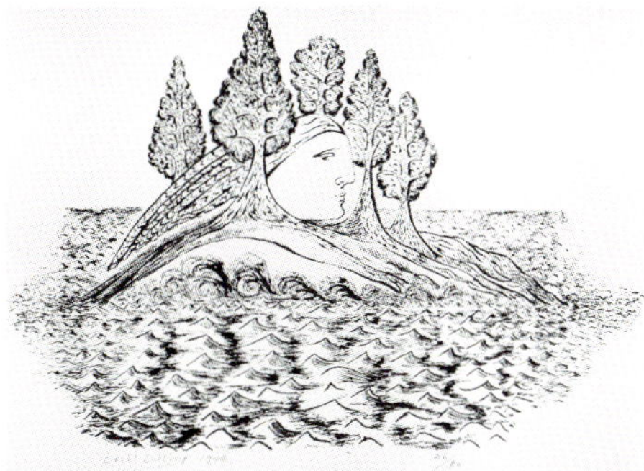

71. Cecil Collins (1908-1989)
The Island, 1944
Roneo print, 285 x 389 mm
Victoria Art Gallery, Bath
(Shown Bath only)

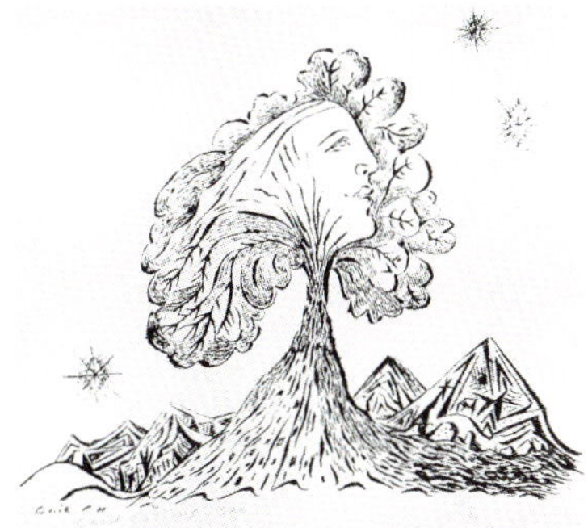

72. Cecil Collins (1908-1989)
Head in a Tree (*Tree and Hills*), 1944
Roneo print, 283 x 389 mm
Victoria Art Gallery, Bath
(Shown Bath only)

scending simple illustration. So this text and these images together project what may be a new understanding of separate arts linking hands under the sun and moon of pastoral tradition. Together the artists and I seek to evoke a creative life lived in landscapes still partly there to see and feel. Elgar himself once said to a young composer: "I am glad you smell the Severn in my music"'.

69

Ravilious produced posters and designs for Wedgwood, including the celebration mug (1936) for the coronation of King Edward VIII, which was withdrawn and revised for the coronations of George VI and Elizabeth II; the Alphabet mug (1937); the Afternoon Tea (1937), Travel (1938), Garden Implements (1939), china sets and the Boat Race Day cup (1938). Garden, introduced in 1938, was considered by many to be the most elaborate of the Ravilious designs.

Although known primarily for her work as a printmaker, Clare Leighton also designed numerous book illustrations, bookplates, engravings, illustrations, mosaics, and stained glass windows over the course of a long and productive career. She wrote seven books, among them *Four Hedges: A Gardener's Chronicle*, illustrated with her own prints, and a treatise on wood engraving, her forte.

70

John Piper (1903-1992)
Green Man Plate
Southampton City Art Gallery
(Book Case)

A Green Man is a representation of a face surrounded by or made of leaves. Foliage may sprout from the nose, mouth, nostrils or other parts of the face and these shoots may bear flowers or fruit. The Green Man motif has many different faces and variations. It is found in many cultures, often being related to natural vegetative deities. It is primarily interpreted as a symbol of rebirth or 'renaissance' representing the cycle of growth, being reborn anew every spring. It is particularly associated with Celtic folklore and the semi-wild man who lives on the edge of the forest. Taken up by the late Victorian Arts and Crafts Movement, 'he is the voice of inspiration to the aspirant and committed artist. He can come as a white light or the gleam on a blade of grass, but more often as an inner mood. The sign of his presence is the ability to work or experience with tireless enthusiasm beyond one's normal capacities.' (William Anderson, *Green Man: The Archetype of our Oneness with the Earth*)

71 - 72

2008 sees the centenary of the birth of Collins, who deserves wider recognition as a poet and a painter. Described as 'a poet who happens to use form and pigment instead of words'[58], Collins in fact wrote poems throughout his life, which closely relate to the visionary atmosphere of his paintings and writings on the theme of the Fool, a theme which dominated his work from 1939: 'The saint, the artist, and the poet are all one in the Fool, in him they live, in him the poetic imagination of life lives.[59] He contrasted the Fool with 'the manifest bankruptcy and sterility of contemporary life'. The Fool rejects modern society, because 'the Fool represents that

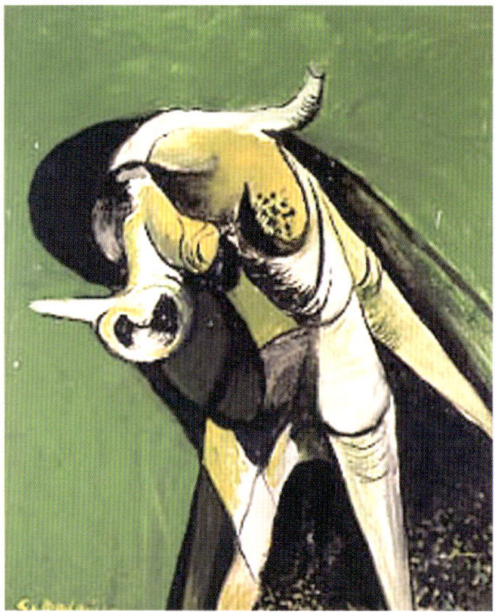

73. Graham Vivien Sutherland (1903-1980)
Green Tree Form, 1940
oil on canvas, 605 x 545 mm
British Council

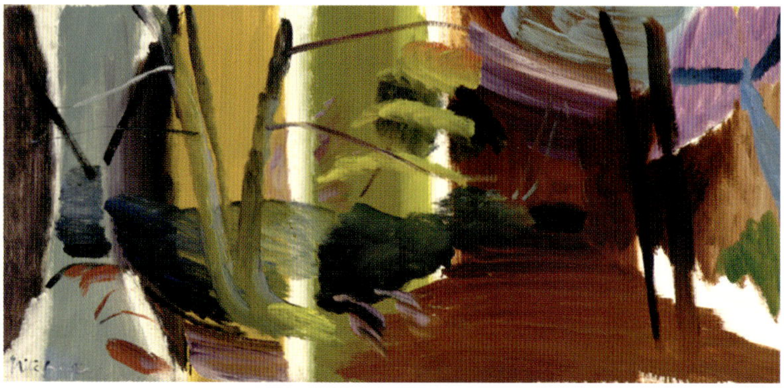

74. Ivon Hitchens (1893-1979)
Oak Tree in Purple Woods
oil on canvas, 435 x 1094 mm
Southampton City Art Gallery, Smith Bequest

profound fertile innocence, down from which we have fallen, into the dirt and filth of mechanical existence'. This 'fertile innocence' is captured in these two works, which also suggest the influence of Art Nouveau and Surrealism on Collins. Here we have metamorphosis, a process that also fascinated Nash, the human head emerging from a tree recalling the Green Man. In *The Island* the female head/tree form is surrounded by water, perhaps designed to suggest creation, as Venus was born from the sea. Both works seem to borrow from the idea of creation myths, denying the slaughter of the war. .

73

Sutherland first visited Wales in 1934 and returned at regular intervals throughout the decade. He made small sketches of natural phenomena that sparked his imagination and nourished his ideas. He began to discern 'personalities' or 'personages' in the organic forms he collected, endowing them in his paintings with human overtones. This work is based on a fallen tree lying on a grassy bank, exposing its roots, at the entrance to a lane. The tree assumes a quasi-human form, resembling a bloated, truncated, corpse. Sutherland has isolated this 'found object' and abstracted its form so that it seems to loom from the lurid green surrounds. *Green Tree Form* bears a striking resemblance to Nash's *Monster Field*, photographed in 1939. *Green Tree Form: Interior of Woods* (1940, Tate Britain) is a related work.

74

There is a musicality about this depiction of a Sussex wood; Hitchens even maintained, 'My paintings are painted to be listened to'. Colour and broad swathes of paint are used to articulate space and shifting forms that evoke the sensuous experience of lush, leafy woodland. The lively brushwork and vibrant colouring suggests a sense of movement and rhythm, the wind rustling in trees and fleeting bird song; the artist is trying to capture the 'essence' of nature. The work itself moves between the abstract and figurative; the divided form on the left echoes Sutherland's 'personages' and 'personalities'.

The scene is animated by creating advancing and receding space, and with the play of light and dark. Hitchens used the Japanese word *noten* to describe this aspect of his art. *Noten* means the harmony of dark and light spaces. Hitchens employs his trademark long horizontal canvas to give a wide vista. There is no conventional single viewpoint to hold the eye, which is allowed to range freely across the canvas.

75

James Sellars (1927-2000)
Tree Creeper Island
mixed media, 350 x 545 mm
Pandora Sellars

This subject was found in the Test Valley. Jim Sellars was Graham Oveden's teacher and mentor at the Southampton College of Art.

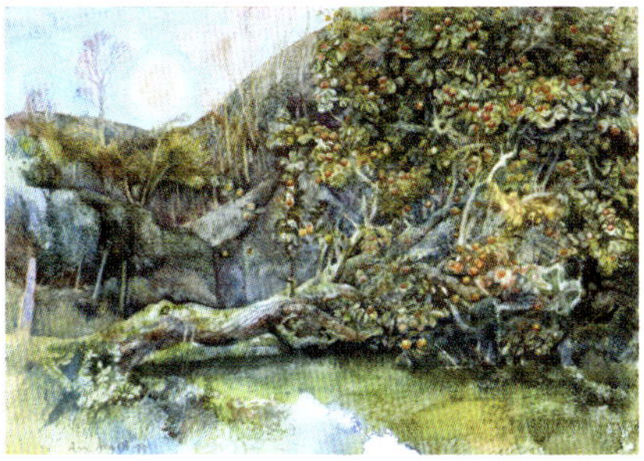

76. Ann Arnold (1936-)
Fallen Tree
watercolour, 229x 343 mm
Christopher Martin

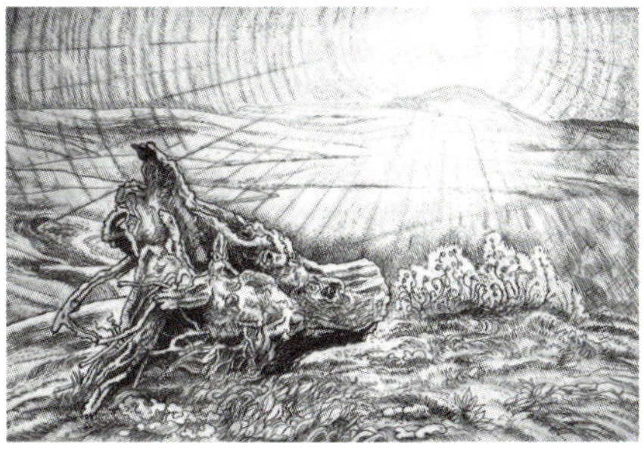

77. Edgar Holloway (1914-)
Wolstonbury (c.1990)
etching on paper, 176 x 264mm
Stuart Southall

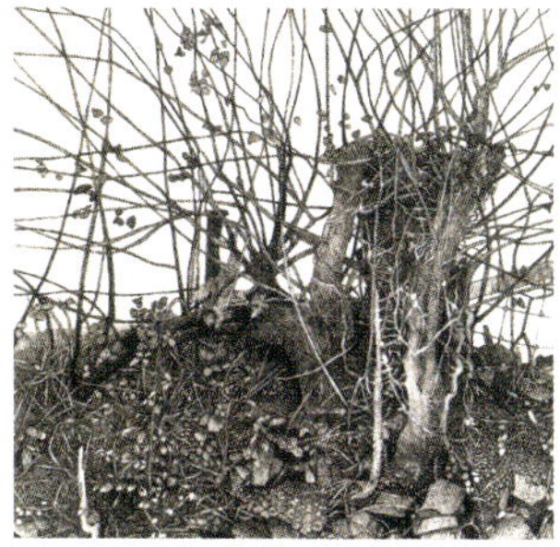

78. Annie Ovenden (1945-)
Tangled Woven Webb
pen and ink, 340 x 355 mm
2006, Anne Anderson

76

The Marches, after centuries of warfare between the English and the Welsh, are resonant with melancholic associations that are very much to Ruralist taste. In front of the Arnold's Shropshire home, rises a formidable hill crowned by an Iron Age hill fort known as Care Caradoc, much painted by Ann; it is one of a system of such forts, 'markers of semi-legendary battles between Romans and Britons'.[60] Ann Arnold's watercolours subtly catch the spirit of this haunted and haunting region.

Here the apple tree has fallen; perhaps toppled over by the weight of its own fruit. The scene is bathed in the mystical light of the full moon; there is that 'pervading sense of fatalism', as detected in *The Sanctuary*.

77

Now in his nineties, Holloway is one of the few surviving artists who enjoyed success during the etching revival of the 1920s and 1930s. Showing his work, from 1931, at the Twenty One Gallery he came into contact with Paul Drury, Joseph Webb and Ernest Lumsden, the author of *The Art of Etching*. Although the market was in decline, Holloway continued to make prints until 1947, when financial pressures led him into commercial design, cartography, lettering and the designing of book jackets. In 1949 he joined the craftsmen of the Guild of St Joseph and St Dominic on Ditchling Common, East Sussex, established by Eric Gill (1882-1940) and Hilary Pepler in 1919. It was reading the work of Gill that precipitated Holloway's conversion to Catholicism at the age of twenty-seven. In 1968 Holloway returned to watercolours and etching, after a hiatus of some twenty years.

Wolstonbury, on the South Downs, was derived from a watercolour of 1982. The dramatically lit recumbent tree trunk is reminiscent of Nash's 'monsters'.

78

One of a series of three works all bearing the same name; the trees around Barley Splat, her Cornish home, would have inspired Annie Ovenden. Still growing out of a dry-stone wall, the stump is throwing out spindly branches. Like Nash's 'monsters' this 'dotard' has taken on a malevolent form; Schama uses the term 'dotard' to describe one of the dead Burham beeches, which looks like an animal writhing in its death throws or, bleached white, the carcass of some pre-historic beast. Dotard describes 'an old person with impaired intellect', as though these trees are still trying to generate life even though they have lost their creative powers.

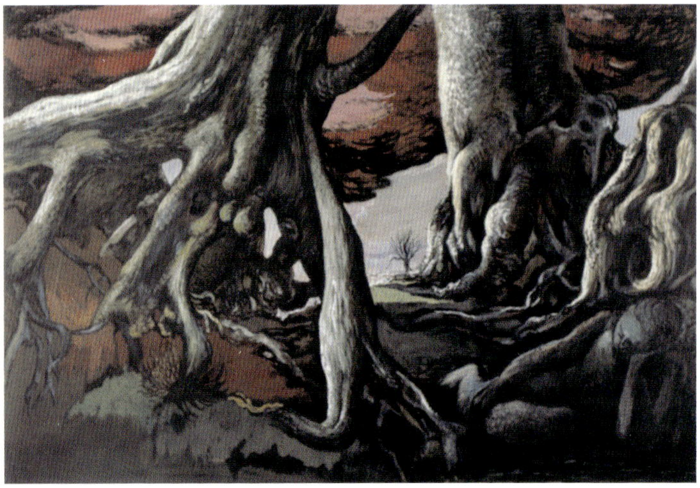

79. John Elwyn (1916-1997)
The Stillness of the Roots, 1946
watercolour incorporating gouache
pencil and crayon
Peter Wakelin and Clive Hicks-Jenkins

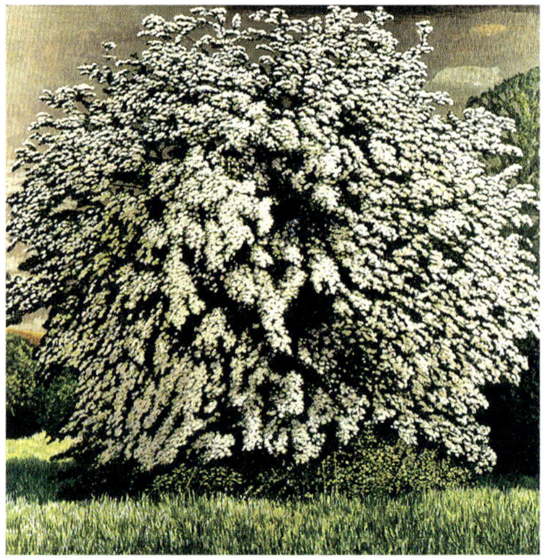

80. David Inshaw (1943-)
May Tree with Grey Sky, 1998
oil on canvas, 1168 x 1168 mm
Ivor Braka

79

Elwyn's wartime drawings recall works by his exact contemporaries John Minton, John Craxton and Michael Ayrton, who are now associated with the Neo-Romantic movement that flourished during Britain's isolation. His paintings of gnarled and twisted roots and menacing tree stumps in scarred and desecrated landscapes, which he discovered whilst a forestry worker above Pont-Rhyd-y-Fen in the Afan Valley, echo Sutherland's Pembrokeshire works. The lone figure that sleeps in a claustrophobic landscape of tangled roots in *The Stillness of the Roots* recalls Craxton's *Poet in Landscape* (1941, the artist) and *Dreamer in Landscape* (1941, Tate Britain). The *Aftermath* drawings of 1945 that depict surreal scenes of chaos and destruction reveal the artist's anxieties about the war (he had been a conscientious objector) and his horror at the atrocities committed at the Belsen concentration camp; these works were clearly cathartic.

80

Inshaw had already achieved a considerable reputation before the forming of the Ruralists. *The Badminton Game* (1972-3) first caught the public's attention; this was presented to Tate Britain in 1980. *The Cricket Match* (1976) set in Little Bredy, West Dorset, captures the very spirit of England. Liking cricket and flower shows, as well as Blake and Elgar made Inshaw an obvious Ruralist candidate; moreover Graham Arnold was his teacher and mentor of old from Beckenham College of Art. However, Inshaw was already in a band of brothers, the Broadheath Brotherhood, so named after Elgar's birthplace, which had come together in 1971, the same year Inshaw moved to Devizes. The Broadheath Brotherhood included Inshaw, the Arnolds and another married couple John and Diana Morley (clearly you need seven to form a brotherhood). John Morley, also a student of Graham Arnold, had already been contaminated with a preference for Palmer. The Broadheath Brotherhood celebrated 'Englishness'; Richard Jefferies, Wordsworth and Milton were on their reading list: 'They immersed themselves in the spirit of Blake's Jerusalem and saw themselves as illuminated by his incandescent vision'.[61] Arnold came up with the idea of getting away to the *real* country; they could pool resources, buy a big house, grown their own vegetables and most importantly give up teaching and get down to painting. But the Morleys had only just bought a cottage in Suffolk and John needed his teaching position. He was also rather suspicious of 'communities'. Shortly after fate intervened, as the Arnolds, via Inshaw met Peter Blake and that dinner party was held at Wellow. The Morleys were not there so they did not become founder members of the Brotherhood of Ruralists.

Looking for his own piece of England, Inshaw settled on Devizes, a small market town in Wiltshire; he acquired a large Georgian house and invited the Arnolds to join him. Devizes was ideally situated as the Wessex landscape, the barrows, the megaliths and particularly Silbury Hill captivated Inshaw. This forty metre high man-made pre-historic hill is still a mystery, as successive excavations have failed to unlock its secrets. It clearly had a purpose, being part of a pre-historic complex that includes Avebury and West Kennet long barrow but it remains 'a stupendous enigma'; the perfect Ruralist motif: 'in painting after painting he evokes a world both recollected and projected, of intimation and

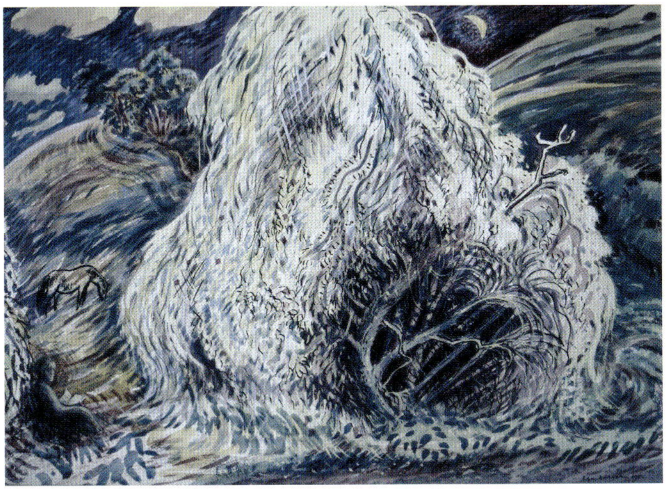

81. Edgar Holloway (1914-)
The Bride, Keymer Bostall, 1982
watercolour, 370 x 520 mm
Edgar and Jennifer Holloway

provocative possibility rather than forthright exposition'.[62]

The *May Tree* appears in the foreground of *Portrait of Silbury Hill, May* (1989, Cat. 99). It is now monumental, looming so large that its seems about to embraced us. It clearly signals spring and rejuvenation but the cascade of white blossom also resembles a bridal veil.

81

Holloway's later watercolours are less concerned with literal transcriptions; *Orchard Moon* (Cat. 122) and *The Bride* are more visionary, lyrical interpretations concerned with the 'spirit of place'. This work is intensely Palmeresque, with its tapestry-like landscape and crescent moon; a solitary figure sits in the moonlight reading. Edward Calvert's *The Bride* (1828, British Museum) depicts a naked female figure in a fruitful landscape; Holloway's bride is more enigmatic, the title referring to the Old Man's Beard covering a hawthorn bush, which conjures up the vision of a veiled bride. The impressive vault-like mass also suggested to him the Church as the Bride of Christ.[63] Holloway was inspired by his impending marriage to Jennifer Boxall, following the death in 1979, after a long illness, of his first wife, Daisy Monica Hawkins. The etching of the same subject dates to 1990.

82

John William North (1842-1924)
The Old Pear Tree 1892
watercolour on paper, 964 x 724
Southampton City Art Gallery
presented by Sir Hubert von Herkomer
(Southampton only)

Painted in 1892, this work is a Victorian interloper. However, it is included to demonstrate the continuity of themes, particularly the fecundity of nature and the desire to band together into artistic collectives as North was an Idyllist. His fellow brothers were Frederick Walker, Boyd Houghton and George Pinwell. As a renowned Victorian book illustrator Graham Ovenden has an obvious affection for him.

> '"North" country, his "spirit of place", lay in Somerset: loveliest region of England which lies between the Quantock Hills and the Severn sea; undulating country that slopes from uplands of pasture and furze common down through orchards and crops to fall into wooded valleys where wind the sweetest fern-fringed streams. Intricate lanes burrow their way in deep grooves between banks of red earth which are overhung with canopies of greenwood festooned with sprays of honeysuckle, dog-rose, and the wild clematis. These cool, shaded ways lead down to thatched farmsteads and hamlets, where in the sheltered gardens grow roses, giant hollyhocks, and all the old-world flowers in a profusion such as elsewhere I have never seen. Here live and toil "amid the peaceful noises of the farm" a sturdy folk of healthy mien, gentle speech, and a most courteous address.' [64]

North had plenty of sympathy with the farmer's life, and was politically active on their behalf, 'but he also admired William Blake, and if he lacked that poet's inspiration he nevertheless saw the countryside with an idealized vision... North was one of the last Ro-

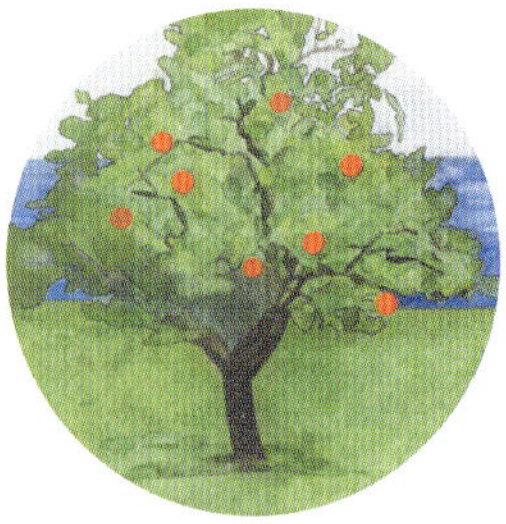

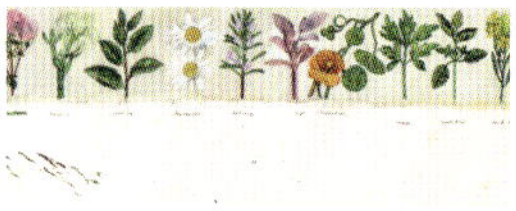

83. Peter Blake (1932-)
The Apple Tree
watercolour, design for top of circular enamel box
The Flowers
watercolour design to go round sides of enamel box
Graham Ovenden

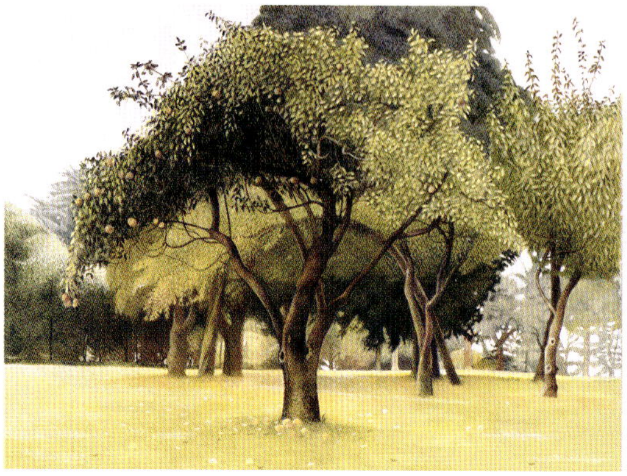

84. Annie Ovenden (1945-)
Rainbow Orchard, Summer, 1996
oil on canvas, 660 x 458 mm
Diana Wilkinson

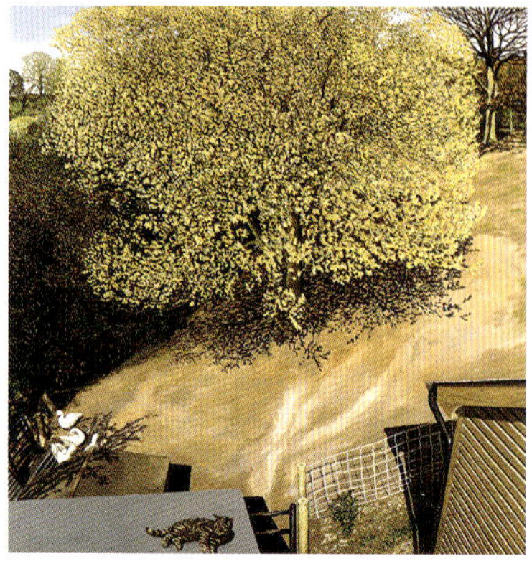

85. David Inshaw (1943-)
Pussy Willow, 1998-2004
oil on canvas, 1524 x 1524 mm
Josie Reed

mantics in the true nineteenth century sense of the term. Much of his work concerns communion with nature'. [65]

North, recognising a weakness, was inclined to avoid figures; *The Old Pear Tree* required amending:

> 'The famous watercolour now called *The Pear Tree* was first shown under the title, *Cupid in the Pear Tree*, and there were then two or three 'amorini' hovering among the branches. The idea is found in Spenser's *Shepherd's Calendar-4th eclogue*, where Cupid is described by a young shepherd as:
> "Entangled in a fowling net
> Which he for carrion crows had set
> That in our peere tree haunted."
> I think North found that his treatment of the cupids did not harmonize with the crisp realism of the tree, and so they have been dissolved in little pink puffs which are still faintly discernible.' [66]

North was more interested in atmosphere and wished to make his drawings tingle and shimmer with light.

83

A miniature version of Samuel Palmer's *Magic Apple Tree* (*c*.1830, Fitzwilliam, Cambridge), 'the supreme expression of Palmer's belief in the abundance of God's gifts in nature, as expressed in Psalm 65':

> 'Thou crownest the year with thy goodness; and thy paths drop fatness. They drop upon the pastures of the wilderness: and the little hills rejoice on every side. The pastures are clothed with flocks; the valleys also are covered over with corn; they shout for joy, they also sing'. [67]

Colin Harrison calls it a 'peculiarly Christian pastoral vision', being 'Palmer's Neoplatonic vision of fecundity, which depended…on the munificence of a bountiful God'.[68] A.H. Palmer also believed his father's passionate love for Ceres, the Roman goddess of the harvest, and Pomona, goddess of fruit trees, gardens and orchards, led him into 'fairy-land'.

84

Painted for Brian Bearne, a great friend and patron of the Ruralists. Bearne was the owner of the Rainbow Auction House in Torquay. This orchard lay behind the salerooms.

85

This monumental willow tree is comically echoed in the tabby cat sunning itself on a nearby roof. The shoots of the Pussy Willow are picked just as the buds expand in spring and are used as religious decoration on Palm Sunday as a replacement for palm branchs in northern climes.

86

Griggs was essentially an etcher of architectural subjects. As Meyrick notes 'one senses in his etchings a lament for the passing of a better world'; he was saddened by 'the war and universal suffering and wickedness, and the moral and material destruction of beauty'.[69] A major figure in the Arts and Crafts revival, Griggs was also a campaigner for the preservation of ancient buildings, a cause close to

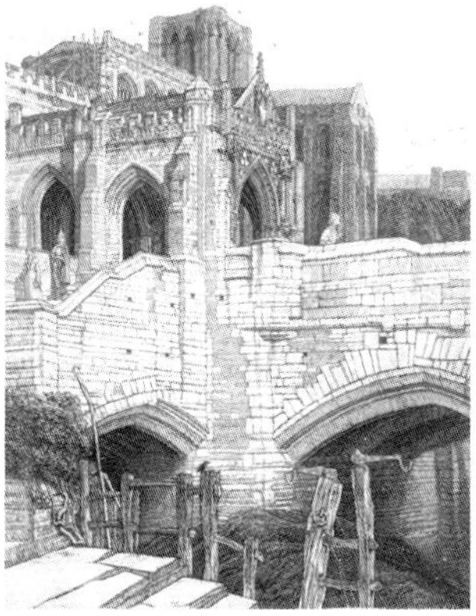

86. FREDERICK LANDSEER MAUR GRIGGS (1876-1938)
Potters' Bow, 1924
etching on paper, seventh state
Comstock 33, 230 x 166 mm
Graham Ovenden

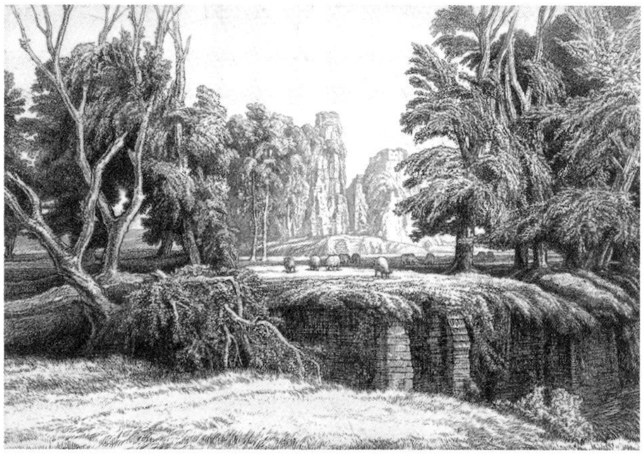

87. FREDERICK LANDSEER MAUR GRIGGS (1876-1938)
Launds, 1928
etching on paper, fifth state
Comstock 39, 173 x 252 mm
Stuart M. Southall

the heart of William Morris. Kenneth Guichard, in *British Etchers 1850-1940*, suggests that Griggs's spirituality, described as austere medieval Roman Catholicism, inhibited the human warmth that is the essence of Palmer's work. Griggs's strong linear detail and architectural design – *Potter's Bow* is described as 'an architectural fantasy', not an actual place– creates a rather stark timelessness. But although 'an indulgence of the imagination – a speculation according to the artist's fancy and affections', the conception is still guided by reason: 'The title suggests that the bridge or "bow" is intended to represent an example of the public spirit of the medieval guilds, when the building of bridges was regarded as a particularly pious act.' [70]

87

Launds was first exhibited at the RA in 1928 as A *Sussex Landscape*. It was reworked by Griggs and dedicated to his great friend Benjamin Martin Chandler, a Bostonian who had settled near Campden. Griggs wrote to Russell Alexander about the work and its progress, giving us a clear idea of his intentions and his indecision concerning its title:

'I'm stumped for a name. It's a jolly scene in warm sunlight, nearly all trees surrounding a mass of ruined old walls (of a castle, or old house partly defensive in character, as an old moat is in the foreground). But it don't look sad. Do you like The Moat? Or The Pleasance? Or an old name like Sedany?' [71]

Griggs derived the motif from his 1916 Irish sketchbook; he had also known a large house in Ireland named 'Rosegarland', which may have suggested an alternative title, *Summer Garland*:

'Very old English! Very Summery too!...An old historic ground, old walls, ivy, trees, and more trees. The sound of jackdaws, and twitter of birds. No figures. Sheep grazing. Thoughts of Dead and gone people of history connected with the place; thoughts of dead loyalties. Some sadness for beauty departed. Some gladness that nature has recompensed the scene with her own tender beauty. And the title (rather hinting of these things) of Summer Garland suggested itself.'

In May Griggs rejected his working title in favour of *Autumn*, which although less allusive was more descriptive, reflecting the fallen bough and bare and withered trunks. With its ruins in mind, Griggs saw autobiographical connotations: 'I was going to say "and my own autumn" but danged if I feel like it, and "a man", dang it, "is as old as he feels."' [72] Finally he hit on the title *Launds* derived from the old word for lawn or sacred ground, which had plenty of connotations 'Launds-All Hallows Summer (Henry V)- Martinmas – Little Summer – St Luke's Summer'. [73] *Launds* reminds us that nature reclaims man's work.

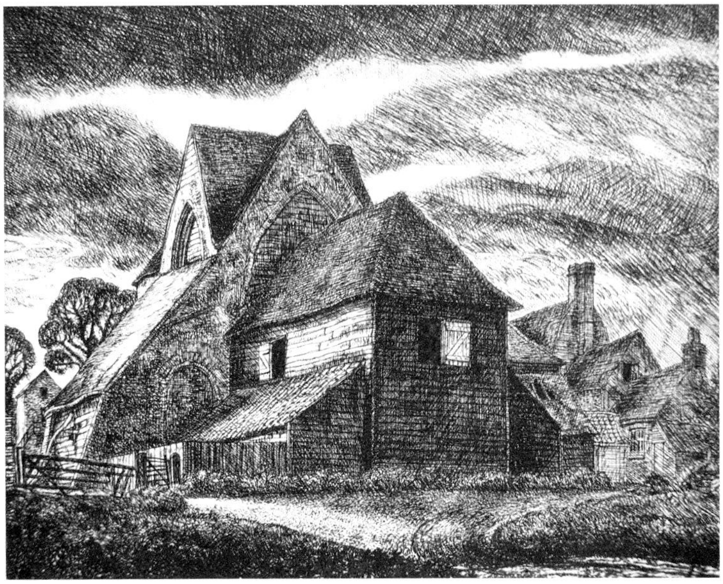

88. Edgar Holloway (1914-)
Latton Priory, Essex (exterior)
etching on paper, 176 x 225 mm, 1936
Edgar and Jennifer Holloway

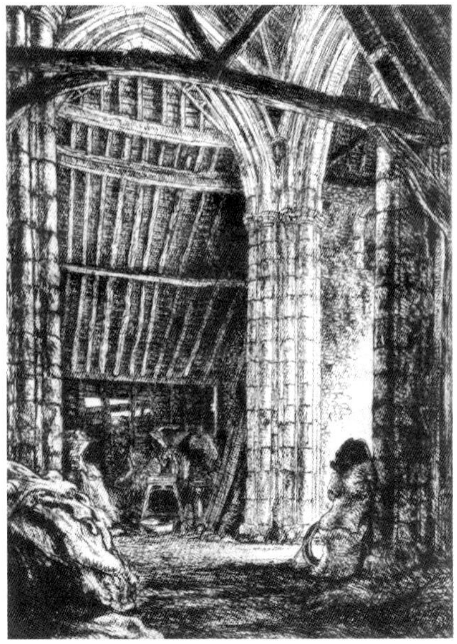

89. Edgar Holloway (1914-)
Latton Priory, Essex (interior)
etching on paper, 275 x 201mm, 1936
Edgar and Jennifer Holloway

88

Falling under the influence of his close friend Scottish painter and etcher William Wilson, Holloway tried to create more 'mood' in his prints of the later 1930s. In *Latton Priory* he achieved mood by building up the image in a densely etched, 'painterly' application of line: 'both in its subject matter and its use of late evening light it is reminiscent of the imagined barns and haunting landscapes of Joseph Webb.' [74]

89

Interior of the Augustinian Priory showing part of the fourteenth century structure forming a barn.

90

This is very much a composite church, Ovenden was inspired by All Saints Dunwich, which did fall into the sea; 'No angel army, saintly horde could stem the blast and gnawing wrath that time has clawed to sea greed's grasp'.[75] But it is Walter de la Mare's short story, *All Hallows*, which provides the key to this work and which also betrays Ovenden's fascination with Elizabethan philosophers like Magus John Dee and Robert Fludd (1574-1637). De la Mare was himself inspired by Richard Hooker (1554-1600), the Elizabethan theologian, who provided the opening quotation:

> 'And because time in itself ...can receive no alteration, the hallowing... must consist in the shape of the countenance which put upon the affaires that are incident in those days.' [76]

All Hallows tells the chilling story of the demonic restoration, taking place virtually unseen, to the fabric of the cathedral of All Hallows. The building is on an isolated spot overlooking the sea, recalling the position of the church at Dunwich before the sea claimed it...

> 'Having at last come limping out upon the green sea-buff beneath which lay its walls – I confess the actuality of it excelled my feeble dreams of it...the cathedral was cruciform. Walls so ancient and so sparsely adorned and decorated could not but be inhospitable in effect. Their stone was of a bleached bone-gray; a gray that none the less seemed as immaterial as flame- or incandescent ash. They were substantial enough, however, to cast a marvellously lucent shadow, of a blue no less vivid but paler than the sea, on the shelving sward beneath them.'[77]

Like Dunwich, All Hallows is threatened by the sea; 'a sea so near at last that I could hear its enormous sallies and murmurings. Indeed I had not realised until that moment how closely the great western door of the cathedral abutted onto the beach'.

Ovenden's poem 'The Sea Cathedral' published in *Satirical Poems and Others* dwells on the invidiously encroaching sea:

> 'All Hallows, hollow Hallow,
> sea stone
> fraught fret
> gaunt gallow
> cliff clung
> loomimg lonely,
> over shelving, sanding shallow.' [78]

Layered into the meaning of *All Hallows* are some real ecclesiastical buildings, Graham being inspired by Albi and St

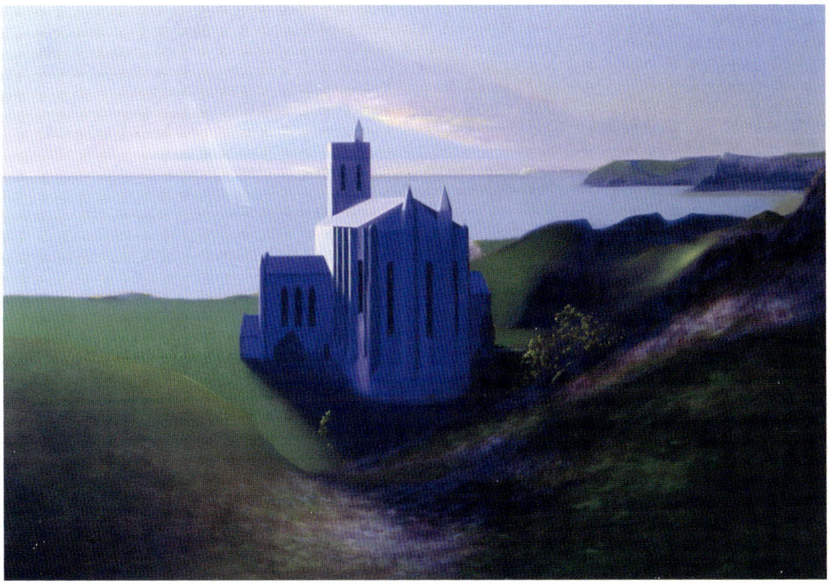

90. Graham Ovenden (1943-)
All Hallows (*The Sea Cathedral*), 1983
oil on panel, 788 x 1142 mm
Jane Wainwright

David's but the real model for the 'cliff clung' church lies at Morwenstow. The Ruralists, who took their annual summer holiday together at nearby Coombe, were undoubtedly attracted to the area by the 1975 centenary celebrations for Robert Stephen Hawker (1803-1875) poet, antiquary, and eccentric Vicar of Morwenstow. Graham could hardly resist such a figure;

'Parson Hawker' was truly wacky, both in his clothes and his habits; he excommunicated his cat for mousing on Sunday. He loved bright colours, the only black he wore being his socks. He built a small hut, now know as Hawker's Hut from driftwood on the cliff looking out to sea; his parishioners had a reputation for 'wrecking'. This is now the National Trust's smallest property. He also built himself a remarkable vicarage, with chimneys modelled on the towers of the churches in his life. Hawker's church stands in an isolated spot, close to the cliffs at Morwenstow. The painting was acquired, rather fittingly, by Clive Wainwright (1942-1999), a great authority on Victorian art, architecture and design and close friend.

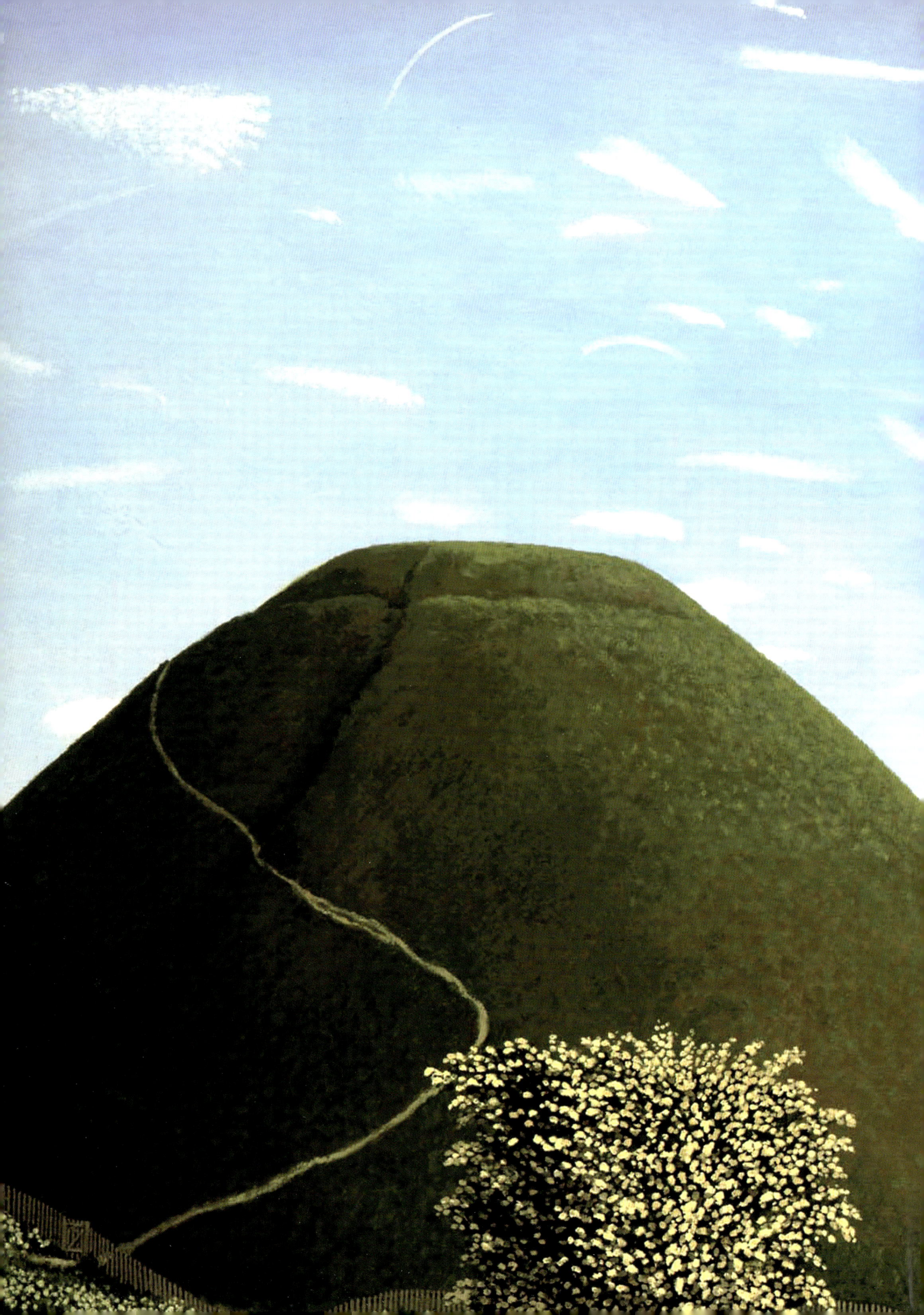

Ancient Landscapes

As Schama observes, 'There have always been two kinds of arcadia: shaggy and smooth; dark and light; a place of bucolic leisure and a place of primitive panic'. The 20th century fascination for pre-historic sites might be viewed as an attempt to connect with our primeval past but one could encounter primitive wildness naturally in Wales. Sutherland went in for 'black' landscapes, provoked by his wartime experiences, while mountainous terrains offered Piper the terror at the heart of the Sublime. Wales was the antidote to the pastoral idyll of Kent and Sussex. Wales also introduces stone as a natural and symbolic motif; the famous 80 blue stones were transported from the Preseli Mountains in South Wales, some 385km (240 miles), to be erected inside the earthen bank of Stonehenge. We are now approaching the original Arcadia, located in the wilds rather than an English landscape garden; Nature could now be identified with a Bronze Age standing stone.[1] Megaliths could be appreciated for their formal, abstract qualities as well as their associations; in effect Stonehenge is still read as a 'ruin', a remnant of a lost civilisation.

The Romantic sensibility makes ruins beautiful to us. Late 18th century taste gauged artefacts and landscape by their pictorial effect; time and the elements made trees and buildings picturesquely rough, with moss, ivy and other encrustations adding variety and tone. Decaying Gothic turrets and pinnacles, laced with all their connotations, became objects of curiosity and places to visit. William Gilpin, a chief exponent of the Picturesque, alongside Sir Uvedale Price and Sir Richard Payne Knight, approved of the visual and decorative effect of Tintern Abbey: 'time has worn off all traces of the chisel; it has blunted the sharp edges of the rule and compass, and broken the regularity of the opposing parts', though a 'mallet judiciously used ...might be of service in fracturing some' of the too regular gable ends![2] Gilpin's eye sought the irregular and the asymmetric, clearly Tintern needed 'improving'; he was not concerned about preserving the fabric of the building, ideally it should crumble some more. Extreme decay, mutilation, discolouration and decomposition allured the artist's eye. Devotees of the Picturesque visited locales like John Dyer's *Grongar Hill* (1761) where amid 'huge heaps of hoary mouldered walls...the pois'nous adder breeds/Concealed in ruins, moss and weeds'.[3] Jane Austin considered this admiration for 'pleasing decay' went too far; surely Henry VIII had not dissolved the monasteries and abbeys just to improve the English landscape. Nature provided the 'ornaments of time', ivy, mosses and lichens, which for Gilpin 'gave those full blown tints, which add the richest finishing to a ruin'.[4] These effects made Fountains Abbey 'a sacred thing. Rooted for ages in the soil, assimilated to it, and become as it were, a part of it; we consider it as a work of nature, rather than of art'.[5] For Ruskin, the encroachments and depredations of time, rampant vegetation and ominous cracks, 'assimilate the architecture with the work of Nature, and bestow upon it those circumstances of colour and form which are universally beloved by the eye of man'.[6] 'The sad spectacle of the works of man slowly being absorbed by the organic forces of nature', to use Robert Rosenblum's words, clearly acted as a *memento mori.* Only the passing of time could bring a ruin to perfection, 'which gives it perfect beauty; and brings it... to a state of nature'.[7] Ruins gain much of their emotive force by being seen as constituent parts of the landscape, being slowly reclaimed and absorbed back into the land. This idea clearly appealed to Nash, who liked his antiquities to be unkempt and abandoned; his depictions of megaliths even suggest that 'these "strange forms" had somehow sprouted spontaneously out of the ground'.[8]

Nash does not appear to have been taken by the conventionally picturesque; the Gothic is distinctly absent from his vision. It was earthworks, Iron Age hill forts, Neolithic long barrows, chalk-cut figures, stone circles and megaliths that gripped his feelings. Remote and uninhabited, these sites link us to a pre-Christian, primeval past. Here:

> 'the constructions of our distant ancestors have long ago been overtaken by the organic attentions of Nature, which has produced tracts of landscape at once poetic and timeless in that traces of prehistory have been all but erased by, on the one hand, an overlay of smooth turf and on the other, enriching woodland'.[9]

These relics are sometimes only just perceptible; continuously ploughed over their remains leave a ghost-like mark on the land; they have been almost completely reabsorbed. This was Nash's 'Unseen Landscape' or 'hidden spirit', which he defined as the *genius loci*: 'Nash was interested in landscapes that had once been made, that had once been subject to the hand of man, but where what had formerly existed was now concealed'.[10] He will take us to 'Unseen Landscapes' that are there to be seen but which, being commonplace, have not pierced out consciousness. Releasing this hidden spirit required representing the passing of time, collapse, decay, forestation or grassing over, 'to stimulate the imagination to re-create the past in its own way'.[11] Nash's Englishness relates to his sense of history, he sought places where the past was visible on the surface but he was just as concerned with the mystery of what lay beneath. He was concerned not 'with the past as past but the accumulated intenseness of the past as present'.[12]

The undulating ramparts and ditches of Maiden Castle and Badbury Rings, in Dorset, both Iron Age hill forts, ripple like waves; an equivalent that would have appealed to Nash. Works like *Circle of the Monoliths* (1937-8, Leeds Museums and Art Galleries) blur land and sea; here the megaliths lie amidst the trenches of the First World War, which savagely cut the landscape like wounds. In a number of works Nash cites Silbury Hill. This 40 metre high pre-historic mound manages to look natural while being artfully constructed. Its purpose is still a mystery, as successive excavations have failed to unlock its secrets. Archaeologists calculate that Silbury Hill was built about 4600 years ago and that it took 18 million man-hours to create its conical shape. Nothing has ever been found under Silbury Hill: at its core there is only clay, flints, turf, moss, topsoil, gravel, freshwater shells, mistletoe, oak, hazel, sarsen stones, ox bones, and antler tines. It clearly had a purpose, being part of a pre-historic complex that includes Avebury and West Kennet long barrow but it remains 'a stupendous enigma'. Inshaw has also formed an attachment to Silbury, its pap-like breast-shaped contour appearing close up and far away, embedded in the landscape. Silbury could be said to be Inshaw's equivalent of Nash's *Wittenham Clumps*. In *Wiltshire Landscape* (1987-88, Cat. 98), Silbury is enfolded by the agricultural landscape, silhouetted by a field of bright yellow; perhaps suggesting that its purpose was to ensure the fecundity of nature. This is also suggested by *Portrait of Silbury Hill, May* (1989, Cat. 99), where a May tree in full bloom is silhouetted by the mound. The sky is a 'carnival of activity- the sky crowded with the shuttlecock vapour trails of clouds, the great green pudding of the hill itself garlanded with a ribbon path, which might have been flung around the maypole, and the attendant may trees clearly poised on the brink of another movement in their eternal Morris dance.'[13] But a full luminous moon hangs over Silbury, joined by squabbling rooks, in *Wiltshire Landscape* suggesting something more sinister; many have imagined the flat top of the mound as a place of execution or sacrifice. The hill becomes even spookier by night; *Silbury Hill on a Starry Night* (1986, Cat. 129). Silbury's possibilities are endless; it is an emblem of timelessness: 'Here, the intersection of the timeless moment/ Is England and nowhere. Never and always'.[14]

Nash was also drawn to the Rollright Stone Circle in Oxfordshire and the great architecture of Stonehenge; but as Henry Moore's chosen site and the destination of so many tourists it had rather lost its mystery. His passion was reserved for the Great Avenue and megalithic circles at Avebury, which up until then had largely been left undisturbed. It is one of the finest and largest Neolithic monuments in

Europe dating to around 5000 years ago. It is older than the megalithic stages of Stonehenge, which is located about 32 km (20 miles) to the south, although the two monuments are broadly contemporary overall. Discovered when his health was rather precarious in 1933, Avebury revived Nash's inspiration:

> 'The great stones were then in their wild state, so to speak. Some were half covered by the grass, others stood up in the cornfields or were entangled and overgrown in the copses, some were buried under the turf. But they were wonderful and disquieting.' [15]

Shortly after Nash's first encounter the work began of reinstating the circles; 'so that to a great extent that primal magic of the stones' appearance was lost'. Our aesthetic appreciation requires maintaining a delicate balance between the monument and nature which must appear uncontrived; the idea that decay has been arrested or the ruin has been restored lessens its emotional impact: 'We need to have the reassurance of accidental creation...if it is known to be preserved the ruination seems no longer the work of pure fate'.[16] Summerson reminds us that ruins should be seen on the 'verge of dissolution', connoting the fragility of life and the passing of all things.

Nash did not find animism in the stones; this was not a case of 'object-personages', 'Monster Field' was yet to come. Nash was attracted by formal qualities, the shapes of the stones; 'Their colouring and pattern, their patina of golden lichen, all enhanced their strange forms and mystical significance'.[17] After Cubism, conventional representation became problematic but Piper identified prehistory as offering one answer to the difficulty; '[Artists] have visited museums, and skidded back through the centuries, across whole continents and civilisations in their search…In this country, for instance we find Paul Nash identifying all nature with a Bronze Age standing stone'.[18] Thereafter Nash hunted stones, by the seashore, on the downs, in the furrows. Initially the stones were 'objects in the landscape', as seen in the *Landscape of the Megalith* Series, but later, as Nash tells us, 'certain stone personages evolved', such as the 'stone birds' in the *Nest of Wild Stones* (1937). Surrealism plays its part in this metamorphosis, as does the state of dreaming. Nash returned to Avebury in 1943; the reconstruction impressed him, he took photographs of the stones and was again moved by their 'disquieting beauty'. He professed a desire to 'live near them for a time to get to know them again'. Inshaw has also sought this proximity to the Wessex landscape.

Cardinal sees Nash's Avebury as 'a realm of inchoate stirrings, in which enough symmetry and design was discernable to prompt intimations of past civilisations; but with a goodly measure of unkempt growth to foster the sense of naturalness'.[19] In contrast Inshaw's *Standing Stone* (1988/89, Cat. 110) belongs to the clipped Avebury of today. Nash's *Druid Landscape* (1934, Cat. 109) makes that inevitable but erroneous connection between Avebury and the Druids; the Celtic Druids came along a great deal later. But Avebury was undoubtedly used for 'rituals' and seems to be associated, like Stonehenge, with sun worship and pantheism; Avebury was recently voted the country's third most spiritual place. The Ruralists could not resist meeting four times a year on the solstice and the equinox.

Nash's catalogue of ancient sites is completed by his interest in figures cut into the chalk: the huge giant at Cerne Abbas in Dorset and the Uffington White Horse on the Berkshire Downs drew his sympathy as 'specimens of primitive artistry, perhaps also moving traces of the vulnerability of human effort, in so far as such endeavours have an air of only just surviving into modern times'.[20] Nash's photographs of the 'dragon-shaped' White Horse show his admiration for the design, its classic sinuous Celtic lines but his close-ups focus on the bands of chalk laid bare, creating abstract, organic forms across the hillside. On the ground the sharp delineation of white on green is lost; edges appear 'eaten', the grass attempting to grow back. Once more Nash seems enchanted by the signs of 'disintegration', savouring the spectacle of Nature reasserting herself. Graham Arnold too has been fascinated by this disintegration, collecting nodules of chalk from the Uffington horse and framing them as relics within his collages.

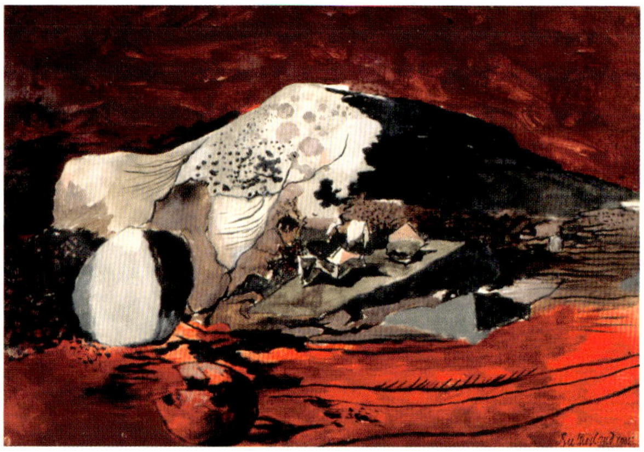

91. Graham Vivien Sutherland (1903-1980)
Red Landscape, 1942
oil on canvas, 998 x 680 mm
Southampton City Art Gallery
Chipperfield Bequest

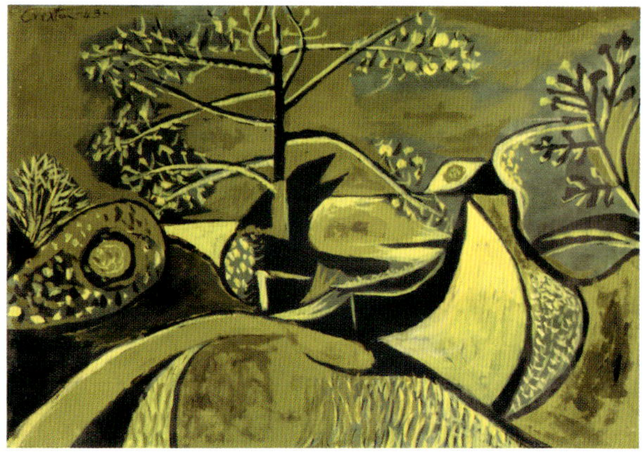

93. John Craxton (1922-)
Dark Landscape 1943
oil on canvas, 552 x 375 mm
Southampton City Art Gallery
donated by the Contemporary Arts Society

91

Sutherland found the quality of the light in Wales magical and 'transforming'. He experimented with a new range of intense colours alien to the countryside – magenta, orange, egg-yellow, lemon, purple, raspberry and lime. The patches of colour 'were looped round and stitched together by a rambling black line and punctuated by jagged black areas of shade – the overall effect being reminiscent of coals in fire'. They also recall Palmer's sepias or 'blacks' in the Ashmolean; Sutherland seems temporarily obsessed with darkness.

Red Landscape appears to be a view of Carnllidi near St David's in Pembrokeshire. Sutherland at this time was in Wales as an Official War Artist to make drawings of bomb damage, mining and quarrying. The use of non-naturalistic colouring evokes an atmosphere of menace and imminent violence that perhaps reflects the artist's feeling about wartime.

92

Graham Vivien Sutherland
Red Hills, 1944
gouache, 380 x 750 mm
on loan to Victoria Art Gallery
Bath from a private collection
(Shown Bath only)

93

The landscapes produced by Craxton in the 1940s, were a personal, poetic vision of nature. At the time such work had patriotic connotations, the English landscape being seen as central to national identity. In this work, Craxton uses the modern idiom of semi-abstract curvilinear forms, flatness and empathic line, suggesting the influence of his friend and mentor Graham Sutherland, as well as Pablo Picasso and Joan Miró. Line was important for Craxton: 'Line, or the definitive borderline, is not unlike speech itself in inflection and tone. For me line is the clearest way I have of saying something in the most direct way'.

94

From 1943 Minton was an enthusiastic teacher at the Camberwell School of Art, the Central School of Art and the RCA; he would teach Graham Arnold. By now he was an acknowledged graphic master, the pen, which allows no second chances, was his favourite tool. His work in black and white looks effortless. Minton's style became the fashionable norm of the late 1940s and early 1950s; many of his ex-students adopted his mannerisms. Minton's drawings are densely worked; *Recollection of Wales* sits alongside other works of this period, like *Harvest Moon* (1944) and *Surrey Landscape* (1944).

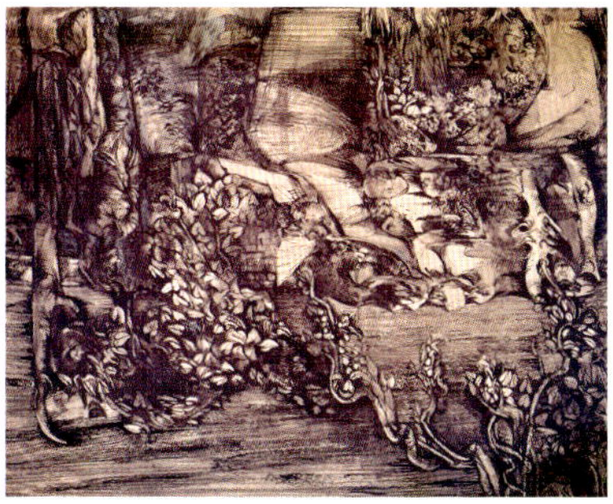

94. John Minton (1917-1957)
Recollection of Wales, 1944
ink and bodycolour on paper
495 x 630 mm
British Council

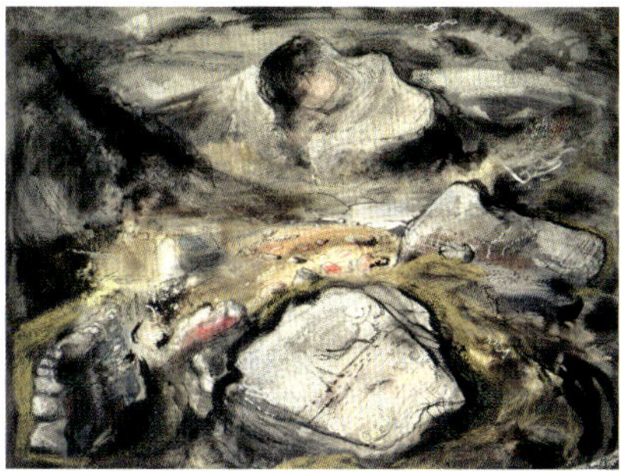

95. John Piper (1903-1992)
Snowdonia, North Wales, 1945-49
watercolour, pen, ink and pencil
380 x 925 mm
Reading Foundation for the Arts

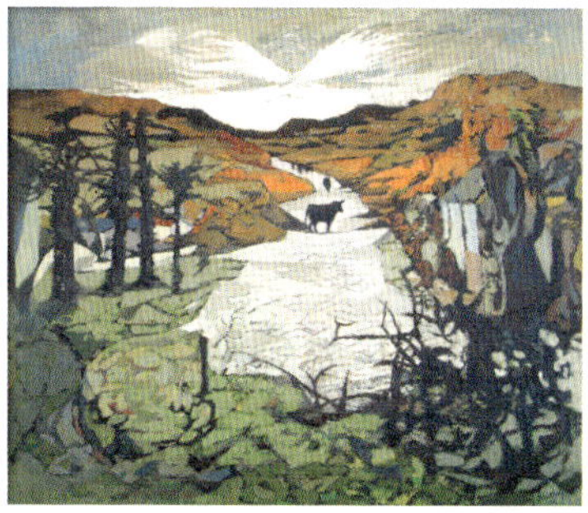

96. John Elwyn (1916-1997)
The Adventurer, 1954
oil on canvas, 200 x 240 mm
Robert Meyrick

95

It was not until he 'abdicated' from abstraction that the Piper that we recognise today emerged. He initially set out to depict the great country houses of England and Wales, a task that no major artist had undertaken since Turner and Constable. By now Piper had formed an alliance with Betjeman, working on the *Shell Guides to the English Counties*. Antiquarianism was in the air; Piper tackled Stowe, Stourhead and Hafod in Wales. It was Vanbrugh's great burnt out Seaton Delaval Hall, Northumberland (1942) which really took his fancy. Piper's limited range of colours was established – black, white, pale yellow, indian red and light blue and his habit of flicking black lines and details on top of colour to pull the design together. His strong brushwork and lighting effects create drama, the final composition being likened to stage sets or ballet curtains. During his time as a war artist Piper recorded many violated churches and bombed-out houses. Researching his book on *British Romantic Artists* seems to have stimulated Piper's interest in the Sublime; inevitably this took him to Wales, which he first visited in 1944. He was conscious of following Palmer, who went there in 1835 and 1836. It was Richard Wilson (1714-82) who had opened English eyes to 'the salutary pleasures of exploring romantic hollows and folds in hills, damp valleys, and distant exciting mountains screened by foreground trees'. [21] The example of Sutherland and Piper had all young artists heading for Wales. Piper was attracted to the ruggedness of Snowdonia; geology gave him a new interest in natural shapes and forms. Evidently he could cope with the rough weather. The acute loneliness did not bother him; Snowdon provided the chance to capture the terror at the heart of the Sublime. These are pictures full of menace and foul weather; but like Ruskin, Piper was looking for the hand of God.

96

In the 1950s Elwyn continued his experimentation with large decorative landscapes. The rhythmic forms often suggest a 'humanised' or 'sexualised' landscape. Analogies are made between the contours of the landscape – mountains spurs, undulating hills, wooded valleys and writhing country lanes-and aspects of the human anatomy, as *In the Hill's Elbow* (1959): 'I am interested in how the inhabitants have dug themselves in-so to speak- to the sheltered corners and elbows of the hills and valleys'.[22] Like an 18th century artist in search of the picturesque, he sought the interesting and sensuous forms of the small-enclosed valleys and 'womb-like enclosures'. Here we see cattle meandering along a Cardiganshire lane; the high horizon provides plenty of space for the stylised forms of the landscape. He wrote:

> 'If one responds to the mood of the surrounding countryside, if one can become aware of the pulsating earth around one, one can get nearer to the essence, the *genius loci* of the place. To arrive at that point and to be able to express the experience of environment and convey it on canvas is what I would like to achieve. It should be a personal and individual synthesis of the chosen subject.' [23]

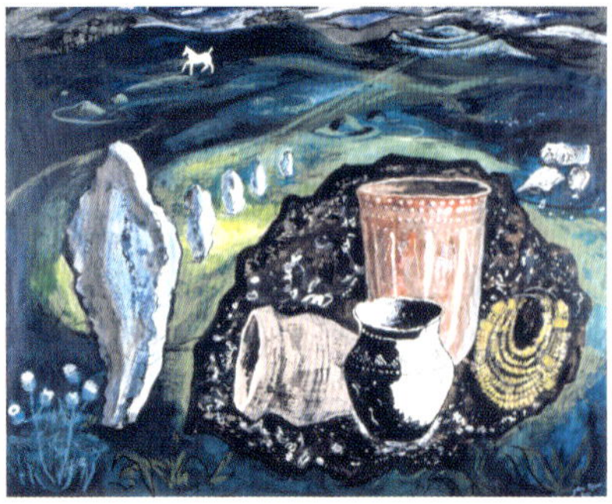

97. John Piper (1903-1992)
Cartoon for the stained glass window in the Art Gallery at Wiltshire Heritage Museum, 1981 gouache, 1108 x 1190 mm
Wiltshire Heritage Museum

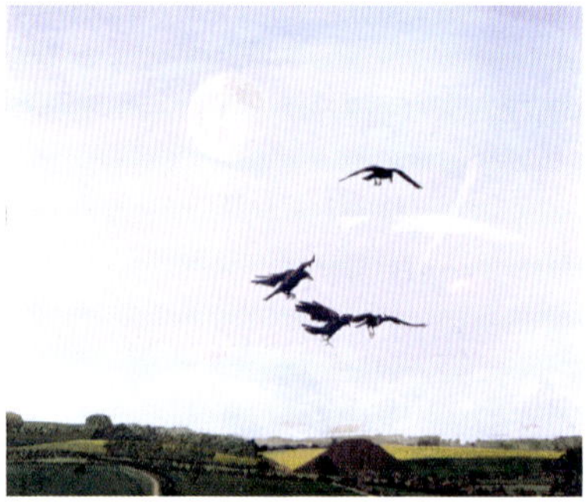

98. David Inshaw (1943-)
Wiltshire Landscape 1987-88
oil on canvas, 1295 x 1524 mm
Edmund Ovenden

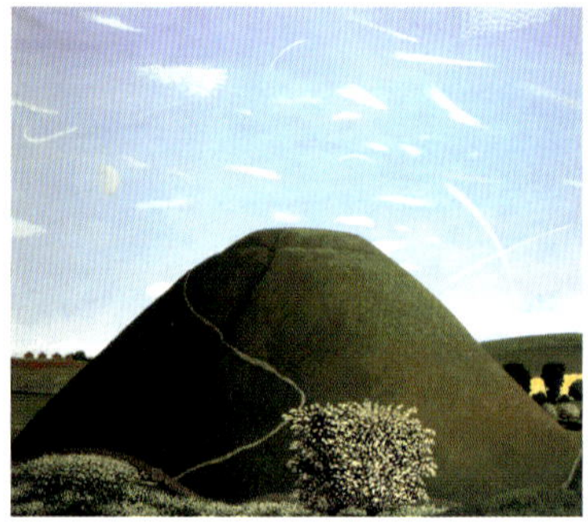

99. David Inshaw (1943-)
Portrait of Silbury Hill, May, 1989
oil on canvas, 1270 x 1447 mm
Lady Rothschild

97

This is an imaginative compilation of the Wessex landscape, encompassing the megaliths, earthworks, barrows and white horses. The cut-away view inside an urn burial recalls Sir Thomas Browne's *Hydriotaphia, Urne-Buriall* of 1658, a favourite of Graham Ovenden.

98

It was not until Inshaw left the RCA in 1966 and went to live and teach in Bristol that landscape made an appearance in his output. Coupled with his weekend forays into Dorset with his friend Alf Stockham, Inshaw began to read Thomas Hardy:

> 'The excitement that he felt on reading Hardy, the chords of feeling and sentiment that Hardy's approach to his subject matter struck in him, only served to confirm his growing instinct that it was in the more conventional theme of landscape with figures that he would find a way of painting best suited to expressing his intense personal feelings.' [24]

Nicholas Usherwood places Inshaw in a direct line of descent from Samuel Palmer in his Shoreham 'Valley of Vision' period. Prophetically Inshaw grew up in the shadow of Palmer, at Biggin Hill, Kent, less than ten miles from Shoreham. His mother introduced him to Palmer's Darenth Valley on family picnics. She even pointed out to him the house where Palmer stayed; this was his first experience of an artist's life and work. Back in the 1950s Biggin Hill was Inshaw's 'childhood landscape', his personal 'valley of vision'. He remembers being out and about all day, bird watching and keeping rooks. In this work the rooks have a frozen stillness, placing them outside time, the 'mysteries and fantasies of his childhood landscapes in Kent' repositioned in Wiltshire (Inshaw moved to Devizes in 1971, thence to Clyro, near Hay on Wye, Wales in 1989 but returned to Devizes in 1995).

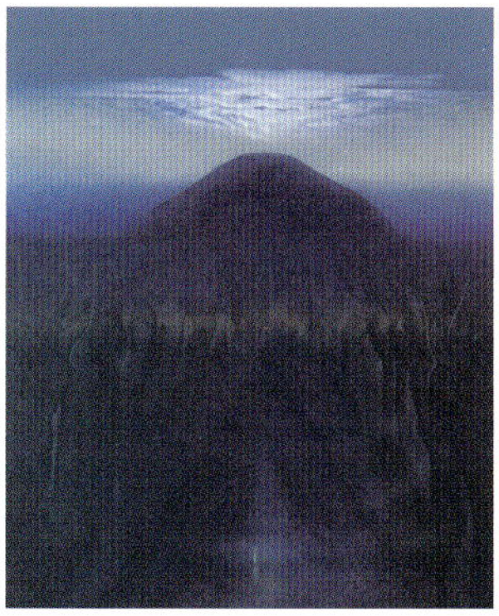

100. Graham Ovenden (1943-)
Sentinels of Silbury
oil on board
300 x 230 mm, 1982
Fred Olsen

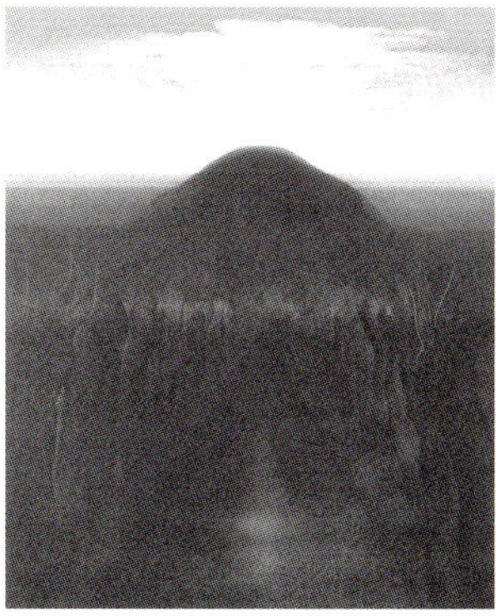

100a. Graham Ovenden (1943-)
Sentinels to Silbury
drawing (private collection)

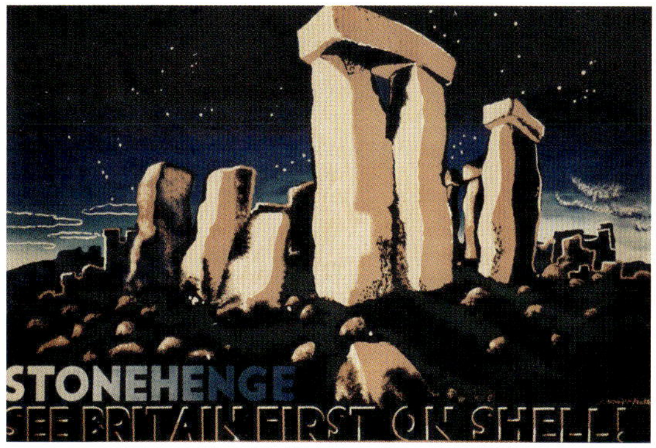

101. Edward McKnight-Kauffer (1890-1954)
Stonehenge, 1931
lithograph, framed dimensions 1175 x 985 mm
Shell Art Collection

99

The title 'portrait' gives Silbury a personality or character; as in the case of Nash, landscape is subtly anthropomorphised. Figures are not necessary to imbue the landscape with humanity; 'landscape forms can be interpreted as covert representations of the feminine, by virtue of physical analogy'. [25] The voluptuous contour of the mound takes on sexual symbolism. But, like Nash, 'the inference should surely be that his anthropomorphic landscapes are not simply an expression of narrow sexuality, but are agile symbolic surfaces across which are inscribed a gamut of human feelings'.[26] Inshaw sees his work underpinned by Thomas Hardy's lesson, 'that beauty of association is far superior to the beauty of the aspect'.[27] In the case of Silbury, Inshaw appear to be captivated by its 'formal features' as well as its 'associative force'.

100

This mystical image implies that the Great Avenue at Avebury may have begun its life as an avenue of trees. The processional way leads our eye to the summit of Silbury Hill, silhouetted by a band of pale sky. The conical shape of the hill is mirrored in a curious cloud formation, which heightens the supernatural qualities of the scene.

101

An iconic image of Stonehenge by one of the most prolific and influential graphic designers of the 20th century; Cubism, Futurism and Surrealism found expression in his posters, translating the complicated language of the avant-garde into accessible commercial design. At the outbreak of the First World War, the American- born Kauffer moved from Paris to London. During the next twenty-five years Kauffer worked for the Shell Oil Company, the Great Western Railway, the Empire Marketing Board and the Post Office. His designs ranged from book jackets and illustrations to stage sets and textiles, but it is for his London Transport posters that he will always be remembered. The image of Stonehenge was adopted by advertisers seeking a 'symbol of Britain'.

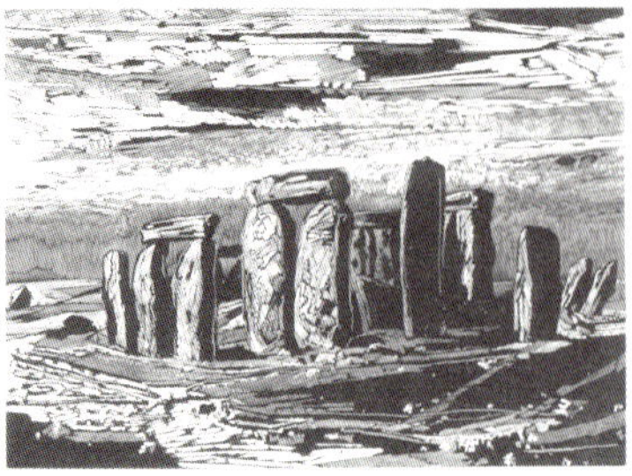

102. Gertrude Hermes (1901-1983)
Stonehenge, 1963
wood engraving, 255 x 355 mm
Southampton City Art Gallery

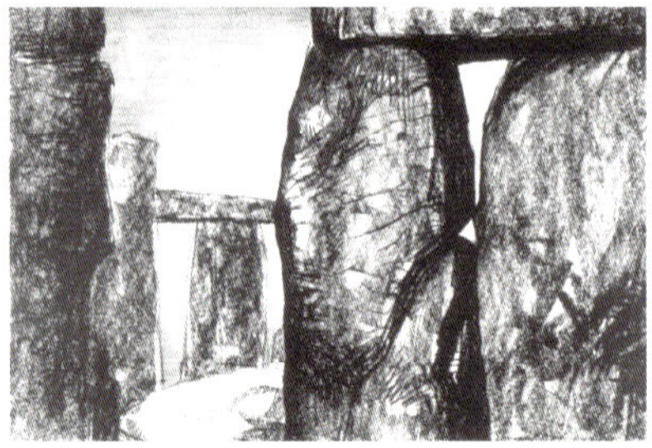

103. Henry Moore (1898-1986)
Stonehenge IV or Inside the Circle
from a set of fifteen, 1971-73
lithograph, 290 x 437 mm
Wiltshire Heritage Museum

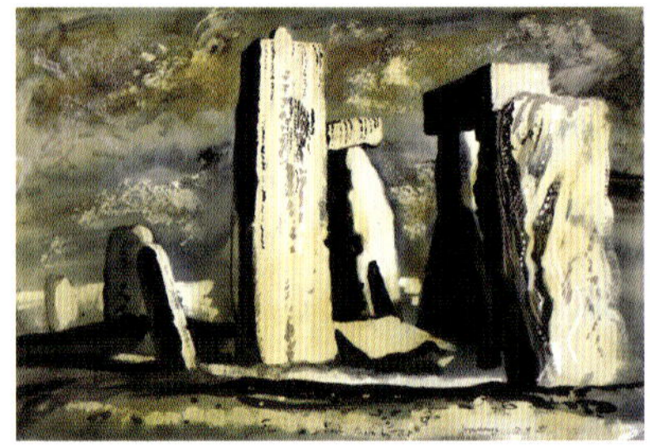

104. John Piper (1903-1992)
Stonehenge, Wiltshire, 1981
illustration from *Piper's Places. John Piper in England and Wales*
London: Chatto and Windus
Hogarth Press 1983
Anne Anderson (Book Case)

102

The distinctive features of Stonehenge, as well as its mysterious origins and use, have guaranteed its position in popular culture. The landmark has become a symbol of British culture and history, being portrayed in art, literature and advertising campaigns, as well as television, film and computer games. The arrangement of the standing stones topped with lintels is unique, not just in the British Isles, but in the world.

103

'As it was a clear evening, I got to Stonehenge and saw it by moonlight;
I was alone and tremendously impressed. (Moonlight, as you know, enlarges everything, and the mysterious depths and distances made it seem enormous).'
Henry Moore.[28]

From the 1920s Moore returned again and again to Stonehenge to sketch and take photographs, resulting in the shadowy, brooding and evocative lithographs of Stonehenge he created in the 1970s.

104

Stonehenge aroused complicated emotions in Piper, its wild and remote character, which had attracted Hearne, Constable and Turner, was long gone and its position was marred by Larkhill Camp and the visitors' car park; today the site is still compromised by fences and busy roads. But he sided with William Long, in feeling the 'very sacred character of the place…and the (probably) long period during which it must have served as a *locus consecratus* to the surrounding people'.[29] Stonehenge was still, in Piper's view 'one of the most beautiful man-made objects in Britain'. It was possible 'to recognise here a giant of visual drama and intensity'. [30]

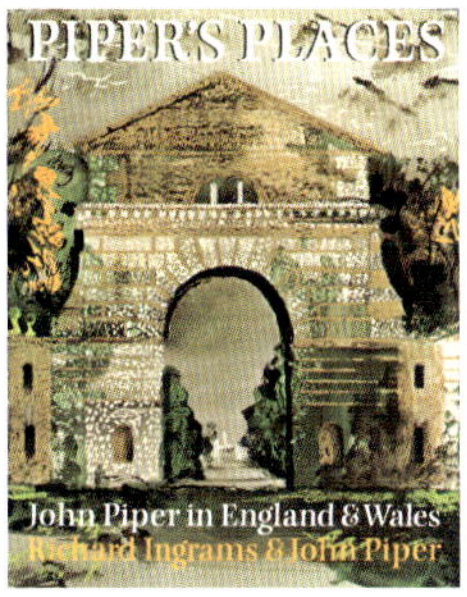

104a. John Piper
Piper's Places, John Piper in England and Wales
London: Chatto and Windus
Hogarth Press, 1983
Anne Anderson
(Book Case)

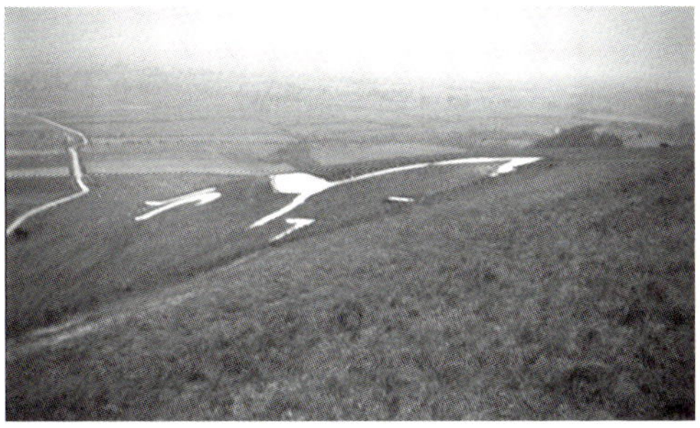

105. Paul Nash (1889-1946)
The White Horse, Uffington, Berkshire 1937
illustration from *A Private World. Photographs by Paul Nash*, Fischer Fine Art, 1978. (Book Case)

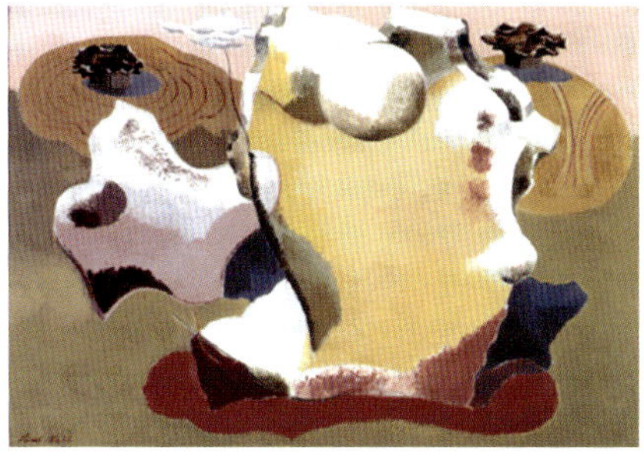

107. Paul Nash (1889-1946)
Landscape of the Megaliths, 1934
oil on canvas, 495 x 730 mm
British Council

105

Nash drew on the imaginative potential of prehistoric sites to produce modern works of art:

> 'Once the rather futile game of "picking out" the White Horse is abandoned, the documentary importance of the site fades, and the landscape asserts itself with all the force of its triumphant fusion of natural and artificial design'. [31]

106

Paul Nash (1889-1946)
Stones at Avebury, 1942
illustration from Andrew Causey
Paul Nash's photographs, Document and Image
London: Tate Gallery, 1973, Anne Anderson (Book: case)

Nash photographed the stones after archaeologist Alexander Keller had reconstituted the circle but felt that preservation had robbed the stones of much of their primeval mystery.

107

Writing about *Equivalents for the Megaliths* (1935, Tate Britain), Nash commented:

> 'These groups [at Avebury] are impressive as forms opposed to their surroundings...they are dramatic also, however, as symbols of their antiquity, as hallowed remnants of an almost unknown civilisation. In designing the picture, I wished to avoid the very powerful influence of the antiquarian suggestion, and to insist only upon the dramatic qualities of a composition.'

Nash wished to unlock their imaginative potential; 'if the suggestiveness of these forms was to bear fruit it would be by liberating them from any safe historical or archaeological understanding, in order for them to work almost as Surrealist *objets trouvés*'.[32] Nash is quite happy to rearrange the topography of Avebury; here the preferred Wittenham Clumps appear to be transposed into the background. Seen obliquely, the clumps of trees cast their shadows onto contour lines or furrows left by a plough. It is

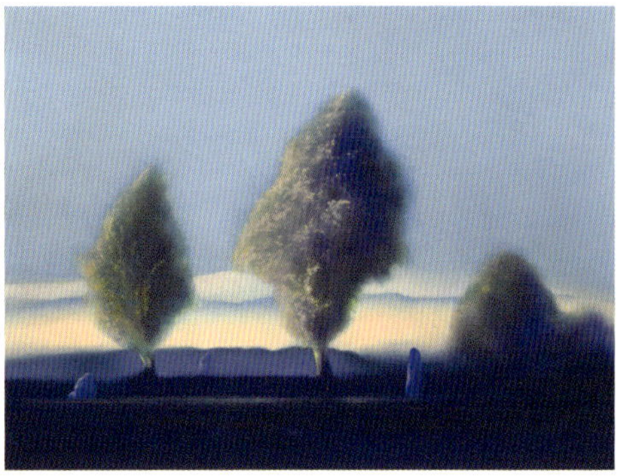

108. Graham Ovenden (1943-)
Spring Morning, Wiltshire, 1984
oil on canvas, 520 x 735 mm
Fred Olsen

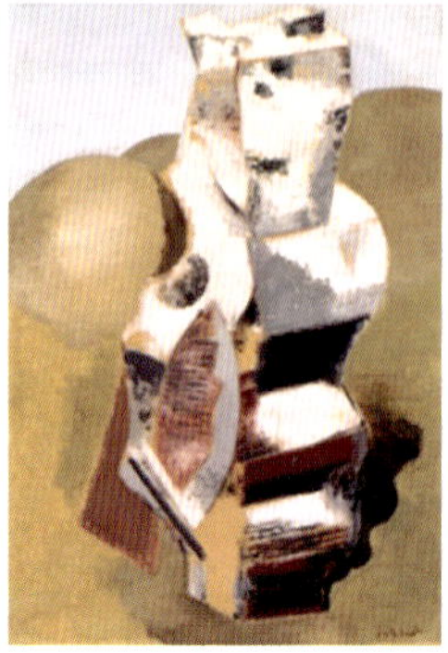

109. Paul Nash
(1889-1946)
Druid Landscape, 1934
oil on cardboard
585 x 405 mm
British Council

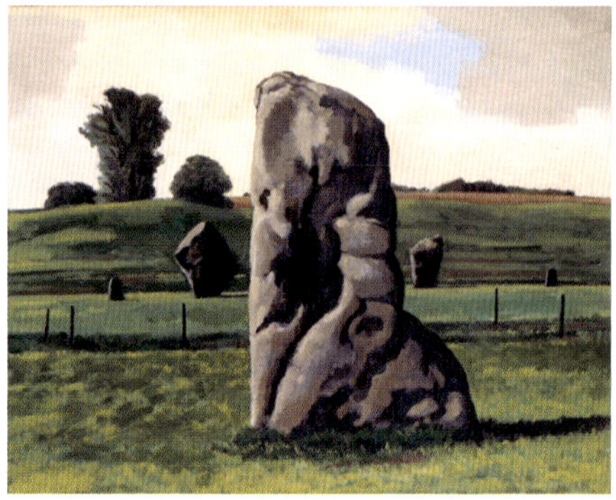

110. David Inshaw (1943-)
Standing Stone, 1988/89
oil on canvas, 558 x 711 mm
Wiltshire Heritage Museum, Devizes

possible that Nash was making the connection between the sacred grove as a precursor or equivalent of the stone circle or henge.

108

In comparison with Nash, Ovenden seems more concerned to catch the mystical spirit of these ancient stones, dawn casting them in an eerie light. On a return journey from Devizes, the luminous effects created by a hoar-frost struck him; the landscape was bathed in shimmering pinks and blues. But this is still a 'landscape of the mind'; the circle is in fact three monoliths, smaller versions of his *Tower of Babel*, interspersed by three verdant trees. These groups of three immediately recall the Trinity and the three crosses at Calvary. Ovenden is implying a continuity of worship, the stones reminding us of our pagan ancestors, while the living trees speak of Christian faith.

Ovenden's interest in antiquities was prompted by Walter de la Mare and Clive Wainwright; Sir Thomas Browne's *Hydriotaphia, Urne Buriall* of 1656 being a favourite work:

> 'Tis opportune to look back at old times, and contemplate our forefathers.
> Great examples grow thin, and to be fetched from the passed world… We have enough to do to make our selves from present and passed times, and the whole stage of things scarce serveth for our instruction.'[33]

109

Avebury is a spiritual centre for those who believe in Paganism, Wicca, Druidry and Heathenry, and for some it is more important than Stonehenge. The pagan festivals all attract visitors, and the summer solstice especially draws large crowds from the religious to the idly curious. Giving the appellation 'druid' to a megalith certainly humanises it but it is totally erroneous in terms of historical fact.

110

A great deal of interest surrounds the stones at Avebury, which people often describe as falling into two categories; tall and slender, or short and squat. This leads to numerous theories relating to the importance of gender in Neolithic Britain, with the taller stones considered 'male' and the shorter ones 'female'. There are two squat stones behind the tall one; perhaps a man sandwiched between two women! The tall stone certainly looks phallic. The stones were not dressed in any way and may have been chosen for their pleasing natural forms.

111

The curious natural rock formations at Brimham in Nidderdale are scattered over some fifty acres of lonely moorland. Erosion has created a great variety of weird and wonderful shapes. Many of the gritty monstrosities suggest all manner of things, including elephants, hippos, bears, mushrooms and some are said to have associations with druids, Mother Shipton and even the Devil himself.[34] The rock featured by Sutherland is probably the two hundred ton *Idol Rock* which balances on a stalk twelve inches in diameter.

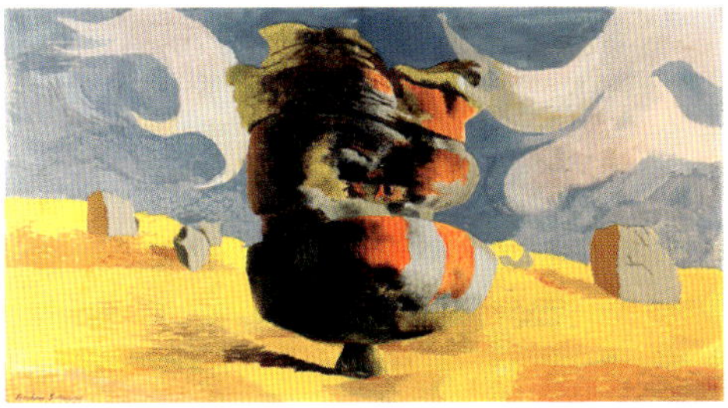

111. Graham Vivien Sutherland (1903-1980)
Brimham Rock, Visit Britain's Landmarks, 1937
Shell advertising campaign
gouache on paper framed dimensions
1130 x 690 mm
Shell Art Collection

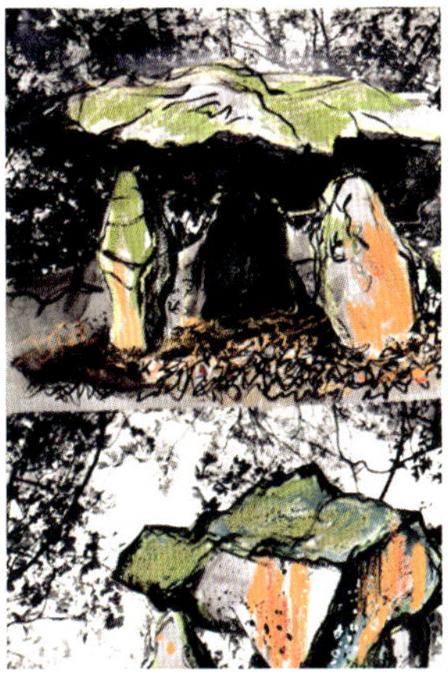

112. John Piper (1903-1992)
Stones and Bones XVI '21'
screen print, 350 x 500 mm
inscribed 'Dolmen near
Login, Carmarthen, 1977'
one of twenty-seven prints
in a portfolio published by
Kelpra Press, 1978, Reading
Art Foundation

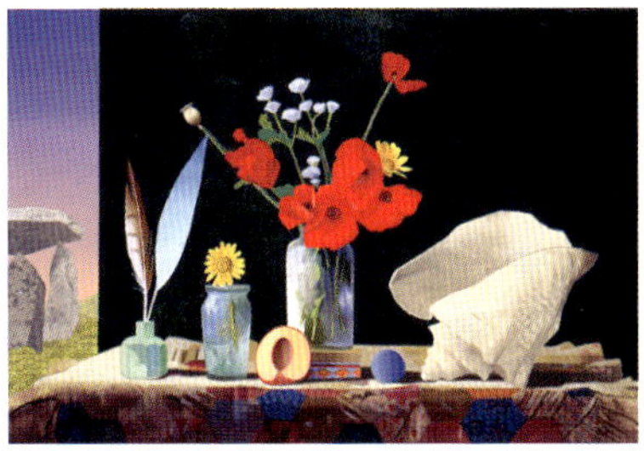

113. Graham Arnold (1932-)
Found Objects
oil on board, 305 x 560
Christopher Martin

112

Dolmen (also known as cromlech, anta, quoit and portal dolmen) is a type of single-chamber megalithic tomb, usually consisting of three or more upright stones (megaliths) supporting a large flat horizontal capstone (table). Most date from the early Neolithic period (4000 BC to 3000 BC). Dolmens were usually covered with earth or smaller stones to form a barrow, though in many cases that covering has weathered away, leaving only the stone 'skeleton'. of the burial mound intact.

113

This still life contains many of Arnold's favourite 'icons' and 'totems', some of which he has painted repeatedly over the last fifty years, ever since his father first arranged them for him when he was just six or seven years old; they include a cloth made from national flags collected from cigarette packets sewn together, seen in *Postcard from Uffington* (*c.*1994). The cloth has faded and aged over the years; here the tablecloth is a patchwork quilt. These ephemeral objects are relics, 'something concrete from the past' which act like a 'touchstone', helping to recall the past. His favourite books function in the same way, *A Week at the Lizard* (1848) and *Flowers of the Field* (1851) by the Revd A.C. Johns (1811-74), a Victorian writer and naturalist. Visits to Cornwall involved expeditions to the locations mentioned in the books. On the left is a dolmen, a repeated motif, like the ones Arnold would have seen in Cornwall. Locally called 'Quoits', there is a group of portal dolmens or portal tombs at West Penwith, Cornwall: Lanyon Quoit near Madron and Trevethy Quoit are also well-known landmarks. The poppies also feature in *Postcard from Uffington*, being homage to Edward Thomas, one of Arnold's favourite writers, who died in the First World War. Arnold's works attempt to trap memories in a tangible form; they are reminiscent of the Renaissance 'wunderkabinet' or Cabinets of Curiosity, which contained curios and natural phenomena. Cabinets of Curiosity, the origins of the modern day museum, were designed to explain the world. Arnold's private 'wunderkabinets' encapsulate his world.

114

The rippling terraces of Maiden Castle, Dorset, look rather like windswept sand dunes, the giant furrows of a ploughed field or even waves lapping on the shore. Sir Mortimer Wheeler's excavations at Maiden Castle (1934) caught the popular imagination and the Iron Age hill fort has become a popular tourist attraction. Thomas Hardy's cottage is only a few miles away. The inclusion of the solitary female figure, which indicates the vast size of the hill fort, also provides a link to Inshaw's *She did not turn* (private collection), which was inspired by Hardy's poem:

> She did not turn
> But passed foot-faint with averted head,
> In her gown of green, by the bobbing fern,
> Though I leaned over the gate that led
> From where we waited with table spread;
> But she did not turn:
> Why was she near there if love had fled?

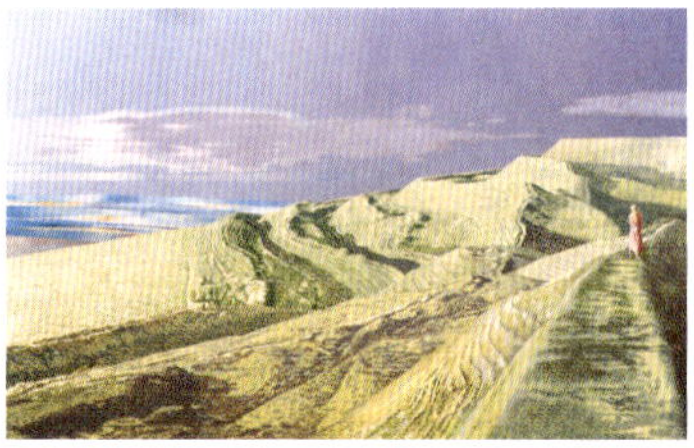

114. Graham Arnold (1932-)
Earthwork or At Maiden Castle
oil on board, 765 x 114
Michael Campbell

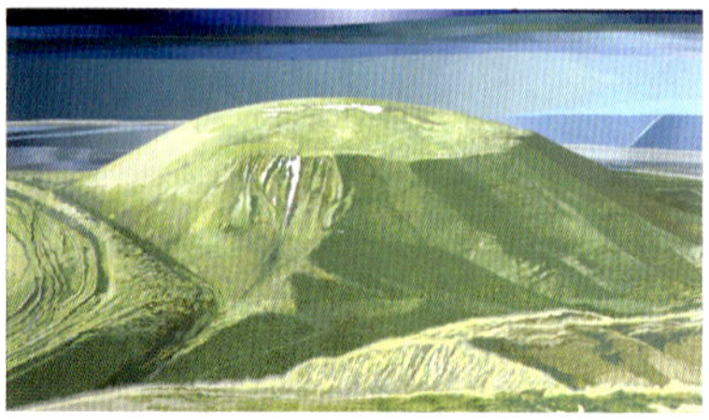

115. Graham Arnold (1932-)
Dragon Hill, Uffington, 1982
oil on board, 330 x 559 mm
Judith Foster

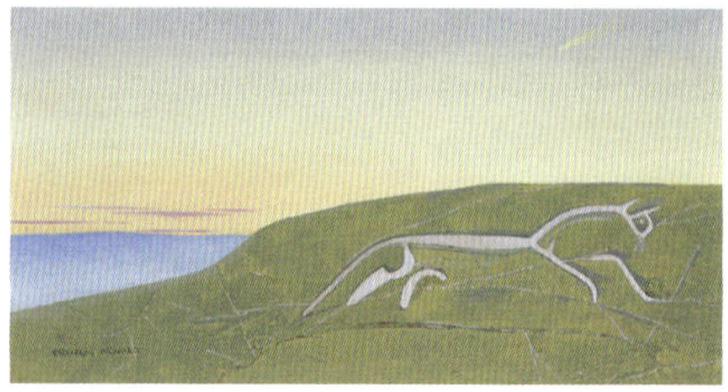

116. Graham Arnold (1932-)
The White Horse, 1997
356 x 178 mm
Mark and Catherine Richards

115

Dragon Hill (also known as St George's Hill) is just below the White Horse at Uffington, the oldest of the white horses cut into the chalk uplands. Sacred, mysterious sites like these have long fascinated the artist; indeed it was a powerful reason for the Arnolds' move to Devizes, close to Avebury, Silbury Hill and Glastonbury – 'landscapes imbued with a rare aura of mystery.'

Dragon Hill is said to be where St George killed the dragon; where the blood was spilled no grass will grow. The subject was brought to Arnold's attention when John and Diana Morley sent a postcard of the hill with an explanation of its supposed magical properties and its connection with St George. Dragon Hill and the White Horse reappear in Arnold's work, with one still-life composition named *Postcard from Uffington* (*c.*1994)

116

A perennial favourite of Arnold, the Uffington White Horse was always thought to be Iron Age, but new evidence suggests a date of *c.*1200-800 BC making the horse Bronze Age. Since the Middle Ages it has been considered a 'horse', though its Celtic stylisation also suggests a dragon. The Celts venerated the horse as the goddess Epona. Alternatively, worshippers of the sun god Belinos or Belenus, who was also associated with horses, could have cut the figure.

It can be seen bottom right in *King's Mirror*. Here it is joined by the Hale-Bopp comet, dubbed the Great Comet of 1997, probably the most widely observed comet of the 20th century, and one of the brightest seen for many decades. It was visible to the naked eye for a record eighteen months. Its inclusion reinforces the timelessness of Uffington and reminds us of Richard Jefferies, one of Arnold's favourite writers, sitting on the 'grass-grown tumuli' and musing on the meaning of time:

> 'There is no separation – no past; eternity, the Now is continuous. When all the stars have revolved they only produce Now again. The continuity of Now is forever'. [35]

117

A persistent theme in Arnold's work is assemblages of objects, which looks back to his father's arrangements and rearrangements of small objects for him to draw and paint. He started making assemblages in the 1960s – in collage combined with painting, reticulated box constructions in mixed media, and as 'postcards' on canvas. This might suggest a surrealist element in Arnold's vision but the Surrealist aim was to create odd juxtapositions and dislocations, like Nash's placing of a tree stump with a tennis ball on the South Downs. While Arnold's assemblages contain many secrets they are designed to be unlocked and he offers us many keys.

King's Mirror, a classic Arnold collage, was a commission on the Celtic theme. The title was taken from the legend of Konungs Skuggsja (Speculum Regale) or the King's Mirror, a Norwegian educational text from *c.*1250 dealing with politics and morality. It was originally intended for the education of King Magnus Lagabote, the son of King Hakon Hakonsson and takes the form of a dialogue between father and son. Arnold was also inspired by a passage in Ruth and Vincent Megaw's *Celtic Art from its beginnings to the Book of Kells*. [36] This tells us about the symbolic value of Celtic art, which sees no

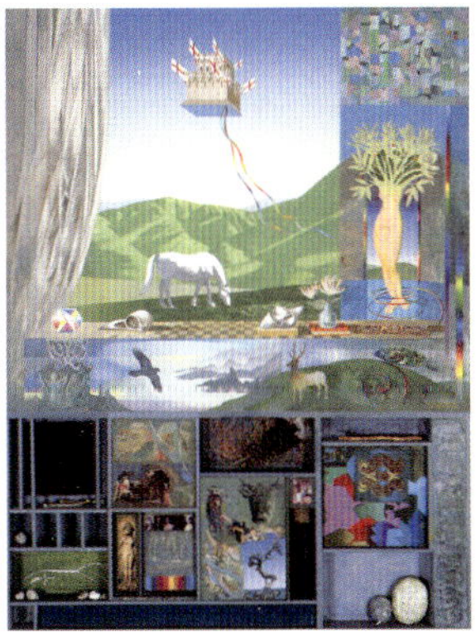

117. Graham Arnold (1932-)
King's Mirror
oil on board, 890 x 685 mm
Jenny Stevens

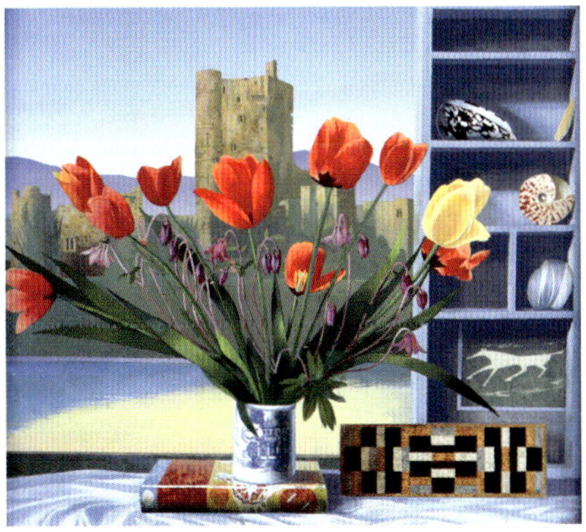

118. Graham Arnold (1932-)
The Strange Game
oil on board, 458 x 408 mm
Mark and Catherine Richards

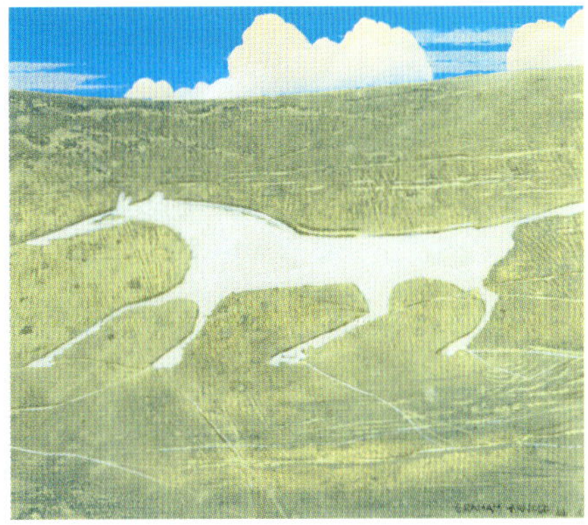

119. Graham Arnold (1932-)
The White Horse, Alton Barnes, 1996
oil on board, 200 x 235 mm
Wiltshire Heritage Museum

boundaries between animals and humans, time and space. Hence, young girls can morph into swans and brave heroes into salmon; shape-sifting or metamorphosis is a commonly held ancient belief. In the painting there is a female figure caught in the act of becoming a tree; as in the story of Apollo and Daphne, who escapes Apollo's unsolicited advances through transformation. The unstable and ambiguous nature of Celtic art allows seemingly abstract decoration to become imbued with human and animal forms. The dragon-like Uffington horse reappears, now joined by fragments of chalk taken from the 'eye' of the horse; bones remind us of the cult of ancestor worship; the crystal is one of Arnold's 'icons' or 'totems', from his father; and there is a reindeer with gigantic horns reminiscent of the petroglyphs or rock drawings of Aalta, northern Norway. But in this microcosm, what is the meaning of the floating flag bedecked tower? Arnold relates an Irish legend or 'wonder' concerning a monastery; seeing a rope and anchor come down from the sky, attaching itself to the church door, the monks are startled to see a man jump overboard from a ship in the sky and 'swim' down to release the anchor. The monks try to hold him back but the abbot forbids this fearing the man will 'drown'. This collapsing of boundaries, ships in the sky, two worlds colliding, adds a surreal element.

118

A classic still life, *The Strange Game* takes its name from the patterned box on the bottom right, found in a book on Canadian folk art, which Arnold considers a 'mystery'. The ruin, a motif that frequently occurs in Arnold's paintings, was seen on holiday in Ireland. The shells are from the artist's collection of 'icons' and 'totems'. The White Horse is the one cut in the chalk at Alton Barnes, in Wiltshire.

119

The Vale of Pewsey is renowned for its White Horses; Wiltshire is *the* county for white horses. There are or were at least twenty-four of these hill figures in Britain, with no less than thirteen being in Wiltshire, and another white horse, the oldest of them all, Uffington, being just over the border in Oxfordshire. 'This horse is a little under a mile north of the village of Alton Barnes, on Milk Hill. The originator was a Mr Robert Pile, of Manor Farm, Alton Barnes. He may have been the same man who was responsible for the first Pewsey horse, or possibly his son. In 1812 Mr Pile paid twenty pounds to a John Thorne, also known as Jack the Painter, to design the white horse and have the work of cutting it carried out. Thorne designed the horse, then sub-contracted the excavation work to a John Harvey of Stanton St Bernard. Before the work was finished Thorne took off with the money, and Mr Pile was left to pay out again. Thorne was eventually hanged, but what crime that was for is not recorded.' [37]

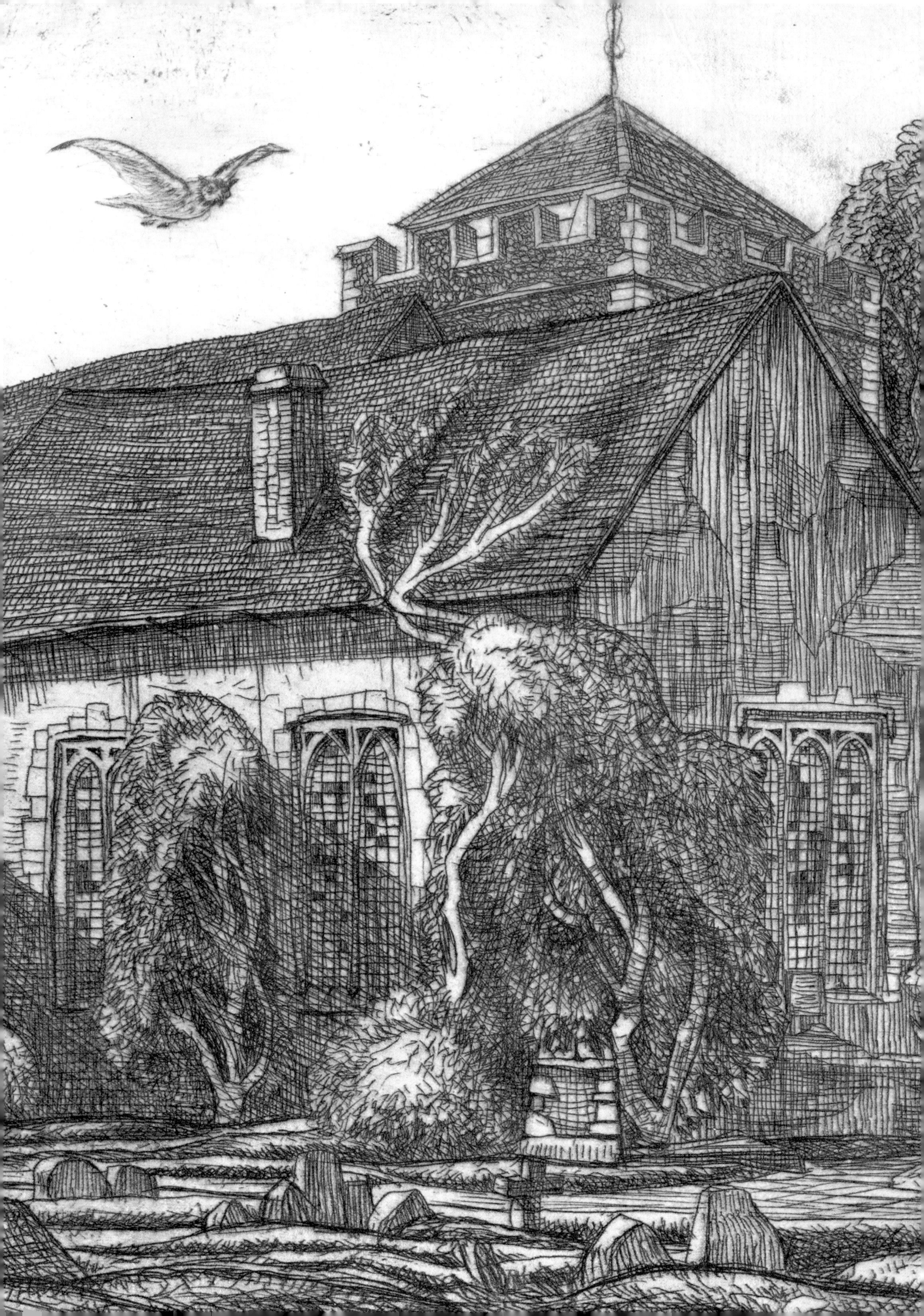

Nocturnes

John Minton joked 'Moons are in! Half-moons are really selling this year'.[1] The full mystery of the British landscape is revealed by moonlight: 'working through the small hours' from the church tower at Castle Combe, Wiltshire, Robin Tanner recalled that 'moonlight lay in sheets of silver so bright and constant that we drew as easily as by day'.[2] The light of the moon is eerie but not malevolent. Palmer used crescent moons and full moons; *Cornfield by Moonlight, with the Evening Star* (*c.*1830, British Museum) is one of Palmer's finest 'moonlights', from the early Shoreham days. The landscape is illuminated by a large waxing sickle moon and evening star; both shine unnaturally brightly: 'The ethereal nature of the work is heightened by the glimmering light, which is stronger than any that could have been cast by a sickle moon and has more of the character of a full-moon'.[3] In mood Palmer's 'moonlights' come close to the paintings of that other great Romantic, Caspar David Friedrich, although Friedrich is more inclined to melancholy. Friedrich dwelt on the isolation of the spiritual man yearning for salvation. His current popularity can be partly ascribed to his ability to convey alienation; like Palmer, Friedrich felt out of tune with his own times. But Palmer's vision of nature is 'ecstatic': 'he celebrated the wonder of nature, though he also indicated a sense of mystery and a mood of contemplation'.[4] In his desire to communicate 'the intimation of a higher reality' light played a major role, as it does in the work of Graham Ovenden, who strives for luminosity. Ovenden achieves this with smoothness, the ultimate reflector, whether hard or soft, of light. 'Light and luminosity', he observes 'are the symbols of our spirituality'. The best translucence and reflective power lies in applying each colour (pure or mixed) as a thin glaze – allowing that to dry thoroughly before applying any further colour (also thinly) over the first. The Pre-Raphaelites achieved their luminous colours in much the same way.

Palmer's higher reality was mysterious and only partly to be perceived; hence his interest in shadows, which heighten the mystery and intimate transience. It was a shadow that awakened Palmer's creative instincts; when he was only four years old, while standing with his nurse Mary Ward, 'watching the shadows on the wall from branches of elm behind which the moon had risen, she transferred and fixed the fleeting image in my memory by repeating the couplet:

> 'Vain man, the vision of a moment made,
> Dream of a dream and shadow of a shade'

I never forgot those shadows and am often trying to paint them'.[5]

Of the creatures of the night, surely the two that harbour the greatest symbolic resonance are the bat and the owl:

> 'The mopeing Owl does to the Moon complain
> Of such, as wand'ring near her sacred Bow'r
> ,Molest her ancient solitary Reign.'

These lines come from Thomas Gray's (1716-71) *Elegy in a Country Churchyard* (1751); when night falls the predatory owl, the 'night hunter', takes to the skies, its screech sending shivers down the spine:

'From cobalt cool through paling pearl
To scarlet on a frozen furl
(floss frost floc filling upper air)
Hangs winter's wan eye chilling glare.

Now falls the afterglow of light,
Each shadow drawn to catch choke night
Where owl holds his silent flight:
Whose ever watchful will sleeps slight…

He seeks the shrouded ice bound waste
as moon maid sheds her brittle wraith…

She casting cruel glamour on the snow:
Spreads over all a heartless glow,
shows the fast her virgin shape…
a whore whose hoaring cold as fate.

The sudden sweep…
his sleek winged taloned swoop
the staggered stoop
of broken breadth …a cry
as wanton wind flakes driven
fly in dance of death.

Life torn, bereft before her hollow sight:
pierced blooded chest on breasted white.'

(Graham Ovenden, *The Night Hunters*)[6]

The owl has been seen as killer, messenger and spirit; hailed as symbols of intelligence, they have also been feared and seen as signs of evil or death. The association with witches is centuries-old, dating to at least the medieval period. People believed that owls were evil spirits in disguise. Alan Garner's *The Owl Service* (1967) is a contemporary interpretation, which Garner described as an 'expression of the myth, of the story of the mythical Welsh figure of Blodewedd, whose story is told in the Fourth Branch of the Mabunogi, the most famous Welsh saga.' The legend concerns a woman created from flowers by a Welsh wizard. Blodewedd betrays her husband, Lleu, in favour of another, Gronw or Goronwy, and is turned into an owl as punishment for inducing Gronw to kill Lleu.

Three teenagers find themselves acting out the old legend of Blodewedd in an isolated valley a few hours drive from Aberystwyth. Alison, the heroine, finds a china service decorated with owls in the attic; as she traces the owls on the plates they disappear. As Alison gets caught up in the rivalry between two boys, Roger and Gwyn, it becomes clear that the legend is being reenacted. At the climax, Alison begins to change into a owl. A storm rages outside, branches smashing through the windows and skylight, the hoot of owls pressing in on them. Feathers swirl in the room and trace owl patterns on the walls and ceiling. Roger shouts that she is flowers, not owls. He yells this at Alison until abruptly all is peaceful, and the room is filled not with feathers but with petals.

Graham Ovenden is particuarly fond of ghost stories by M.R James (1862-1936), Sheridan La Fanu (1814-73) and Vernon Lee (1856-1935 Violet Paget).

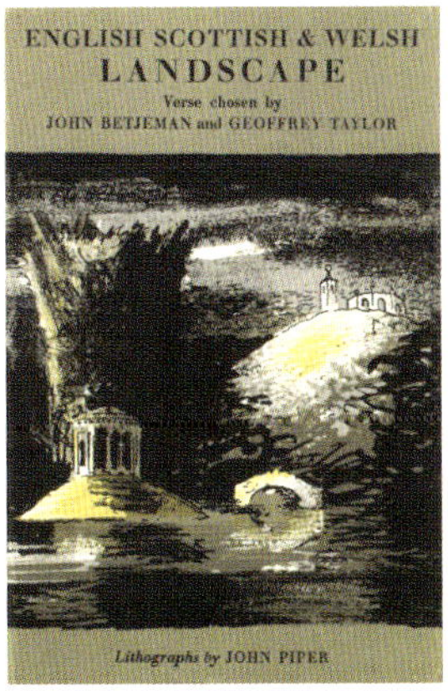

120. John Piper (1903-1992)
English, Scottish and Welsh Landscape Verse 1700-c.1860
chosen by John Betjeman and Geoffrey Taylor with Original Lithographs by John Piper
1944, Lithography on paper
210 x 143 mm, Pallant House Gallery, Chichester

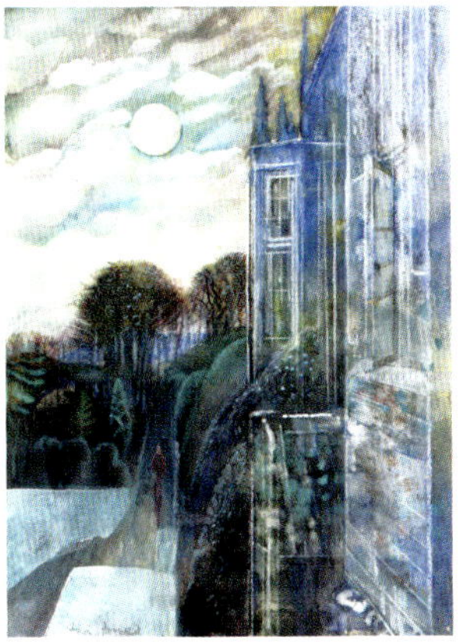

121. Ann Arnold (1945-)
Manor by Moonlight, 2001
watercolour, 225 x 160 mm
Edmund Ovenden

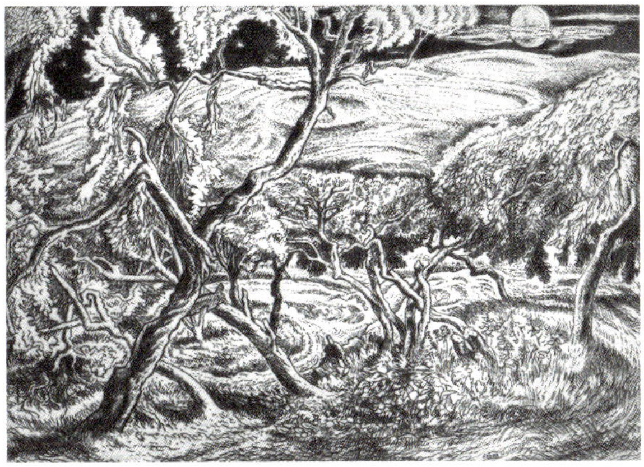

122. Edgar Holloway (1914-)
Orchard Moon, 1990
etching on paper, 177 x 253 mm
Edgar Holloway

120

In 1944 Sheila Shannon and W.J. Turner, the editors of the *Britain in Pictures* series commissioned Piper to produce lithographs to decorate an anthology of English, Scottish and Welsh Landscape verse. The well-known poets selected included John Clare, Samuel Coleridge Taylor, William Collins, William Cowper, Alfred Lord Tennyson, James Thompson and William Wordsworth. But Betjeman and Taylor also included numerous poems by 'unknown clergymen'. Their criteria were 'that the poet should have obviously looked at and loved what he described'. Piper's twelve three-colour lithographs were intensely atmospheric, with dark skies over landscapes devoid of figures. Several featured picturesque buildings and ruins: Rievaulx in Yorkshire, Talland Church in Oxfordshire and Grongar Hill, Carmarthenshire.

121

This is reminiscent of many Victorian ghost stories involving haunted houses; the Ovendens and Arnolds are especially fond of M.R. James (1862-1936). James's ghost stories were published in a series of collections: *Ghost Stories of an Antiquary* (1904); *More Ghost Stories* (1911); *A Thin Ghost and Others* (1919), and *A Warning to the Curious and Other Ghost Stories* (1925). Many of the tales were penned as Christmas Eve entertainments and read aloud to select gatherings of friends. The classic Jamesian tale usually includes the following elements:

1. A characterful setting in a small English village or country estate, an ancient town or a venerable abbey.
2. A rather naïve and nondescript gentleman-scholar as protagonist.
3. The discovery of an old book or other antiquarian object that somehow calls down the wrath, or at least the unwelcome attention, of a supernatural menace, usually from beyond the grave.

According to James, the story must 'put the reader into the position of saying to himself: 'If I'm not careful, something of this kind may happen to me!'

122

After a watercolour (1982), of an old orchard at Burnt House, Bostal, near Ditching on the South Downs. A luminous full moon hangs over an orchard that is being reclaimed by nature. The limbs of the ancient untended trees form distorted patterns; this 'spooky' image provides a contrasting foil to Ovenden's tranquil *Orchard Moon*.

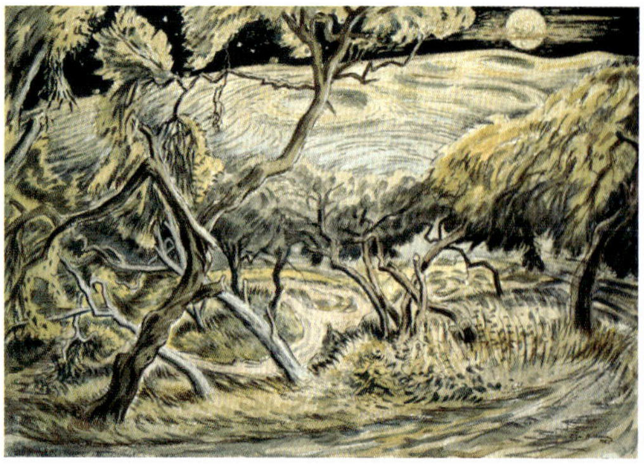

122a. Edgar Holloway (1914-)
Orchard Moon, 1982
watercolour, private collection

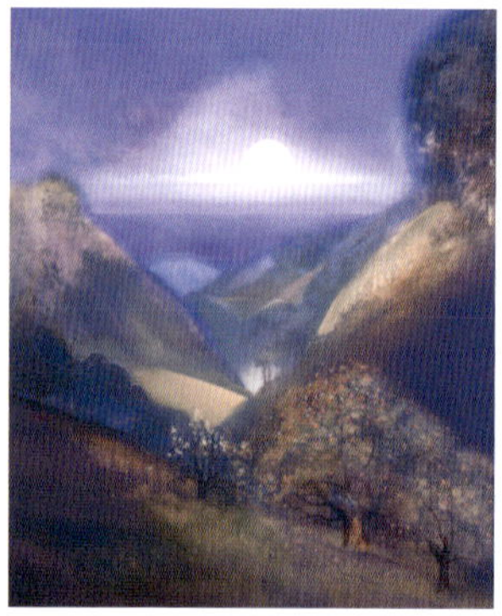

123. Graham Ovenden (1943-)
Orchard Moon, 2004
oil on canvas, 435 x 360 mm
Diana Wilkinson

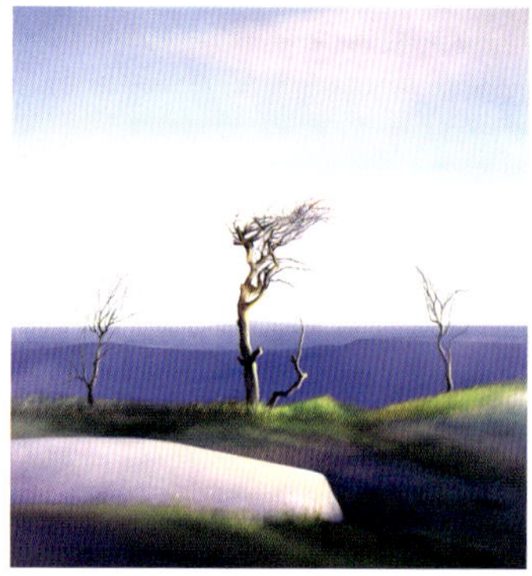

123a. Graham Ovenden (1943-)
Trinity
oil, private collection

123

Orchard Moon is especially Palmer-like, with its luminous moon floating on vaporous white clouds. The eye is taken through the folds of the landscape, a natural tunnel extending to the horizon where the moon rises and casts its slivery light. The image is peaceful but melancholic, suggestive of loss. There are inevitably three apple trees, one being less mature, almost child-like. The religious significance of the Trinity immediately springs to mind, while apple trees recall Palmer's *Magic Apple Tree*, painted during the Shoreham period, as well as a time of innocence before the Fall.

Graham writes that his works are:

> '…a synthesis of the landscapes we encounter in actuality (Cornwall and Shropshire) and that half dream state which can engulf our emotions at the experiencing of a higher reality. Despite deprivations and inconsideration for our environment Britain's landscapes are still that of enclosed gardens leading onto and into the greater nature. Light which is the symbolism of our spirituality still moulds and caresses form, unifying both structure and emotion with its benediction.' [7]

124

Warleggan is a small village close to the Ovenden's home at Barley Splatt, near Bodmin. For many years the parish had to cope with an eccentric rector, Frederick Densham, who upset the locals so much that they refused to go to church: Densham made a reputation for himself by preaching to the empty church, filling the pews with cardboard figures of previous rectors of the parish. Annie Ovenden visited Warleggan soon after she and Graham moved to Cornwall:

> 'I went early one evening with a friend to look around the graveyard. Warleggan is an isolated parish of the edge of Bodmin Moor; tall beech trees in which dozens of cawing rooks have made their nests surround the ancient church. The combination of the eerie sound of the birds and the dark gradually descending imbued the whole place with an extremely spooky atmosphere from which my friend and I eventually fled.' [8]

125

With War increasingly likely, Webb focused on pastoral subjects and nocturnes. *Pippin Lane*, is a moonlit subject of Webb's own invention, although 'Pippin' may allude to Webb's visits to the apple orchards of Kent. The meandering road was used to suggest the traveller; Webb is known to have admired the poetry of Francis Thompson (1859-1907) who, living the life of an addicted vagrant, hoped to emulate the drug-induced creative visions of de Quincey's *Confessions of an Opium Eater*. In danger of relapse, Thompson spent an extended retreat at the Norbertine Monastry of Sorrington, Sussex, in 1889, where he composed his most famous poem, the autobiographical *Hound of Heaven* that tells of God, who does not abandon, but pursues, the most wayward soul:

> 'I fled Him, down the nights and down the days;
> I fled Him, down the arches of the years;

124. Graham Ovenden (1943-)
Moon Rise over Warleggan or Autumn Moon, 2007
oil on canvas, 420 x 585 mm
Peter and Renata Nahum

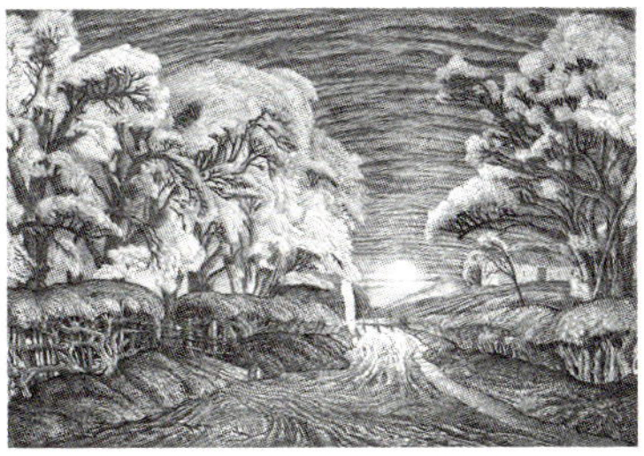

125. Joseph Webb (1908-1962)
Pippin Lane, 1938
etching on paper, 172 x 240 mm
Stuart Southall

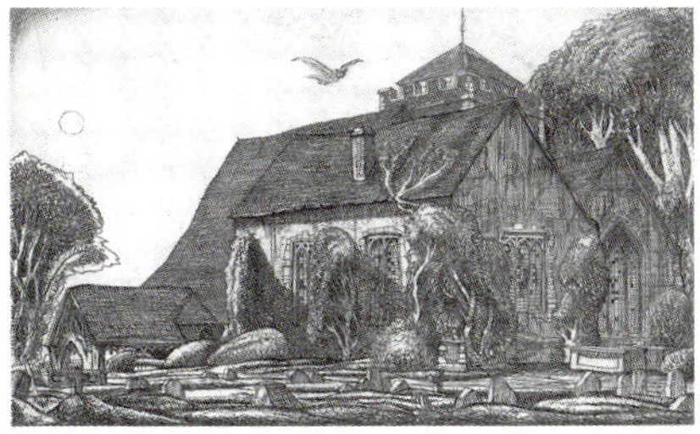

126. Joseph Webb (1908-1962)
Stoke Poges, 1931
etching on paper, 200 x 303 mm
The School of Art, University of Wales Aberystwyth

> I fled Him, down the labyrinthine ways
> Of my own mind; and in the mist of tears
> I hid from Him, and under running laughter.' [9]

126

In the summer of 1931 Webb was on the road again, in Buckinghamshire, drawing sites with literary associations (*Milton's Cottage*, 1931). *Stoke Poges* shows the graveyard and twelfth century Church of St Giles, where it is thought that Thomas Gray (1716-71) set *Elegy in a Country Churchyard* (1751); the poet is buried here under the Tudor-style mullioned windows of the Hastings Chapel. Grigg's had depicted the fourteenth century porch, which stands on the south side. The first state of Webb's etching bore the inscription 'Where heaves the turf in many a mouldering heap'. Rather than lamenting great national heroes, Gray's *Elegy* commemorates the commonplace country folk buried in the churchyard, honouring their 'useful toil, their homely joys and destiny obscure':

> 'Far from the madding Crowd's ignoble Strife,
> Their sober Wishes never learn'd to stray;
> Along the cool sequester'd Vale of Life
> They kept the noiseless Tenor of their Way.'

The *Elegy* is replete with pastoral imagery, from lowing cattle to weary ploughmen, so familiar to us from Palmer's Shoreham days:

> 'The *Curfeu* tolls the Knell of parting Day,
> The lowing Herd winds slowly o'er the Lea,
> The Plow-man homeward plods his weary Way,
> And leaves the World to Darkness, and to me.' [10]

But Webb's image conjures up the melancholic moonlight, with the 'moping owl' disturbed by the presence of the poet, who, encroaching on her 'sacred Bow'r', molests her private domain:

> 'Now fades the glimmering Landscape on the Sight,
> And all the Air a solemn Stillness holds;
> Save where the Beetle wheels his droning Flight,
> And drowsy Tinklings lull the distant Folds.
> Save that from yonder Ivy-mantled Tow'r
> The mopeing Owl does to the Moon complain
> Of such, as wand'ring near her sacred Bow'r,
> Molest her ancient solitary Reign.'

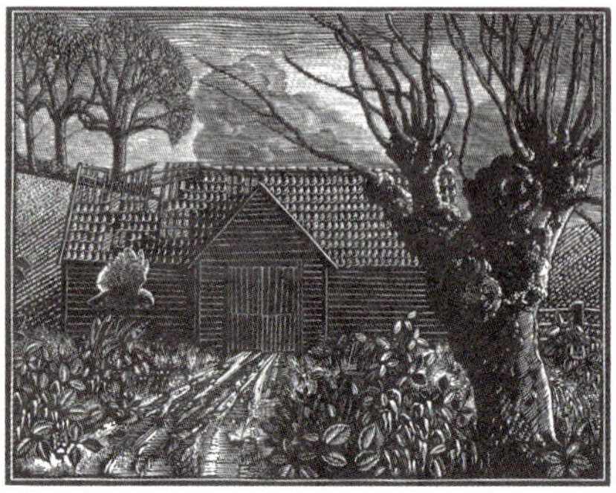

127. John Morley (1942-)
Barn Owl, 1993
woodcut, 85 x 114 mm
John Morley

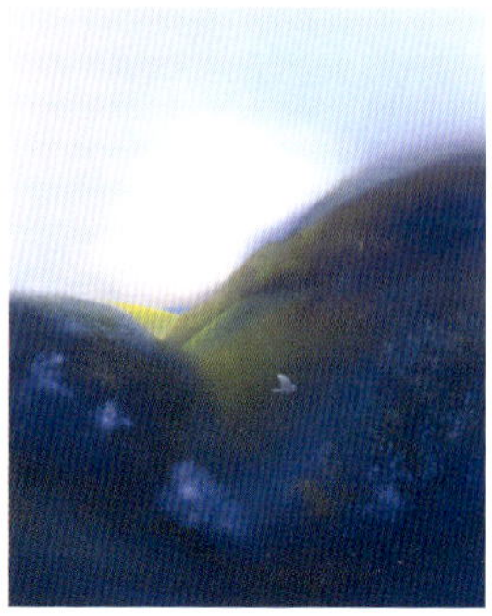

128. Graham Ovenden (1943-)
May Day Eve, 2000-01
oil on board, 440 x 365
Peter and Renata Nahum

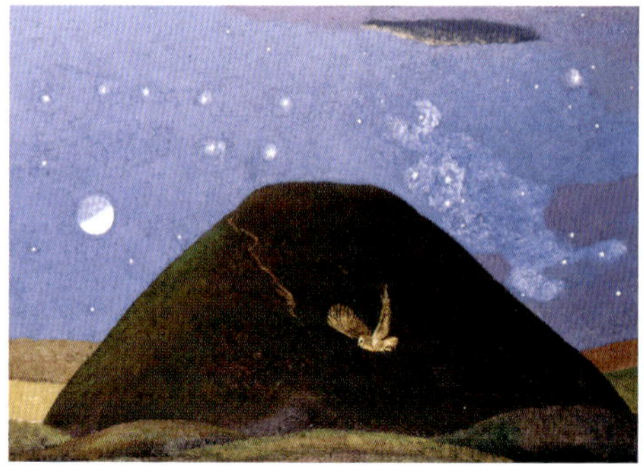

129. David Inshaw (1943-)
Silbury Hill on a Starry Night, 1986
oil on canvas, 584 x 813 mm
Tom Stoppard

127

Morley's works depict the Suffolk countryside, around his home near Beccles. This image follows in the traditions of Griggs and the Class of 21. In addition to the owl scouting for prey, there is a wonderfully gnarled and pollarded tree on the right.

128

In pagan times, May Day celebrations marked the first spring planting. The Celts and Saxons celebrated 1st May as the day of Beltane or the day of fire; Bel was the Celtic god of the Sun. More recently we think of it as 'the people's holiday or labour day'. The Saxons began their celebrations on the eve of May, 30th April. It was an evening of games and feasting commemorating the end of winter and the return of the sun; it was a fertility ritual. Torch bearing peasants would climb to the top of the hills and ignite wooden wheels that cascaded down to the fields below (rather like Catherine Wheels; also referenced in Nash's *Eclipse of the Sunflower*).

May eve celebrations were eventually outlawed by the Catholic Church but were still celebrated in rural communities until the late 1700s. Those unafraid of papal authority, or more concerned to appease the ancient gods, would don animal masks and other fancy dress, as on Halloween. The revellers led by the Goddess of the Hunt, Diana and the Horned God, Herne would take to the hills chanting or singing, accompanied by the clarion call of the hunting horn. Over the years Diana and Herne came to be seen as fertility deities of the crops and fields. Diana became Queen of the May and Herne became Robin Goodfellow, Shakespeare's Puck, the legendary faerie or the Green Man (latterly equated with Robin Hood); the Queen of the May was equated with the life of the fields, while Robin reflected the hunting traditions of the woods. May Day Eve became known in Europe as Walpurgisnacht, or night of the witches.

Ovenden took as his starting point Algernon Blackwood's (1869-1951) *May Day Eve* (1907):

> 'It was a calm, windless evening, just after sunset, the air warm and scented, and delightfully still. The train, already sinking into distance, carried away with it the noise of crowds and cities and the last suggestions of the stressful life behind me, and from the little station on the moorland I stepped at once into the world of silent, growing things, tinkling sheep-bells, shepherds, and wild, desolate spaces…
>
> 'Moreover, at the same time the deep sadness of beauty had entered

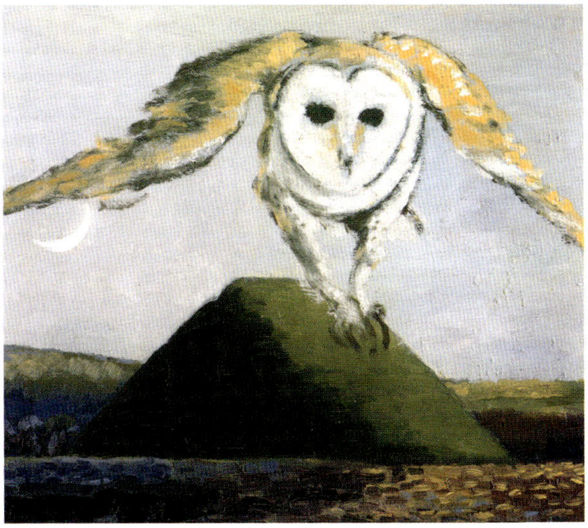

130. Inshaw (1943-)
Owl and Silbury, 1988
oil on canvas, 270 x 35 mm
Geoff and Mary Haydon

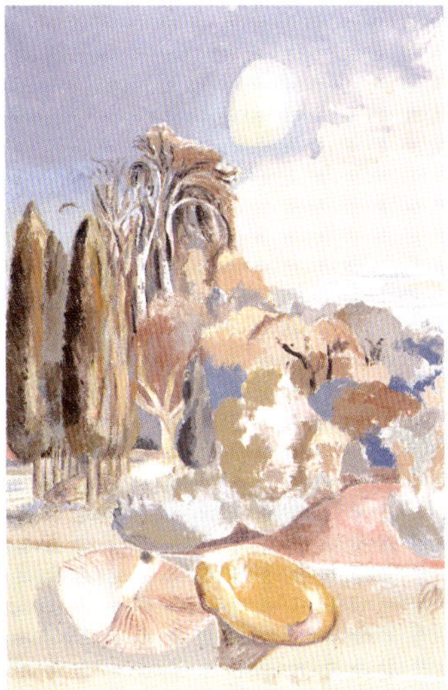

131. Paul Nash (1889-1946)
November Moon, 1942
oil on canvas
Syndics of the Fitzwilliam, Cambs

my heart like a stroke; for all this mystery and loveliness, I realized poignantly was utterly independent and careless of me, as me; and that while I must pass, decay, grow old, these manifestations would remain for ever young and unalterably potent.'

129

Silbury looks like Nash's 'green pyramid' in this work by Inshaw. The stars twinkle in the night sky with an unnatural brightness. The owl swoops majestically through the scene.

130

Heading straight towards the viewer, its talons unfurling, you feel this owl is about to swoop on you, rather than on some unsuspecting mammal.

131

'Call it, if you like, a transcendental conception; a landscape of the imagination'...Paul Nash, *Picture History*, 1945.

Nash was referring here to his Boar's Hill cycle, the works created in the garden of Sandlands, in Boar's Hill, Oxfordshire, that belonged to Hilda Harrison. Nash's imagination has been caught by the phenomenon of the moon appearing in daylight on a clear autumn evening; it is where the sun should be, as in Ovenden's *Poplars*, high and full in a crisp, blue sky. One senses that winter is not far way (it is spring in Ovenden's work). On the left there is an avenue of tall leafy cypresses, an evergreen long associated with immortality, often to be found flourishing in cemeteries. This tree also connotes death itself, cypresses being connected with the Underworld in Greek and Roman mythology. The contrast between the living and the dying is vividly expressed throughout the painting. Nash was fascinated by the cycle of death and rebirth in nature, by the rhythm of the seasons, and there is a general intimation of mortality in *November Moon*: a sense that the end of nature's cycle has been reached. For now the cold moon and the autumn colours hold sway over the garden.

The foreground is filled with a gigantic mushroom and a convolvulus, or Morning Glory, which are extremely swollen in size.[11] Nash is constructing another 'equation'; the autumnal mushroom, which signals death, and the summer flower. The convolvulus flower twists from left to right, following the daily rotation of the sun, while its stalk twists elliptically from right to left. These details show Nash's deepening concern with time, with daily and annual cycles and, since the mushroom and the flower will shortly wither, with the 'transition from individual time to the timelessness of death'. [12] Due to his declining health, Nash sensed his impending death, describing this period of his life as his 'last phase'.

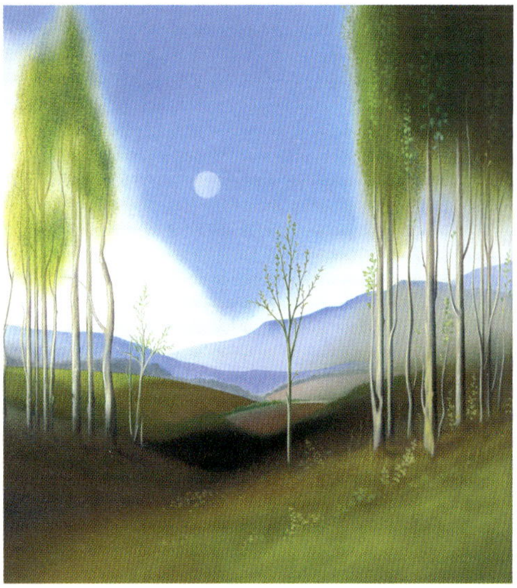

132. Graham Ovenden (1943-)
Poplars, 1991
oil on board, 308 x 275mm
Diana Wilkinson

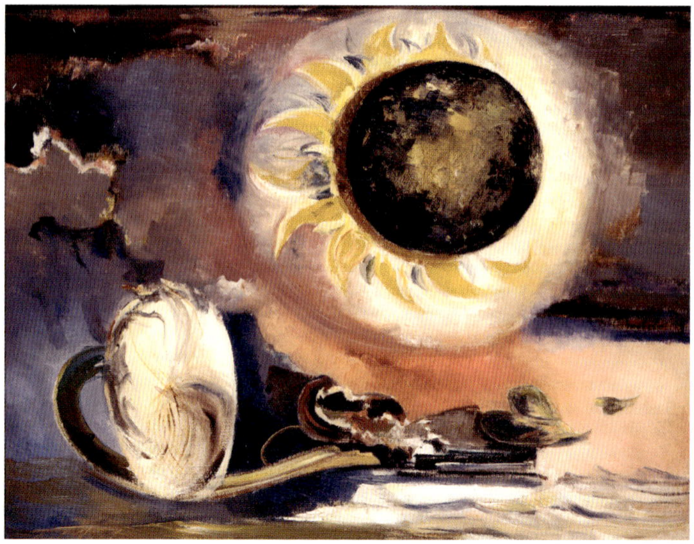

133. Paul Nash (1889-1946)
Eclipse of the Sunflower, 1945
oil on canvas, 711 x 914
British Council

132

In this tranquil image 'imagination is tempered by objective observation'; like Nash's *November Moon* this work is 'a transcendental conception'.[13] *Poplars* uses the Trinity theme, with a sapling protected by mature trees. Nature is rejuvenating, with the sapling just coming into leaf: 'It's no coincidence that most of my landscape paintings deal with spring: ecstasy burgeoning forth'.

Echoing diagonals, the position of the sapling off-centre, his preferred asymmetry, creates a sophisticated composition given depth by tonality. The forms of the landscape are echoed in the sky, a favourite device of Ovenden's, which he admits to borrowing from Friedrich. Ovenden discovered Friedrich by chance; passing a bombed-out church in Portsmouth, he and his father were drawn to explore the ruined vicarage. Here under the staircase Graham found a bookcase that had evaded destruction ironically filled mostly with German books, including Karl Robert Langewiesche, *Der Blumenkorb* (1924) on German painting of the first and second quarters in the 19th century. Graham encountered for the first time not only the intensity of Friedrich but also Otto Runge (1777-1810) and the Nazarenes. This chance find seems in hindsight prophetic.

133

Towards the end of his life, due to both the war and the serious decline in his health, Nash turned to 'elegiac' symbols, particularly the sunflower. This flower bears an exceptional degree of symbolism from Blake's poem *Ah! Sun-Flower*, with its sunflower weary of time to Tennyson's *A Spirit haunts the year's last hours* (1830):

> 'Heavily hangs the broad sunflower
> Over its grave I' the earth so chilly.'

In the Victorian *Language of Flowers* the sunflower stood for adoration or constancy.. The origin of this meaning was the classical myth of Clytie who was punished by Apollo for causing her sister's death. Transformed into a 'flower that turns with the sun and reflects its colour', Clytie, forever rooted to the earth, was doomed to follow the sun god's course across the sky. In the 1870s the sunflower became the emblem of the Aesthete Oscar Wilde; it now signified yearning or unrequited love and sorrow. Above all the Sunflower embodied longing, a hopeless desire for Beauty that was by definition unobtainable. The flower could simultaneously signify hope and hopelessness. Nash seems to be aware of all these permutations of meaning. Nash had also read Frazer's *The Golden Bough* (1922), where he came across the story of the midsummer fire festival, when lighted fire wheels were rolled down the hill to imitate the course of the sun across the sky, as on the May Day Eve festival. In the *Eclipse of the Sunflower*, Nash fuses the flower's petals with the fiercely burning aureole of an eclipsed sun-disc, 'an image that for all its mystical meaning also reflected the infernal calamity of a global conflict'.[14] Nash saw himself in the sun-disc, 'escaping "into vast lonely spaces in complete freedom of bodily action", escaping the land, but in death, returning to it'. [15]

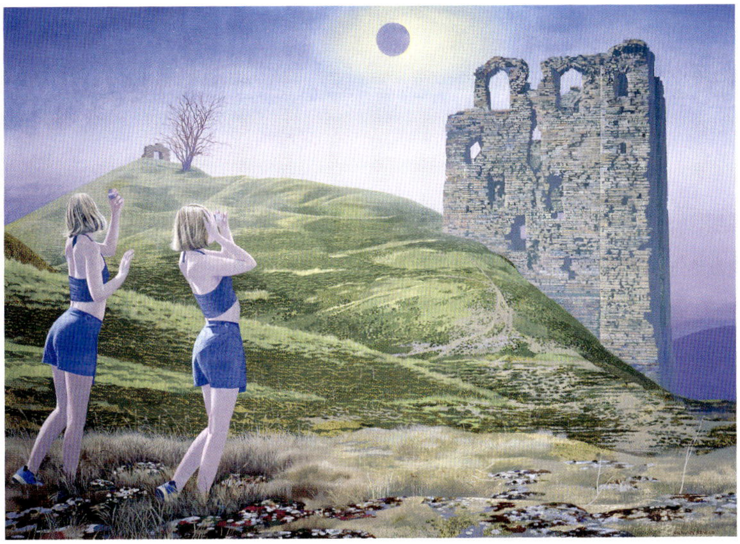

134. Graham Arnold (1943-)
The Twins watching the Eclipse at Clun Castle, 2001
oil on wood panel, 1219 x 1813 mm
Mike and Rosemary Lambert

134

Arnold writes:

> 'I took a long time coming to the final composition of this painting. Everything in the painting is undergoing a cycle of change. Some of the cycles are very long term-hundreds of years- some of them very short- one year- and locked into these cycles are our own brief vulnerable lives. I saw the youthfulness and the beauty of the twins as something of infinite preciousness and fragility set in a cosmos of cold indifference.' [16]

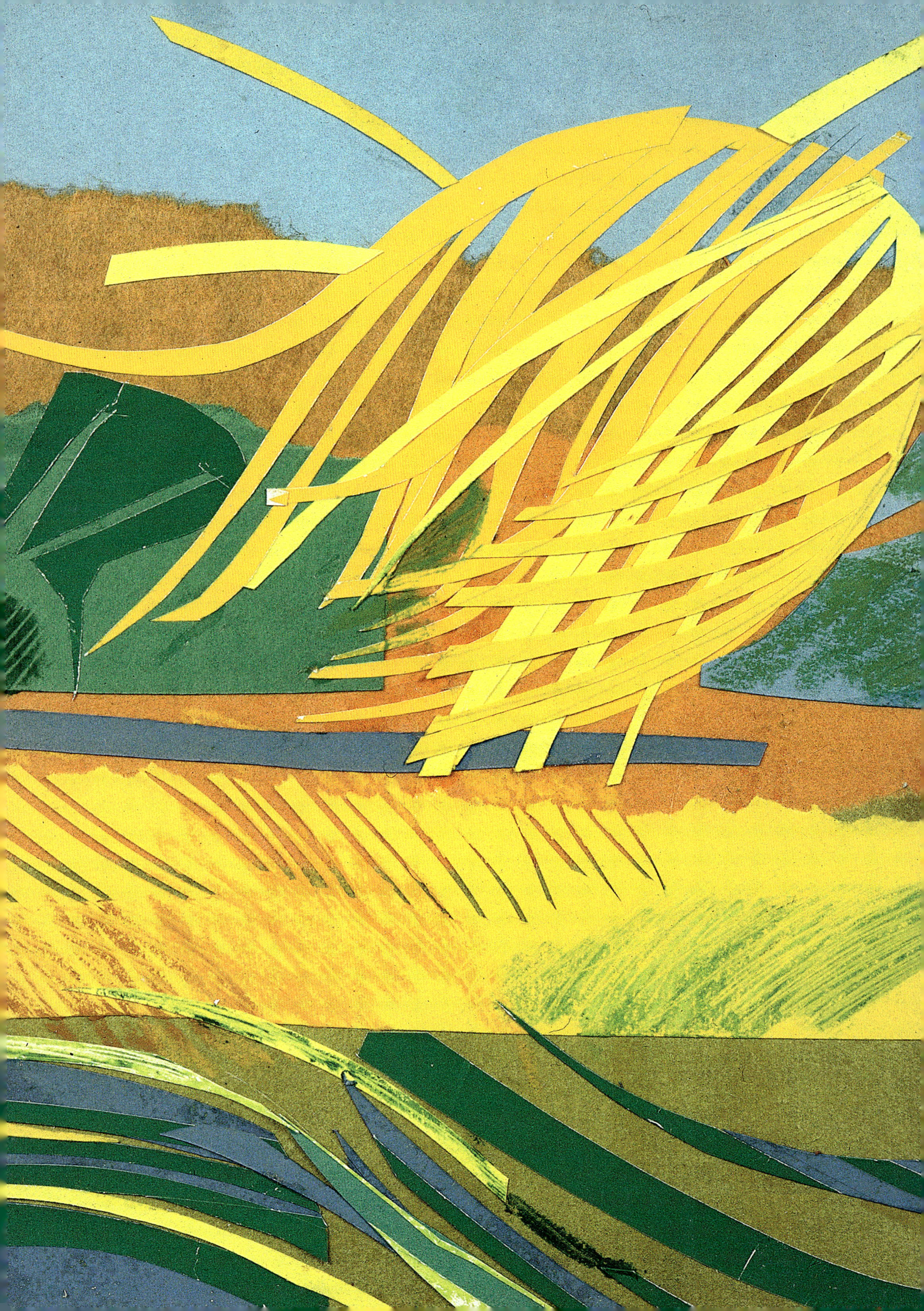

James Sellars (1927-2000): Artist and Teacher

Ovenden recollects an enjoyable and fruitful period at the Southampton College of Art[1] (1960-64), where the 'solid academic training based on direct observation suited him admirably'.[2] He could have opted for Winchester School of Art, which had a reputation for Fine Art teaching. The strength of the College, ever since the days of the Southern College of Art, lay in Printing, Fashion and Illustration. However, although the main emphasis was on 'industrial and applied arts', there was also 'a small but strong core of Fine Art work, incorporating Painting and Sculpture, Embroidery, Printmaking and Ceramics'.[3] The College was able to offer fine art teaching alongside more practical, 'commercial' courses.

Ovenden was able to benefit from the 'strong core' of students and teachers, with Bill Smith as Principal and Sydney Greenwood as Vice-Principal. [4] He recalls that 'we loved it. All the students did'. He describes an 'intimate' atmosphere and working conditions to which 'there was no comparison', and a 'substance' which is lacking today, for all our glamorous buildings and high ideas. He credits the life-drawing master at the time, David Richards, as 'an absolute master draughtsman', but reserves the highest praise for his teacher James Sellars, of whom he comments 'with Jim you got more – you got an inkling of what art is really about':

> 'In all probability a great teacher is as rare a being as the great artist. A willingness to communicate self selflessly, enthuse nature without cynicism or personal gratification is a true gift. This gift James Sellars bestowed upon his pupils with a stern but kindly benediction. We, his pupils, will be forever grateful for such matters and the many kindness' which this intriguing and inspiring man brought, not only to our studentships, but equally into maturity.' [5]

It was Sellars who introduced an already opinionated Ovenden to Palmer and Blake, and then to Paul Nash and Stanley Spencer. Sellars and his pupils would cycle westwards, into Dorset, and the moorlands of the Purbeck peninsula about Swanage (Hardy and Nash territory). Such encounters helped Ovenden to find his direction as a distinctly rural painter in the English mould.

Ovenden formed a life-long friendship with Sellars, 'a truly cultivated and immensely accomplished man'. His knowledge extended to all areas of great art, and was always given freely and accurately. Periods of full- and part-time teaching enabled Sellars to pass on his knowledge and skills. He was certainly a dedicated teacher who enhanced the learning experience of his pupils. His passion for landscape painting and the English Tradition was 'injected into all who came into contact with him':

> 'Like all artists of true substance, James Sellars held to his inner visions, enriching them with dynamic observations of what was best in twentieth century art. The richly and intensely observed 'portraits' of the Test Valley temperas (a medium much favoured by Sellars) are as seen and felt as any in the English landscape. His intellect was well-honed both in writing[6] and in teaching, yet there was no dry formality. He always did his own work with us, so you became part and parcel. Quite stern; that was something I thrived on, because I was always a hard worker. He would take criticism – because I didn't stand shoulder to shoulder with him in certain areas like Matisse, which he deeply loved.' [7]

After winning a scholarship to the RCA, where he joined the Fine Art Printmaking Department, Sellars was able to work with such artists as Graham Sutherland and John Piper. He was closely associated with 'The Kitchen Sink Painters' of the 1950s. This group of young men, fresh from the strictures of National Service and ready to separate themselves from the Academicians of the time, drew inspiration from their informal domestic environment. For Sellars, however, it was the English landscape, with its diversity and romanticism that held an enduring appeal. He is described as 'plainly heir to the long tradition of English Pantheism'. He observed and painted the landscapes in and around the places where he lived. To begin with the 'rugged gritstone country' close to his home city of Sheffield, then the lush water meadows of the Lower Test Valley, Hampshire and finally in retirement the Wye Valley: 'Just as Constable was at one with his East Anglian water meadows of the River Stour, likewise James Sellars was at one with his Valley of the Test and its water meadows in Hampshire'.[8] Ovenden holds Sellars' work in high regard: 'I think they are very important. They fit absolutely within the context of English pastoral tradition, and I think that Southampton will probably end up being embarrassed that they didn't realise what they had on their doorstep'.

But it was as an educator, 'in all probability the foremost teacher of his generation', that Sellars really left his mark. John Griffin, former Southampton Student, valued both the artist and the teacher:

> 'Integrity, honesty, humility, observation, accuracy, craftsmanship are just a few of the words relevant to the teaching of Jim Sellars...The influence of Blake, Palmer, Nash, Sutherland, Sellars, continues in all of us today, but we must not forget that his interests lay not only in the English school. He was very much aware and appreciative of most, if not all, movements in great Art, a veritable encyclopaedia on the subject, a deep and rich mine of information, profoundly respected by all of us who have had the privilege to draw upon it. His vast store of knowledge into which he delved from time to time was always given freely and accurately...No amount of words can sum up his visual passion; the paintings speak for themselves and always will. I am indebted to him.' [9]

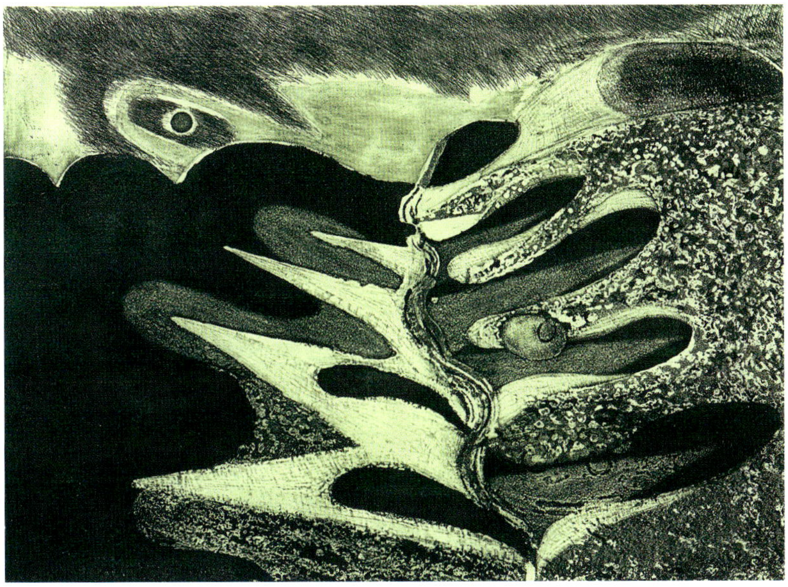

1. James Sellars (1927-2000)
Yorkshire Valley, 1966
etching and acquatint, 220 x 305 mm
edition of 20

Experimental printmaking was Sellars' life-long discipline. This early work has the intensity of Blake, seen through the lens of the Neo-Romantics. There are traces of Sutherland and Minton. It shows a good eye for design, while holding an intensity of vision.

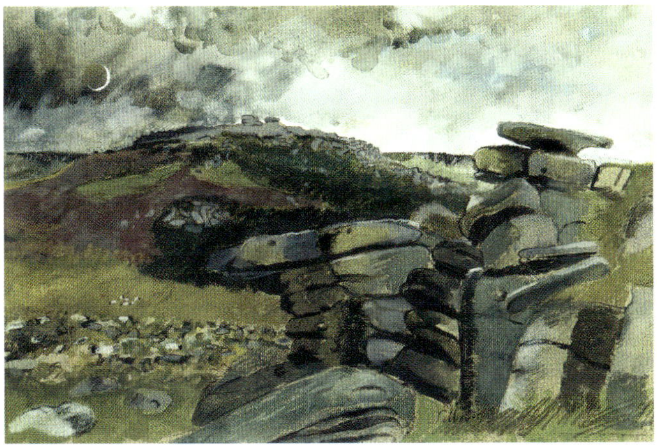

2. James Sellars (1927-2000)
Yorkshire, 1955/60
gouache and pastel, 295 x 455 mm

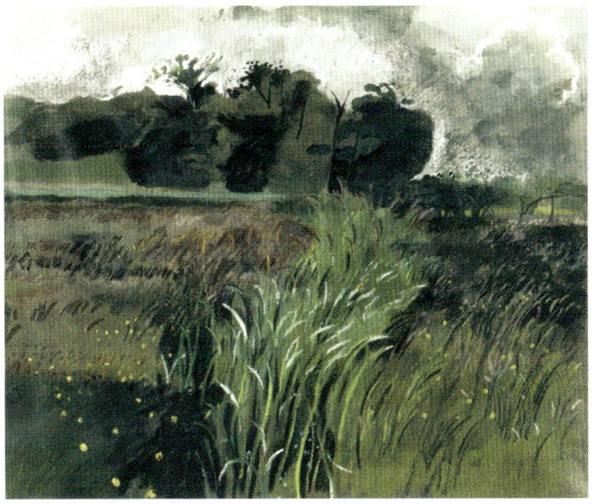

3. James Sellars (1927-2000)
Strong Winds, 1974
pastel and tempera, 355 x 445 mm

The Test Valley proved to be one of the most fertile sources for Sellars' vision. The series of pastels and tempera paintings he created in these lush surrounding are an important contribution to the English pastoral tradition. While Sellar's essays on the Test Valley capture the actuality of the landscape, they also transcend objectivity and reveal a deep understanding of the mysteries of nature. Ovenden comments: 'The richly and intensely observed portraits of his Test Valley temperas are surely as seen and felt as any in the English landscape.'

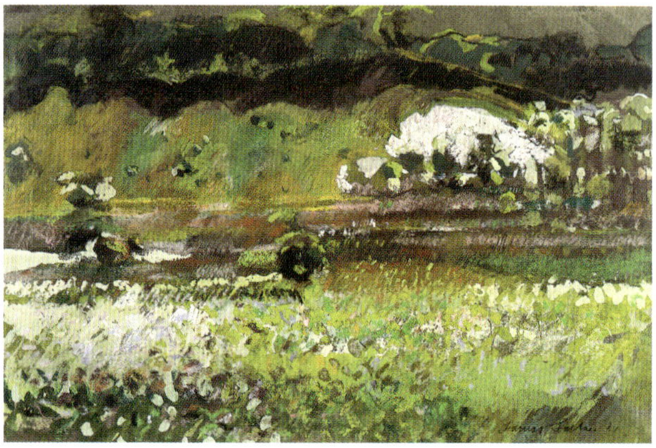

4. JAMES SELLARS (1927-2000)
Test Valley - Mottifont, 1964
pastel, 360 x 547 mm

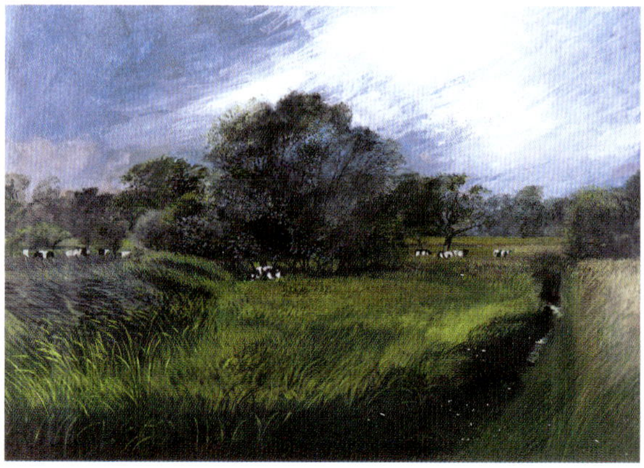

6. JAMES SELLARS (1927-2000)
Test Valley, the Hard, 1976
tempera, 380 x 540 mm

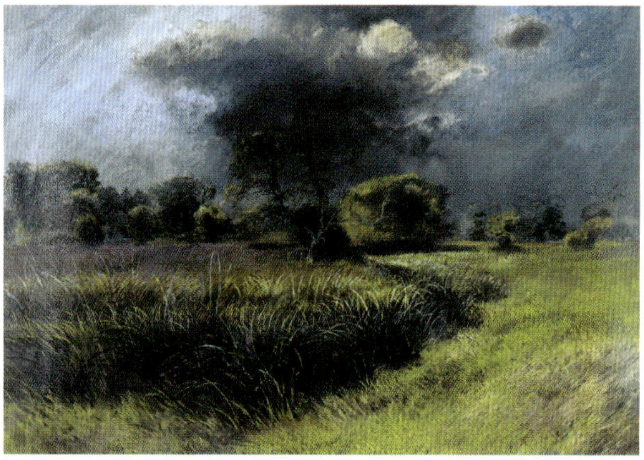

7. JAMES SELLARS (1927-2000)
Test Valley, Oncoming Storm, 1978
tempera, 370 x 540 mm

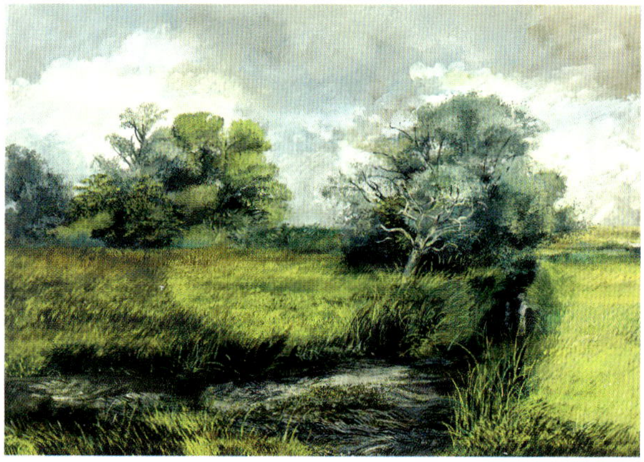

8. JAMES SELLARS (1927-2000)
Test Valley, 1977
tempera, 383 x 550 mm

5. JAMES SELLARS (1927-2000)
Test Valley, 1975
pastel and tempera, 350 x 550 mm
not illustrated

9. JAMES SELLARS (1927-2000)
Moccas Park, Duck Pond, 1986
tempera, 350 x 540 mm
not illustrated

10. JAMES SELLARS (1927-2000)
The Blue Road, 1981
not illustrated

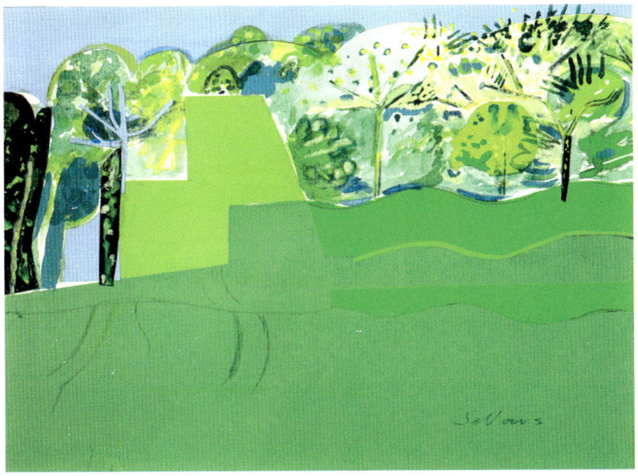

11. James Sellars (1927-2000)
Fieldscape, 1986
collage, 260 x 310 mm

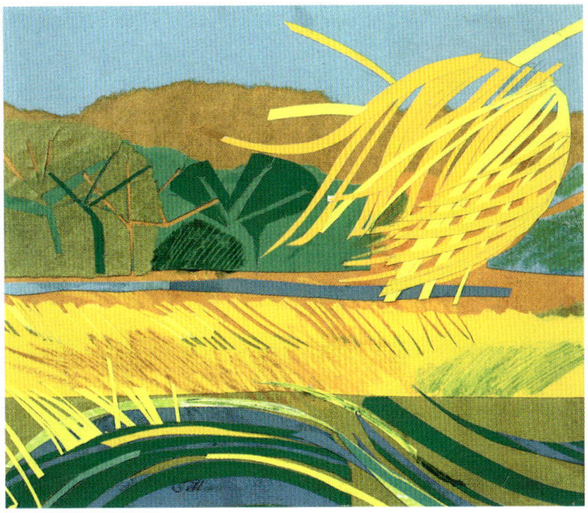

12. James Sellars (1927-2000)
Cornfield, c. 1990
collage and body colour, 250 x 295 mm

The later collages are joyful in colour and masterful in design. They were often given as presents or even used to wrap gifts.

13. James Sellars (1927-2000)
Owl 1, 1961
lithograph, edition 20, 470 x 330 mm
not illustrated

14. James Sellars (1927-2000)
Owl 2, 1961
lithograph, edition 20, 420 x 600 mm
not illustrated

All works lent by Pandora Sellars.

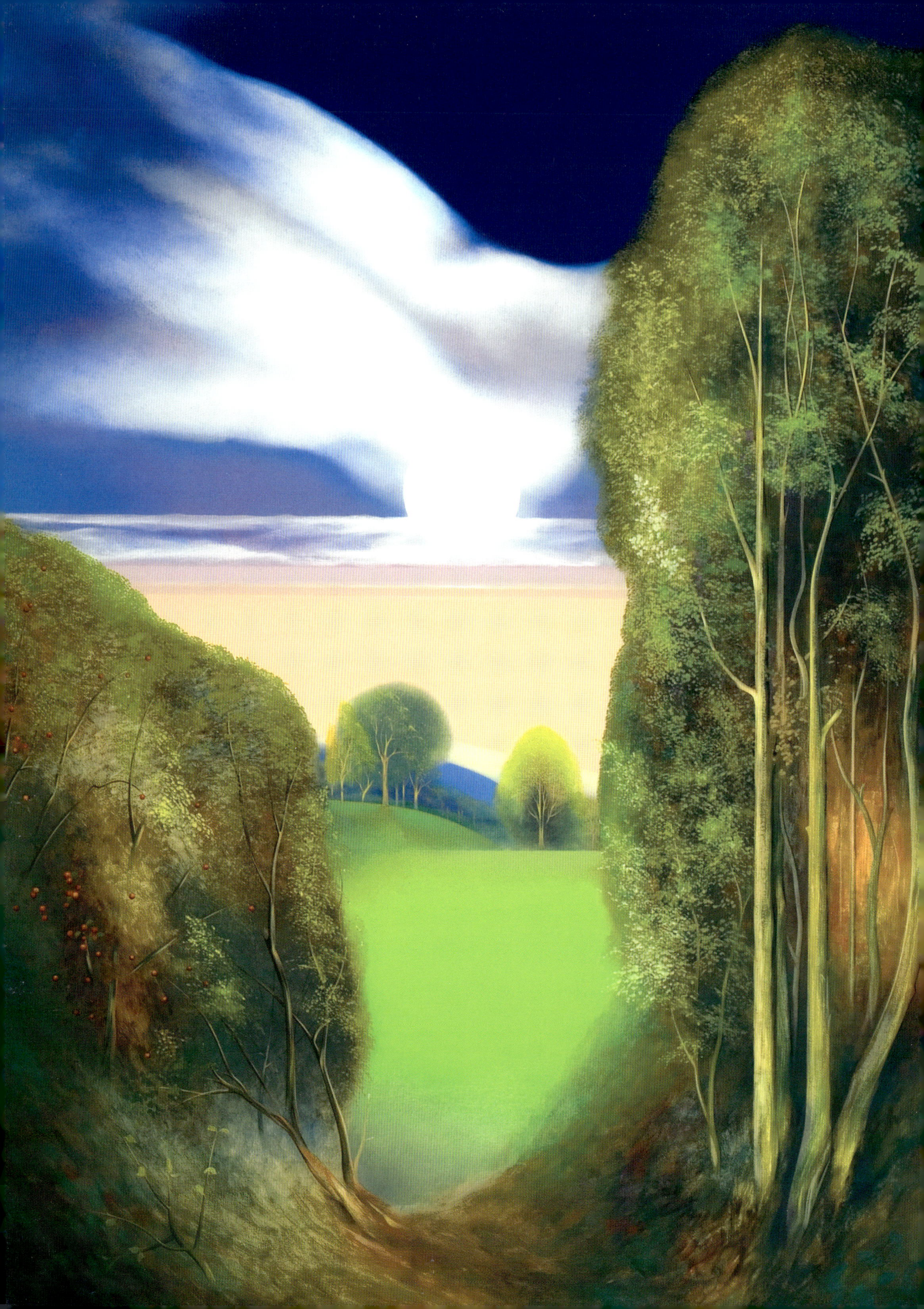

Afterword: Graham Ovenden

Peter Nahum

Countries, like dogs, have their day: inspired artistic movements emerge to bloom as a poetic vanguard. Japan, India, Germany , France, Britain, Scandinavia or the USA, for instance, have all, in different eras, been the focus of, and influence on the international *à la mode*. What may have been obvious to fewer in the know at the time becomes manifestly conspicuous to the majority in retrospect.

It is clearly arguable that the most consistent and important contribution that Britain has made to the world's artistic endeavours and connoisseurship over the last three centuries has been inspired by a joyous observation of nature, which emerges in all three arts: painting, music and poetry. And this flowering of painting in the eighteen and nineteenth centuries of an intimate and somewhat mystical expression of the humbling beauty of the artists' rural surroundings echoes the illuminated manuscripts uniquely created in Irish and Northern British monasteries over a thousand years before.

Graham Ovenden is a traditional landscape painter in the sense that he makes no attempt to be avant-garde. In the same fashion, he is a man of his time and his images are unlikely to have been created in any previous era. He is, as were his antecedent muses, at one and at peace with the landscape and awed by its gentleness, its power, its spirituality and in wonder at the poetry within a transient snowflake or its dramatic and overpowering presences. This, in itself, does not make great art. To see and feel deeply is one thing, but to have the gift of the gods and the application to express those feelings in a manner which enhances the life of us mere mortals and draws us deep within our private emotions, is quite another.

For to be gifted one great talent is not nearly enough – in Graham's case a photographic memory, an ability to absorb a visual moment in time with all its subtleties and detailed nuances, as Turner did – a turn in the light that takes your breath away before, in the blink of an eye, it has been lost forever. No, nor added to that the ability to draw and paint, making poetic marks and lines that form an entity that can be read and felt by all. No, not even enough is it to hear and play and be moved by the most lyrical composers, nor enough again to read and absorb and revel in the poets – for those talents may be held lightly by those that have them, but they are not given to all. Combine all these with an intellectually curious brain and these are still not enough. For it is only consistent dedication and application to the artist's craft over a lifetime that hones and coalesces these talents into fragile objects of purity, that are imbued with the power to communicate with the viewer to the profoundest level.

Graham calls this process, from conception to completion of a finished painting, alchemy. And I cannot think of a better expression. Making a painting from the first idea, setting down the initial composition in small mono-tonal brushstrokes on a chosen prepared board, and then building the subtleties of mysterious colour balance to reflect a magical moment of atmospheric bliss, to emerge finally over three to nine months later. The paint is laid on with pure glazes, mostly with tiny brushes, using four primary colours of oil paint, but that is not exclusive. There may well be watercolour and almost certainly places where precise draughtsmanship has been laid down in pencil or outlined finely in oil. As the translucent diaphanous layers are laid, over a period of time, one over another they fashion, as in Pre-Raphaelite painting, multicoloured surfaces through which light may pass, to then bounce off the pure white ground, returning to produce, for the viewer, elusively ever changing combinations of colour balance as the quality of daylight brightens and wanes. Each diaphanous glaze must take its time, over a day or more, to dry before another may be applied. But this lengthy process is not as simple as it may seem, for as the layers build they are rubbed back and added to again, not just with brushes, but fingers and other chosen instruments. Throughout the process, moods materialise, are gently tuned, transformed and balanced with other emerging tonalities. Alchemy indeed; a moon may receive ten or more applications of white glazes before it shines with the definitive intensity or the glow of dusk. Light changes with each new application of layered colour, from gentle to misty to mysterious.

Each one of Graham Ovenden's paintings reflects a differing degree of light and atmosphere; just as those that nature infinitely creates. When we, those that know his work and those that are seduced for the first time, have the privilege of seeing a group of his landscapes, there will always be one to favour our mood and transport us. The evocation of one of these momentary encounters may conjure up an intimate memory, a descriptive passage from Thomas Hardy, a movement by Elgar or a sonnet by Shakespeare. For our perception of nature and its poetic celebration by others must by necessity be interwoven, and these entwined elements are as much part of the lyrical components of Graham's paintings as is his glory in its actuality. A short conversation with him on Romanticism in Britain and Germany produces a rapid fire check-list interwoven with inspiring commentary:

A E Housman
Wordsworth
Robert Burns
Walter Scott
Thomas Hardy
M.R. James
Richard Jefferies
Gilbert White
George Herbert
Elgar
Vaughan Williams
Frank Bridges
Edmund Rubbra
Peter Maxwell Davis
Benjamin Britten
John Clare
Walton
Percy Grainger
Delius
Henry Purcel
Handel
Denton Welsh
William Morris
Samuel Palmer
William Blake
Blake – Thornton's *Virgil* – woodcuts –
The Corn Laid Waste
Paul Nash

Children's Songs and Poems
by Walter de la Mare
A Prisoner in Fairyland by
Algernon Blackwood and
set to music by Elgar as
The Starlight Express (1916)
The rediscovery of Folk culture in
the1840s and 1850s
Music & songs & dances of Britain and
middle Europe
Emily Bronte's *Wuthering Heights*
High Romanticism
Wagner
Shakespeare and Goethe and Heine's
poems
Goethe: *Erlkönig* 1782, set to music by
Schubert aged 18 in 1815
Loewe
Otto Beamish
Caspar David Friedrich
Rembrandt landscape drawings and
etchings
Rubens landscapes
Ruisdael
Dürer's Landscape study of water, sky
and pine trees (British Museum)
The Book of Kells

And these are only jumping-off points to explore the rich hinterlands of interpretation, influence and counter-inspiration where poetry and reality intermingle. For conversation with Graham Ovenden is always enlightening and revealing. He wears his self-made scholarship lightly and donates it freely and without condescension. To while away a few hours with him is always an enriching delight. I once remarked that when I thought about his out-of-focus edges, where the leafy outline of a tree is seen *contra-jour* against a gentle evening sky that it reminded me of Vermeer, whose softly myopic and mysterious interiors result perhaps from previewing his subject in the *camera obscura*. Whereupon Graham replied by beginning to describe his in-depth observations drawn from studying Vermeer's techniques first-hand. His small studio is always alive with music played from his extensive collection of early recordings, where pastoral symphonic idylls counterpoint with the soulful tones that originated in the sugarcane fields of slavery. The very first 78 recording that he chose for me from his extensive collection was 'Careless Love', a long-held favourite of mine which I first listened to in the 1960s; an extraordinarily perceptive and unprompted choice on his part. However, my version, which I play often, is by Ottilie Patterson & Chris Barber recorded in the late 1950s, whereas his, the original of 1925, is by Bessie Smith and Louis Armstrong.

Early recording is only one of Graham's scholarly interests. He was one of the first academics with a comprehensive knowledge of the Arts & Crafts Movement, from Augustus Pugin to Ernest Gimson, not only revelling in *The Grammar of Ornament* (1856), but its antecedents and influences. His library burgeons with original publications not only on these subjects, but also early photography, his first love. As a young and lauded photographer in the 1960s, he developed the tools of his trade in the darkroom as well as the fresh air. These skills have re-emerged in the new millennium in his use of the computer, where he creates enchanted imagery which materialises as elegiac giclée prints on archival paper or lettered and bound publications, all "hand-made" by the artist. This contemporary manipulation of his classic photography and draughtsmanship, combining his knowledge of Owen Jones' *The Grammar of Ornament* with contemporary design, has spilled back into his more recent landscape painting, where the dreamlike qualities of the landscape are enhanced by a contemporary vision. (*Autumn Moonrise* 2007)

I had long coveted owning a landscape by Graham Ovenden, from the days when my miserly 1970s Sotheby's pay failed to stretch that far. In fact my first purchase was his iconic *Ophelia* (1979-81) which I bought in 2000. My wife's first reaction to this honest and revealing portrait was one of slight shock and incomprehension, which, on better acquaintance, was soon replaced by one of admiration and respect. This is a common initial reaction which many people fail to overcome, for what we require from our greatest artists is a deep dug honesty of thought that we are often in denial of ourselves, such as Lucien Freud's female nudes, both vulnerable and post-coital. Graham's young girls, on the other hand, reveal the intermingling of the vulnerability of innocence and the very first learnt behaviour; that of discovering and exploiting the cracks in their parents' armour, a determined seductive manipulation of their love and weaknesses. *Ophelia* is all the more initially shocking as its carefully applied Pre-Raphaelite detail and glazes are displayed in the language of contemporary advertising, thus making perhaps too raw and immediate a statement to the contemporary viewer, who almost certainly expects to be protected by the familiar artificial and sugary language of Victorian genre painting. But perceptive modern statements nearly always take their time to mature in the viewing public's eyes.

This purchase and the next, a glowing little landscape entitled *The Secret Valley*, which we covert, led to our first meeting, and since that time he and his family have enriched our lives on so many levels. Not only do my wife and I intimately live with many of his paintings, but his artistic perceptions and far reaching scholarship have enhanced our appreciation of our own artistic world. And so, in turn, have his fellow Brotherhood of Ruralists: his wife Annie, Graham and Ann Arnold, David Inshaw and Peter Blake. Graham Ovenden's masterpiece, *Sentinels to Paradise* (2002-3), homage to Paul Nash, hangs in our bedroom. Its inherent and intangible spirituality not so much waxes and wanes, but deepens, enlightens and transforms as the light changes from early morning clarity through evening softness to deep night enigma.

Our world at The Leicester Galleries is populated as thickly as we can make it with symbolist and visionary artists, those whose perceptions, however subtle, travel far beyond the merely decorative, and so Graham becomes not just a perfect piece in the jigsaw, but a real inspiration. We have handled works by Turner, Constable, Palmer and Blake, the Pre-Raphaelites: Millais, Holman Hunt and Madox Brown and their symbolist brothers, Rossetti and Burne-Jones, along with their European Symbolistes counterparts, Gustave Doré, Gustave Moreau, Paul Gauguin, Eugène Carrière, Léon Frédéric and Odilon Redon, the forefathers of the Surrealists, who we also handle. Those monumental 19th century British landscape painters who dig so deep into their poetic vision, inspired by 'England's Green and Pleasant Land', have many followers in the 20th century, but the two giants who stand head and shoulders above their admirable colleagues are Paul Nash in the first half of the century and Graham Ovenden in the second.

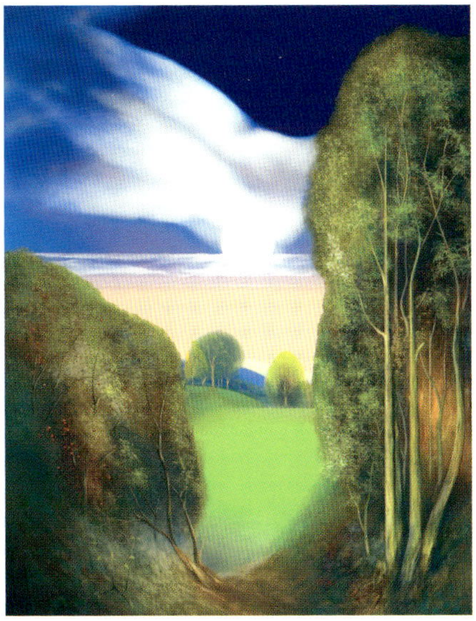

135. Graham Ovenden (1943-)
Through the Window of Mine Eyes or the Communion of the Trees
oil on canvas, 950 x 1220 mm
Peter and Renata Nahum

135

Graham Ovenden describes his work thus:

Fugue – 'The flight of the parts' – within the severest architectonic structure we may achieve the greatest spiritual freedom, and thus the intertwining pillars of vigorous growth stand as portals framing the infinite domain of Eden…

The intense luminous deepening of the night sky, the symbol of our ever-future search into the greater mystery of our universe.

The full moon and attendant sky being the symbol not only of unsullied grace but also the fecund benediction of the reflected sun, thus our sensuality is made whole.

The lower light of the evening sky tells of the journey towards paradise, the 'garden of grace', which lays always just beyond attainment: an unrequited longing touched by the edge of anguish.

The soft luminous sward that is the garden of our spirit, cultivated through light out of the coming darkness – the compassion of Pan's domain ever loving in its fulfilment.

Notes

Ancient Landscapes, Pastoral Visions: Motifs and Meanings

1. Michael Ayrton, *British Drawings*, London: William Collins, 1946, p. 34.
2. Ayrton quoted in Malcolm Yorke, *The Spirit of Place: Nine Neo-Romantic Artists and their times*, London: Constable, 1988, p. 210.
3. Laurie Lee, 'Understanding the Ruralists' in Jerrold Northrop Moore, Laurie Lee, Peter Nahum, *The Ruralists: A Celebration*, Bodmin: Ruralist Fine Art, 2004, p. 109.
4. Bernard-Smith, *The Times*, 1928, quoted in Robert Meyrick, 'In Pursuit of Arcadia: British Print Makers in the 1920s', in Martin, Butlin and Meyrick, *Poets in the Landscape: The Romantic Spirit in British Art*, p. 64.
5. Lee, *Understanding the Ruralists*, p. 111.
6. Simon Martin, 'Poets in the Landscape: The Romantic Spirit in British Art', in Simon Martin, Martin Butlin and Robert Meyrick, *Poets in the Landscape: The Romantic Spirit in British Art*, Exhibition Catalogue, Pallant House, Chichester, 2007, p.14.
7. Yorke, *The Spirit of Place*, p. 84.
8. Larkin in Yorke, *The Spirit of Place*, p. 83.
9. Yorke, *The Spirit of Place*, p. 74.
10. *Poets in the Landscape: The Romantic Spirit in British Art*, Pallant House Gallery, Chichester, 31 March-10 June, 2007 and Simon Martin, Martin Butlin and Robert Meyrick, *Poets in the Landscape: The Romantic Spirit in British Art*, Exhibition Catalogue, Pallant House Gallery, Chichester, 2007.
11. Graham Sutherland, 'Thoughts on Painting', *The Listener*, 6 September 1951, pp. 376-78.
12. John Piper, *British Romantic Artists* (Britain in Pictures Series), London: William Collins, 1942, p. 7.
13. Hugh Cumming, 'Post-Modern Landscape: The Art of Graham Ovenden' in 'Post-Avant-Guarde: Painting in the Eighties', *Art and Design*, Vol 3, 7/8, August 1987, p. 80.
14. Reynolds in Martin, 'Poets in the Landscape', p. 10.
15. William Blake, *Descriptive Catalogue*, London 1809, in Yorke, *The Spirit of Place*, p. 73.
16. Yorke, *The Spirit of Place*, p. 44.
17. Hulme quoted Yorke, *The Spirit of Place*, p. 41.
18. Cumming, 'Post-Modern Landscape: The Art of Graham Ovenden', p. 77.
19. Cumming, 'Post-Modern Landscape: The Art of Graham Ovenden', p. 78.
20. Keith Vaughan in Martin, 'Poets in the Landscape', p. 11.
21. Martin, 'Poets in the Landscape', p. 12.
22. John Minton quoted in Martin, 'Poets in the Landscape', p. 12.
23. Eric Fitch Daglish, 'Foreword', *The Heart of England by Edward Thomas*, London and Toronto: J.M. Dent and Sons, 1932, p. XIII.
24. Daglish, 'Foreword', *The Heart of England*, p. IX.
25. Daglish, 'Foreword', *The Heart of England*, pp. IX-X.
26. Daglish, 'Foreword', *The Heart of England*, p. XI.
27. Daglish, 'Foreword', *The Heart of England*, pp. XI-XII.
28. Daglish, 'Foreword', *The Heart of England*, p. XII-XIII.
29. Samuel J. Looker, 'Introduction', *The Life of the Fields by Richard Jefferies*, London: Lutterworth Press, 1947, p. 12.
30. Looker, 'Introduction', *The Life of the Fields*, p. 11.
31. Looker, 'Biographical Notes', *The Life of the Fields*, p. 280.
32. Looker, 'Introduction', *The Life of the Fields*, p. 16.
33. Richard Jefferies, 'The Pageant of Summer' in Looker, *The Life of the Fields*, pp. 80-81.
34. John Powell Ward, *The English Line Poetry of the Unpoetic from Wordsworth to Larkin*, London: Macmillan, 1991, p. 4.
35. Ward, *The English Line*, p. 4.
36. Walter Pater in Ward, *The English Line*, pp. 4-5.
37. Wordsworth in Ward, *The English Line*, p. 49.
38. Ward, *The English Line*, pp. 126-27, 131-32.
39. Ward, *The English Line*, p. 130.
40. Edward Thomas in Looker, *The Life of the Fields*, p. 286.
41. Schama traces the origins of Aracdia, in *Landscape and Memory*, back to a primordial past; the mark of the original Aracdians was their bestiality but this was tempered by the fecundity of nature. Simon Schama, *Landscape and Memory*, London: Harper Collins, 1995, pp. 526-27.
42. Martin, 'Poets in the Landscape', p. 13.
43. Schama, *Landscape and Memory*, p. 11.
44. Schama, *Landscape and Memory*, p. 11.
45. Schama, *Landscape and Memory*, p. 12.
46. Schama, *Landscape and Memory*, p. 12.
47. Judy Egerton, *Wright of Derby*, London: Tate Gallery, 1990, p. 117.
48. Martin, 'Poets in the Landscape', p. 14.
49. Robert Burton, *Anatomy of Melancholy*, Everyman Edition, 1964, I, p. 246.
50. Paul Fussell, *The Great War and Modern Memory*, Oxford: Oxford University Press, 1977, p. 246.
51. Fussell, *The Great War and Modern Memory*, p. 253.
52. Virgil in Schama, *Landscape and Memory*, p. 516.
53. Fussell, *The Great War and Modern Memory*, p. 231.
54. Fussell, *The Great War and Modern Memory*, p. 232.
55. Ronald Blythe quoted in Fussell, *The Great War and Modern Memory*, p. 232.
56. Julian Moynahan, 'Pastoralism as Culture and Counter-Culture in English Fiction, 1800-1928", *Novel*, VI, No .I, Fall 1972, p. 20.
57. Schama, *Landscape and Memory*, p. 6.
58. Schama, *Landscape and Memory*, pp. 6-7.
59. Schama, *Landscape and Memory*, p. 16.
60. Graham and Ann Arnold, *Exhibition of Work inspired by Gerald Finzi, English Song and Thomas Hardy*, June-July 2001, exhibition leaflet, Silk Top Hat Gallery, Ludlow.
61. Robert Stephen Hawker (803-1875) poet, antiquary, and eccentric Vicar of Morwenstow.
62. Lee, 'Understanding the Ruralists', p. 109.
63. Lee, 'Understanding the Ruralists', p. 111.
64. Lee, 'Understanding the Ruralists', p. 111.
65. Lee, 'Understanding the Ruralists', p. 112.
66. Schama, *Landscape and Memory*, p. 14.
67. Schama, *Landscape and Memory*, p. 15.
68. Palmer, *Letters*, pp. 695-6, William Vaughan, 'The Lonely Tower (c. 1865-

1881)' in William Vaughan, Elizabeth E. Barker and Colin Harrison, *Samuel Palmer: Vision and Life*, Exhibition Catalogue, British Museum, 2005, p. 233. These stones were removed on the Holloway re-print.

69. Cumming, 'Post-Modern Landscape: The Art of Graham Ovenden', p. 79.
70. Cumming, 'Post-Modern Landscape: The Art of Graham Ovenden', p. 79.
71. Yorke, *The Spirit of Place*, p. 18.
72. Tassi quoted in Meyrick, 'In Pursuit of Arcadia', p. 82.
73. Malcolm Yorke, 'English Neo-Romantics', in 'The New Romantics', *Art and Design*, Vol. 4, No. 11/12, 1988, p. 40.
74. Schama, *Landscape and Memory*, p. 517.
75. Graham Ovenden, 'Ruralism and the New Romanticism', 'The New Romantics', *Art and Design*, Vol. 4, No. 11/12, 1988, p. 52.
76. Walter de la Mare in Clive Wainwright, 'Architecture and Antiquities', Victor Arwas, Clive Aslet, Laurie Lee, Robert Melville and Clive Wainwright, *Graham Ovenden*, London: Academy Editions, 1987, p. 108.
77. Yorke, *The Spirit of Place*, p. 18.
78. Paul Nash, 'The Life of the Inanimate Object', *Country Life*, 1 May 1937, in Jemima Montagu, *Paul Nash. Modern Artist, Ancient Landscape*, London: Tate Britain, 2003, p. 93.
79. Yorke, 'English Neo-Romantics', p. 38.
80. Paul Nash, 'Aerial Flowers', *Outline. An Autobiography and Other Writings*, London: Faber 1949, p. 260; Yorke, *The Spirit of Place*, p. 32.
81. Yorke, *The Spirit of Place*, p. 36.
82. Nash, letter to Bottomley, 1 August 1912, in C.C. Abbott and A. Bertram (eds) *Poet and Painter: Correspondence between Gordon Bottomley and Paul Nash*, London, 1955, p. 42.
83. Yorke, *The Spirit of Place*, p. 36.
84. Nash in Yorke, *The Spirit of Place*, p. 36.
85. Yorke, 'English Neo-Romantics', p. 38.
86. Yorke, 'English Neo-Romantics', p. 39.
87. Nash in Roger Cardinal, *The Landscape Vision of Paul Nash*, London: Reaktion Books, 1994, p. 7.
88. Paul Nash, *Picture History*, 1943-5 (Nash's unpublished notes about his work since 1933) in Cardinal, *The Landscape of Vision of Paul Nash*, p. 118.
89. Yorke, 'English Neo-Romantics', p. 39.
90. Yorke, 'English Neo-Romantics', p. 39.
91. Cumming, 'Post-Modern Landscape: The Art of Graham Ovenden', p. 80.
92. Nash, *Outline*, p. 122.
93. Ovenden, 'Ruralism and the New Romanticism', p. 51.
94. Natalie Rudd, *Peter Blake*, Modern Artists, London: Tate Modem, 2003, p. 7.
95. Lee, 'Understanding the Ruralists', p. 111.
96. Meyrick, 'In Pursuit of Arcadia', p. 61.
97. Meyrick, 'In Pursuit of Arcadia', p. 60.
98. Graham Sutherland, 'Welsh Sketchbook', *Horizon* V., April 1942, pp. 225-335.
99. Yorke, *The Spirit of Place*, p. 204.
100. Raymond Mortimer, 'New Movements in Art', *The New Statesman*, 28 March 1942, p. 208.
101. Palmer quoted in Martin, 'Poets in the Landscape', p. 13.
102. Wordsworth quoted in Yorke, *The Spirit of Place*, p. 16.
103. Roberta Smith, 'A Tree-Hugger Ahead of His Time', *New York Times*, 17 March 2006.
104. Yorke, *The Spirit of Place*, p. 17.
105. Edward Calvert in William Vaughan, 'Brothers in art, brothers in love': The Ancients as an Artistic Community', in Vaughan, Barker and Harrison, *Samuel Palmer: Vision and Landscape*, Exhibition Catalogue, British Museum, 2005, p. 17.
106. Cumming, 'Post-Modern Landscape: The Art of Graham Ovenden', p. 78.
107. Cumming, 'Post-Modern Landscape: The Art of Graham Ovenden', p. 78.
108. Cumming, 'Post-Modern Landscape: The Art of Graham Ovenden', p. 78.
109. Cumming, 'Post-Modern Landscape: The Art of Graham Ovenden', p. 77.

Pastoral Revisions: 'Little Englandism' in British Printmaking, 1915-1935

1. Uncredited review of an exhibition of etchings by F. L. Griggs at the XXI Gallery, Adelphi *Colour*, September 1920.
2. Walter Millard 'Mr. Griggs' Drawings and Etchings' *Journal of the Royal Institute of British Architects* 22 May 1915, p. 372.
3. A. H. Palmer *The Life and Letters of Samuel Palmer*, London: Seeley, 1892, p. 16.
4. John Piper *British Romantic Artists*, London: Collins, 1941, p. 7.
5. David Lillington *Time Out London*, 20-27 January 1993.
6. Charles Marriott 'Sources of Art' *Outlook*, 20 September 1919.
7. Uncredited review of an exhibition of etchings by F. L.Griggs at the XXI Gallery, Adelphi *Colour*, September 1920.
8. Uncredited review of an exhibition of etchings by F. L.Griggs at the XXI Gallery, Adelphi *Morning Post*, 28 September 1920.
9. C. M. 'A Constructive Artist' *Evening Standard*, May 1915.
10. Graham Sutherland *The English Vision*, exhibition catalogue, William Weston Gallery, October 1973.
11. Robin Tanner *Double Harness*, London: Impact, 1987, p. 47.
12. Robin Tanner *Double Harness*, p. 47.
13. Uncredited 'Art Exhibition, Mr. Graham Sutherland' *The Times*, London, 28 September 1928.
14. H.H.C. *Times of India* Bombay, 23 October 1928.
15. Uncredited review of 'Etchings and Drawings by Graham Sutherland at the Twenty-One Gallery *Apollo*, November 1928.
16. Uncredited 'Poetic Vision' review of Graham Sutherland's exhibition of drawings and paintings at the XXI Gallery, Adelphi *The Morning Post*, 28 September 1928.
17. Uncredited review of Sutherland's exhibition *The Scotsman* 27 September 1928.
18. *Fine Prints of the Year* Malcolm Salaman (1933 & 1934) and Campbell Dodgson (1938).
19. Beryl Gascoigne *Joseph Webb* (manuscript for a speech delivered on the occasion of the opening of an exhibition) Leighton House, London 1985
20. Edgar Holloway *Printmakers Journal*, Royal Society of Painter-Printmakers, London 1992, No. 13, p. 12.
21. Malcolm Yorke *Spirit of Place: Nine Neo-Romantic Artists*, London: Constable 1988, p. 22.
22. 'In conversation with John Craxton.' *Artists and Illustrators Magazine*, May 1988, p. 18.
23. Peter Woodcock *The Enchanted Isle: The Neo-Romantic Vision from William Blake to the New Visionaries*, Glastonbury: Gothic Image, 2000.
24. John Elwyn 'John Elwyn: Four Works with Notes' *Anglo-Welsh Review* Vol.9, No. 23, 1958, p. 44.
25. John Elwyn, notes on an exhibition in a letter to the author, 1994.
26. Peter Woodcock 'Re-Enchanting the Land' in *This Enchanted Isle*, p.141.

Pastoral Visions

1. Palmer in Kathleen Raine, *William Blake*, London, 1951, p. 183.
2. Laurence Binyon, *The Followers of William Blake: Edward Calvert, Samuel Palmer, George Richmond and their Circle*, London, 1925.
3. Yorke, *The Spirit of Place*, p. 112.
4. Yorke, *The Spirit of Place*, p. 110.
5. During the mid-1920s Palmer's name seemed to be everywhere in the English art world, with the publication of Lawrence Binyon's *The Followers of William Blake* in 1925. After Sutherland and his generation had worked through their Palmer periods, Geoffrey Grigson's *Samuel Palmer: the Visionary Years* (1947) brought his works to a younger generation.
6. Robin Tanner, *Double Harness: An Autobiography*, London: Impact Books, 1987, p. 41.

7. Vaughan, 'The Lonely Tower', p. 224; F.G.Stephens, *Notes by Mr F.G.Stephens on a Collection of Drawings, Paintings and Etchings by the Late Samuel Palmer*, London, 1881, pp. 15-16.
8. Palmer, *Letters*, p.868, in Vaughan, 'The Lonely Tower', p. 242.
9. Colin Harrison, 'The Artistic Rediscovery of Samuel Palmer' in Vaughan, Barker and Harrison, *Samuel Palmer: Vision and Landscape*, p. 56.
10. Yorke, *The Spirit of Place*, p. 109.
11. Edward Bouverie-Hoyton had enrolled in 1918, William Larkins in 1920, Sutherland in 1921; they gelled into a group in 1921.
12. Letter to Berthoud, January 1980 in Roger Berthoud, *Graham Sutherland: A Biography*, London, 1982, p. 52.
13. Douglas Cooper, *The Work of Graham Sutherland*, London, 1961, p. 7.
14. Letter to Berthoud, in *Graham Sutherland: A Biography*, p. 52.
15. 'Landscape and Figures' Graham Sutherland discusses his art with Andrew Forge, *The Listener*, 26 July 1962, pp.132-5.
16. Tanner, *Double Harness*, p. 47.
17. Meyrick, 'In Pursuit of Arcadia', p. 71.
18. Christopher Wood, *Fairies in Victorian Art*, Woodbridge: Antique Collectors' Club, 2000, p. 15.
19. Wood, *Fairies in Victorian Art*, p. 19.
20. Marina Vaizey, *Peter Blake*, London: Weidenfeld and Nicolson, 1986, p. 37.
21. Natalie Rudd, *Peter Blake*, (Modern Artists), London: Tate Publishing, 2003, p. 67.
22. Vaizey, *Peter Blake*, p. 37.
23. Blake in Rudd, *Peter Blake*, p. 62
24. Rudd, *Peter Blake*, p. 62.
25. Blake in Rudd, *Peter Blake*, p. 67.
26. Vaizey, *Peter Blake*, p. 57.
27. Yorke, *The Spirit of Place*, p. 113.
28. Roberto Tassi, *Graham Sutherland: The Complete Graphic Work*, London: Thames and Hudson, 1978, p. 21.
29. Yorke, *The Spirit of Place*, p. 113.
30. Gordon Cooke, 'Introduction', *Graham Sutherland Early Etchings*, London: privately printed,1993, n.p.
31. Sutherland in Martin, *Poets in the Landscape*, p. 47.
32. Martin Butlin, 'The Pastoral Vision: Blake, Palmer and the Ancients 1805-1850' in Martin, Butlin and Meyrick, *Poets in the Landscape*, p. 44.
33. Vaughan, 'The Lonely Tower', p. 242.
34. Griggs in Jerrold Northrop Moore, *F.L.Griggs: The Architecture of Dreams*, Oxford: Oxford University Press, 1999, p. 124.
35. Martin, *Poets in the Landscape*, p. 76.
36. Griggs in F.A Comstock, *A Gothic Vision: F.L. Griggs and His Work*, Boston and Oxford: Boston Public Library and Ashmolean Museum, 1966, No. 36, pp. 167-8.
37. Griggs in Northrop Moore, *F.L.Griggs: The Architecture of Dreams*, p. 200.
38. Comstock, *A Gothic Vision: F.L.Griggs and His Work*, No. 36, p. 168
39. Sutherland in Northrop Moore, *F.L. Griggs: The Architecture of Dreams*, p. 192.
40. Meyrick, 'In Pursuit of Arcadia', p. 71.
41. *James Sellars: Artist-Writer-Teacher*, Exhibition Catalogue, Bodmin, 2003.
42. *As You Like It*, Act II, Scene I, lines 15-18.
43. Ann Arnold, 'Graham Arnold and The Brotherhood of Ruralists', *Graham Arnold; A Retrospective*, Exhibition Catalogue, The Tabernacle Cultural Centre, Machynlleth, 1992, p. 20.
44. Richard Jefferies, *The Story of My Heart*, Harmondsworth: Penguin, 1938, pp. 49-50.
45. Jefferies, *The Story of My Heart*, p. 44.
46. Graham Ovenden, 'Viriditas, the greening power of the Divine', *Graham Arnold; A Retrospective*, Exhibition Catalogue, The Tabernacle Cultural Centre, Machynlleth, 1992, p. 13.
47. Graham Ovenden, 'Viriditas, the greening power of the Divine', p. 13.
48. *Graham Arnold; A Retrospective*, Cat. 21, p. 31.
49. R.G.Alexander, *A Catalogue of the Etchings of Samuel Palmer*, London: The Print Collectors' Club, 1937, p. 27.
50. Jerrold Northrop Moore, *Graham Ovenden: Anatomies of Innocence*, unpublished essay, p. 24.
51. Clive Wainwright, 'Architecture and Antiquities', *Graham Ovenden, Essays by Victor Arwas, Clive Aslet, Laurie Lee, Robert Melville and Clive Wainwright*, London and New York: Academy Editions, 1987, p. 97.
52. Clive Wainwright, 'Architecture and Antiquities', p. 100.
53. Alexander, *A Catalogue of the Etchings of Samuel Palmer*, p. 26.
54. Alexander, *A Catalogue of the Etchings of Samuel Palmer*, p. 26.
55. Palmer to P.G.Hamerton in A.H.Palmer, *The Life and Letters of Samuel Palmer, Painter and Etcher*, London, 1892, p. 970.
56. Alexander, *A Catalogue of the Etchings of Samuel Palmer*, p. 26.
57. Meyrick, 'In Pursuit of Arcadia, 'p. 70.
58. Tanner, *Double Harness*, p. 31.
59. Tanner, *Double Harness*, p. 30.
60. Tanner, *Double Harness*, p. 47.
61. Robert Meyrick, *Joseph Webb 1908-1962. The light that flits across my brain*, exhibition catalogue, Aberystwyth University, School of Art Gallery and Museum and National Library of Wales, 2007, p. 26.
62. Meyrick, 'In Pursuit of Arcadia', p. 69.
63. Chris Beetles, *S.R.Badmin and the English Landscape*, London: HarperCollins, 1985, p. 47.
64. *The Times* review of the 1932 Winter Exhibition at the R.E, in Beetles, *S.R.Badmin and the English Landscape*, p. 47.
65. Beetles, *S.R.Badmin and the English Landscape*, p. 48.
66. Beetles, *S.R.Badmin and the English Landscape*, p. 52.
67. Meyrick, 'In Pursuit of Arcadia', p. 69.
68. Robert Meyrick, *John Elwyn*, an exhibition to celebrate his 80th birthday, National Library of Wales, Aberystwyth, 1996, p. 5.
69. Elwyn in Meyrick, *John Elwyn*, p. 14.
70. Meyrick, *John Elwyn*, p. 34.
71. Meyrick, *Joseph Webb 1908-1962*, p. 33.
72. Yorke, *The Spirit of Place*, p. 168.
73. Yorke, *The Spirit of Place*, p. 168.
74. Yorke, *The Spirit of Place*, p. 173.
75. John Rothenstein, 'Introduction', *John Minton 1915-1957: Paintings, Drawings, Illustrations and Stage Designs*, Exhibition Catalogue, Reading Museum and Art Gallery, 1974, p. 2.
76. Ayrton, *British Drawings*, p. 47.
77. Minton in Simon Martin, 'The Balm of Culture: Romantic Art and Literary Publications of the 1940s, in Martin, Butlin and Meyrick, *Poets in the Landscape*, p. 95.
78. Minton in Frances Spalding, *Dance till the Stars Come Down; A Biography of John Minton*, London: Hodder and Stoughton, 1991, p. 31.
79. Yorke, *The Spirit of Place*, pp. 178-79.
80. Usherwood in Christopher Martin, *The Ruralists*, London: Academy Editions, 1991, p. 91.
81. Alan Dodd, *Diana Howard-Recent Work*, associate of the Brotherhood of Ruralists, exhibition card, 1991

In Search of England

1. Christopher Martin, 'In the Secret Garden; Autumn with the Ruralists', *The Ruralist's*, London: Academy Editions, 1991, p. 25.
2. Martin, 'In the Secret Garden; Autumn with the Ruralists', 31.
3. See Schama, 'Arcadia Redesigned' in *Landscape and Memory*, pp. 517-545.
4. See Schama, 'Hearts of Oak and Bulwarks of Liberty?' in *Landscape and Memory*, pp. 153-174.
5. The Viking God Ulla lived in a yew grove and was the protector of archers.
6. One of the four yews went down in a great storm in 1883, though the three others still survive. The Borrowdale Yew is female and boasts a large hollow that fits four people. Although it was damaged in a storm in 2005, the tree still thrives.
7. Gilpin, *Remarks on Forest Scenery and Other Woodland Views* (1794), in David Lownethal, *The Past is a Foreign Country*, Cambridge: Cambridge University Press, 1985, p. 175.

8. James Stevens Curl in Lownethal, *The Past is a Foreign Country*, p. 179.
9. Gilpin, *Remarks on Forest Scenery*, in Lownethal, *The Past is a Foreign Country*, p. 168.
10. Gilpin's *Three Essays: On Picturesque Beauty; On Picturesque Travel;* and on *Sketching Landscape* to which is *Added a Poem On Landscape Painting*, London, 1792.
11. Martin, 'In the Secret Garden: Autumn with the Ruralists', p. 7.
12. Sutherland in John Hayes, *The Art Of Graham Sutherland*, London, 1980, p. 20.
13. Dylan Thomas, 'The force that through the green fuse drives the flower', *Collected Poems 1934-1952*, London, 1952, p. 8.
14. Yorke, *The Spirit of Place*, p. 118.
15. Graham Sutherland, 'Welsh Sketch Book', *Horizon*, April 1942, in Martin, 'The Balm of Culture', p. 91.
16. Sutherland in Martin, 'The Balm of Culture', p. 90.
17. Martin, 'The Balm of Culture', p. 85,
18. Graham Sutherland, 'Thoughts on Painting', *The Listener*, 6 September 1951, pp. 376-8.
19. Cardinal, *The Landscape Vision of Paul Nash*, p. 7.
20. Cardinal, *The Landscape Vision of Paul Nash*, p. 21.
21. Cardinal, *The Landscape Vision of Paul Nash*, p. 7.
22. Jewson in Moore, *Gothic Visions: The Architecture of Dreams*, p. 249.
23. Comstock, 'F.L. Griggs', No. 52, p. 25.
24. Yorke, *The Spirit of Place*, p. 115.
25. Sutherland in Yorke, *The Spirit of Place*, p. 116.
26. Sutherland in Yorke, *The Spirit of Place*, p. 119.
27. Sutherland in Yorke, *The Spirit of Place*, p. 126.
28. Jolyon Drury, *Revelation to Revolution: The Legacy of Samuel Palmer. The Revival and Evolution of Pastoral Printmaking by Paul Drury and the Goldsmith's School in the 20th Century*, Ashford, Kent: Jolyon Drury, 2006, p. 154.
29. Paul Drury in Drury, *Revelation to Revolution: The Legacy of Samuel Palmer*, p. 155.
30. Michael Blaker in Drury, *Revelation to Revolution: The Legacy of Samuel Palmer*, p. 157.
31. Cardinal, *The Landscape Vision of Paul Nash*, p. 22.
32. Martin, *The Ruralists*, p. 89
33. Graham Ovenden, 'The Great Beech (Fosbury Camp)' *The Marble Mirror*, Cornwall: The Einna Press, 1984, p. 8.
34. Martin, 'In the Secret Garden; Autumn with the Ruralists', p. 21.
35. Martin, 'In the Secret Garden; Autumn with the Ruralists', p. 21.
36. Usherwood in Martin, *The Ruralists*, p. 91.
37. Gordon Cooke, *Graham Sutherland Early Etchings*, London, 1993, np.
38. Beetles, *S.R. Badmin and the English Landscape*, p. 49.
39. Beetles, *S.R. Badmin and the English Landscape*, p. 49.
40. http://www.osbornesamuel.com/pages/biography/hermes.
41. Richard Jefferies, 'August Days', Samuel J. Looker (ed), *The Spring of the Year and other Nature Essays by Richard Jefferies*, London: Lutterworth Press 1946, p. 80.
42. Richard Jefferies , 'Clematis Lane', J. Looker (ed), *The Life of the Fields by Richard Jefferies*, London: Lutterworth Press, first edition 1947, pp. 98-100.
43. John Fowles, 'Introduction', *Richard Jefferies, Round About A Great Estate*, Special Centenary Edition, Bradford on Avon:Ex Libris Press, 1987, p. 9.
44. Eric Fitch Daglish, *The Heart of England by Edward Thomas*, London: J.M. Dent, 1932, Chapter XXXIX, 'A Harvest Moon', p. 193.
45. Alan Horne, *The Dictionary of Twentieth Century British Book Illustrators*, Woodbridge: Antique Collectors' Club, 1999, pp.162-163.
46. Susan Bruxvoort Lipscomb, 'Introducing Gilbert White: an exemplary natural historian and his editors', *Victorian Literature and Culture*, Vol. 35, Issue 2, 2007,Cambridge: Cambridge University Press, pp. 551-567.
47. Martin, 'In the Secret Garden; Autumn with the Ruralists', p. 21.
48. Paul Nash, *Monster Field: A Discovery Recorded by Paul Nash*, Oxford: Counterpoint Publications, 1946, pp. 3-4.
49. Paul Nash, *Monster Field: A Discovery Recorded by Paul Nash*, Oxford: Counterpoint Publications, 1946, pp. 4-5.
50. Cardinal, *The Landscape Vision of Paul Nash*, p. 25.
51. Craxton in Byran Robertson, *John Craxton: Painting and Drawings 1980-1985*, exhibition catalogue, London: Christopher Hull Gallery, June-July, 1985, p. 22.
52. Craxton in Robertson, *John Craxton: Painting and Drawings 1980-1985*, p. 21.
53. Craxton in *John Craxton; Paintings and Drawings 1941-1966*, exhibition catalogue, Whitechapel Art Gallery, London, 1967, p. 6.
54. Craxton in Yorke, *The Spirit of Place*, p. 309.
55. Craxton in Robertson, *John Craxton: Painting and Drawings 1980-1985*, p. 21.
56. Ayrton in Yorke, *The Spirit of Place*, p. 313.
57. Robertson, *John Craxton: Painting and Drawings 1980-1985*, p. 4.
58. Yorke, *The Spirit of Place*, p. 313.
59. Brailsford in Martin, 'The Balm of Culture', p. 94.
60. Cecil Collins, *The Vision of the Fool*, London: Grey Walls Press, 1947.
61. Martin, 'In the Secret Garden; Autumn with the Ruralists', p. 23.
62. Martin, 'In the Secret Garden; Autumn with the Ruralists', p. 13.
63. Simon Rae, *David Inshaw*, exhibition catalogue, privately printed, 2004, n.p.
64. Jennifer Holloway, *Capel-y-ffin to Ditchling: Watercolours and Drawings by Edgar Holloway*, exhibition catalogue, 2001, Cat No. 32.
65. Herbert Alexander, 'John William North ARA RWS 1842–1924', *Old Water-Colour Society's Club Fifth Annual Volume*, 1927-8.
66. R.M. Billingham, 'A Somerset Draw for Painters - Victorian Artists at Halsway Manor', *Country Life*, 18 August 1977, pp. 428-30
67. Herbert Alexander, 'John William North ARA RWS 1842–1924', *Old Water-Colour Society's Club Fifth Annual Volume*, 1927-8.
68. Colin Harrison, 'Later Shoreham (1830-35)', in Vaughan, Barker and Harrison, *Samuel Palmer: Vision and Landscape*, Cat No. 69, p. 141.
69. Harrison, 'Later Shoreham (1830-35)', Cat No. 69, p. 144.
70. Meyrick, 'In Pursuit of Arcadia', p. 62.
71. Comstock, *A Gothic Vision*, No. 33, p. 149.
72. Griggs in Comstock, *A Gothic Vision*, No. 39, p. 181.
73. Griggs in Comstock, *A Gothic Vision*, No. 39, p. 182.
74. Griggs in Northrop Moore, *F.L Griggs: The Architecture of Dreams*, p. 210.
75. Robert Meyrick, 'Introduction,' *Edgar Holloway at 80*, a retrospective exhibition, Wolesley Fine Art, London 1994, p. 9.
76. Graham Ovenden, 'All Saints Dunwich', *The Marble Mirror: Thirty Poems by Graham Ovenden*, Cornwall: The Einna Press, 1984, p. 14.
77. De la Mare in Wainwright, 'Architecture and Antiquities', p. 105
78. De la Mare in Wainwright, 'Architecture and Antiquities', p. 105.
79. Graham Ovenden, *Satirical Poems and Others*, St Columb, Cornwall: Turangalila Press, 1983, p. 35.

Ancient Landscapes

1. See Sam Smiles, 'Equivalents for the Megaliths: Prehistory and English Culture, 1920-50' in David Peters Corbett, Ysanne Holt and Fiona Russell (eds.) *The Geographies of Englishness: Landscape and the National Past 1880-1940*, New Haven and London: Yale University Press, 2002, pp. 199-223.
2. Gilpin, *Observations on the River Wye*...1770, pp. 47-8 in Lowenthal, *The Past is a Foreign Land*, p. 156.

3. Lowenthal, *The Past is a Foreign Land*, p. 157.
4. Gilpin, *River Wye*, p. 48 in Lowenthal, *The Past is a Foreign Land*, p. 157.
5. Gilpin, *Observations …made in the year 1772, on…the Mountains, and Lakes of Cumberland, and Westmorland*, p. 88 in Lowenthal, *The Past is a Foreign Land*, p. 157.
6. Ruskin, Seven Lamps of Architecture, 1849, p. 183 in Lowenthal, *The Past is a Foreign Land*, p. 157.
7. Gilpin, *Observations …made in the year 1772, on…the Mountains, and Lakes of Cumberland, and Westmorland*, p.67-8 in Lowenthal, *The Past is a Foreign Land*, p. 158.
8. Cardinal, *The Landscape Vision of Paul Nash*, p. 21.
9. Cardinal, *The Landscape Vision of Paul Nash*, p. 20.
10. Andrew Causey, 'Paul Nash and Englishness' in Jemima Montagu, *Paul Nash: Modern Artist, Ancient Landscape*, London: Tate Publishing, 2003, p. 45.
11. Causey, 'Paul Nash and Englishness', p. 25.
12. Myfanwy Evans in Causey, 'Paul Nash and Englishness', p. 24.
13. Rae, *David Inshaw*, n.p.
14. T.S. Eliot in Rae, *David Inshaw*, n.p.
15. Nash in Montagu, *Paul Nash: Modern Artist, Ancient Landscape*, p. 76.
16. John Summerson, 'The past in the future' in Lownethal, *The Past is a Foreign Country*, p. 169.
17. Nash in Montagu, *Paul Nash: Modern Artist, Ancient Landscape*, p. 76.
18. Piper in Sam Smiles 'Ancient Country: Nash and Prehistory' in Montagu, *Paul Nash: Modern Artist, Ancient Landscape*, p. 33.
19. Cardinal, *The Landscape Vision of Paul Nash*, p. 21.
20. Cardinal, *The Landscape Vision of Paul Nash*, p. 22.
21. Yorke, *Spirit of Place*, p. 97.
22. Meyrick, *John Elwyn*, p. 34.
23. Meyrick, *John Elwyn*, p. 34.
24. Nicholas Usherwood in Martin, *The Ruralists*, p. 81.
25. Cardinal, *The Landscape Vision of Paul Nash*, p. 30.
26. Cardinal, *The Landscape Vision of Paul Nash*, p. 31.
27. Nicholas Usherwood, *David Inshaw: Moments of Vision (Between Fantasy and Reality)*, exhibition catalogue, Agnews, 2004, n.p.
28. http://www.bbc.co.uk/wiltshire/entertainment/arts/henry_moore_exhibition.shtml.
29. Richard Ingrams and John Piper, *Piper's Places. John Piper in England and Wales*, London: Chatto and Windus, Hogarth Press, 1983, p. 123.
30. Ingrams and Piper, *Piper's Places*, p. 127.
31. Paul Nash, 'Unseen Landscapes', 1938 in Smiles, 'Ancient Country: Nash and Prehistory', p. 32.
32. Smiles 'Ancient Country: Nash and Prehistory', p. 32.
33. Wainwright, 'Architecture and Antiquities', p. 104.
34. http://www.brimhamrocks.co.uk.
35. Richard Jefferies, *The Story of My Heart*, Harmondsworth: Penguin, 1938, pp. 49-50.
36. Ruth and Vincent Megaw, *Celtic Art from its beginnings to the Book of Kells*, London and New York: Thames & Hudson, 1989.
37. http://wiltshirewhitehorses.org.uk/altonbarnes.html

Nocturnes

1. Minton in Martin, 'The Balm of Culture', p. 95.
2. Tanner, *Double Harness*, p. 47.
3. William Vaughan, 'Shoreham and the Ancients (1825-30)' in Vaughan, Barker and Harrison, *Samuel Palmer: Vision and Landscape*, p. 125.
4. William Vaughan, 'Introduction', in Vaughan, Barker and Harrison, *Samuel Palmer: Vision and Landscape*, p. 13.
   Palmer in Vaughan, 'Introduction', p.14.
6. Graham Ovenden, 'The Night Hunters', *The Marble Mirror*, p. 29.
7. Graham Ovenden, 'Walk to Paradise', *Ruralist 2001, Barley Splatt*, exhibition catalogue, 2001, p. 11.
8. Annie Ovenden, 'Moments before the incident in the forgotten garden', *Ruralist 2001, Barley Splatt*, exhibition catalogue, 2001, p. 7.
9. Francis Thompson, *The Works of Francis Thompson. Poems*, 2 vols, New York: Charles Scribner's Sons, 1913, Vol I, pp. 107-13.
10. Thomas Gray, *An Elegy in a Country Church Yard* (1751) *and The Eton College Manuscript*, Project Gutenberg, Etext-No. 15409, Los Angeles: Williams Andrews Clark Memorial Library, University of California, 1951, n.p.
11. The yellow, trumpet shaped plant next to the mushroom has also been identified as another sort of fungus known as a chanterelle.
12. Cardinal, *The Landscape Vision of Paul Nash*, p. 114.
13. Paul Nash, *Picture History*, 1943-5 (Nash's unpublished notes about his work since 1933) in Cardinal, *The Landscape of Vision of Paul Nash*, p. 118.
14. Simon Grant, 'Paul Nash: War Artist, Landscape Painter' in Montagu, *Modern Artist, Ancient Landscape*, p. 46.
15. Grant, 'Paul Nash: War Artist, Landscape Painter', p. 46.
16. Graham Arnold, 'The Twins Watching the Eclipse at Clun Castle', *Ruralist 2001, Barley Splatt*, exhibition catalogue, 2001, p. 9.

James Sellars (1927-2000): Artist and Teacher

1. The Art and Technology Colleges were merged in 1978, under the auspices of cost- effectiveness, to form the Southampton College of Higher Education. The story of the College of Art as a separate entity ends with the merging of various institutions into Southampton Institute of Higher Education in 1984, the year Jim Sellars retired.
2. Victor Arwas, 'Introduction', in Arwas, Aslet, Lee, Melville and Wainwright, *Graham Ovenden*, pp. 13-16
3. *Official Opening of the Southampton College of Art by Roy Hattersley MP, Friday 15th March 1974*, p. 3.
4. From a personal interview by Sophie Callaway, 25 February 2005.
5. Graham Ovenden, 'Preface', *James Sellars: Artist-Writer-Teacher*, Exhibition Catalogue, Bodmin: Ruralist Fine Art, 2003.
6. James Sellars, *Samuel Palmer*, London: Academy Editions, 1974.
7. Jerrold Northrop Moore in consultation with the artist, *Graham Ovenden: Anatomies of Innocence*, unpublished essay.
8. *James Sellars: Artist-Writer-Teacher*, n.p.
9. *James Sellars: Artist-Writer-Teacher*, n.p.

Bibliography

General

Ayrton, Michael, *British Drawings*, London: William Collins, 1946.

Egerton, Judy, *Wright of Derby*, London: Tate Gallery, 1990.

Fussell, Paul, *The Great War and Modern Memory*, Oxford: Oxford University Press, 1977.

Lownethal, David, *The Past is a Foreign Country*, Cambridge: Cambridge University Press, 1985.

Martin, Simon, Martin Butlin and Robert Meyrick, *Poets in the Landscape: The Romantic Spirit in British Art*, exhibition catalogue, Pallant House Gallery, Chichester, 2007.

Martin, Simon, 'Poets in the Landscape: The Romantic Spirit in British Art', in Martin, Butlin and Meyrick, *Poets in the Landscape: The Romantic Spirit in British Art*.

Megaw, Ruth and Vincent, *Celtic Art from its beginnings to the Book of Kells*, London and New York: Thames & Hudson, 1989.

Northrop Moore, Jerrold *The Green Fuse, Pastoral Vision in English Art 1820–2000*, Woodbridge: Antique Collectors' Club, 2007.

Piper, John, *British Romantic Artists* (Britain in Pictures Series), London: William Collins, 1942.

Schama, Simon, *Landscape and Memory*, London: Harper Collins, 1995.

Smiles, Sam, 'Equivalents for the Megaliths: Prehistory and English Culture, 1920–50' in David Peters Corbett, Ysanne Holt and Fiona Russell (eds.) *The Geographies of Englishness: Landscape and the National Past 1880–1940*, New Haven and London: Yale University Press, 2002, pp. 199-223.

Wood, Christopher, *Fairies in Victorian Art*, Woodbridge: Antique Collectors' Club, 2000.

Woodcock, Peter, *The Enchanted Isle: The Neo-Romantic Vision from William Blake to the New Visionaries*, Glastonbury: Gothic Image, 2000.

Pastoral Authors

Burton, Robert, *Anatomy of Melancholy*, New York: Everyman Edition, 1964, Vol. I.

Daglish, Eric Fitch, 'Foreword', *The Heart of England by Edward Thomas*, London and Toronto: J.M. Dent and Sons, 1932.

Gray, Thomas, *An Elegy in a Country Church Yard* (1751) *and The Eton College Manuscript*, Project Gutenberg, Etext-No. 15409, Los Angeles:Williams Andrews Clark Memorial Library, University of California, 1951.

Jefferies, Richard, *The Story of My Heart*, Harmondsworth: Penguin, 1938.

Lipscomb, Susan Bruxvoort, 'Introducing Gilbert White: an exemplary natural historian and his editors', *Victorian Literature and Culture*, Vol. 35, Issue 2, 2007, Cambridge: Cambridge University Press, pp. 551-567.

Looker, Samuel J. (ed.), *The Spring of the Year and other Nature Essays by Richard Jefferies*, London: Lutterworth Press, 1946.

Looker, Samuel J., *The Life of the Fields by Richard Jefferies*, London: Lutterworth Press, 1947.

Moynahan, Julian, 'Pastoralism as Culture and Counter-Culture in English Fiction, 1800–1928', *Novel*, VI, No. I, Fall 1972, pp. 20-35.

Richard Jefferies, Round About A Great Estate, Special Centenary Edition, Bradford on Avon: Ex Libris Press, 1987.

Thomas, Dylan, *Collected Poems 1934-1952*, London: J.M. Dent and Sons, 1952.

Thompson, Francis, *The Works of Francis Thompson. Poems*, 2 Vols., New York: Charles Scribner's Sons, 1913.

Ward, John Powell, *The English Line Poetry of the Unpoetic from Wordsworth to Larkin*, London: Macmillan, 1991.

Etchers/Engravers

Beetles, Chris, *S.R. Badmin and the English Landscape*, London: HarperCollins, 1985.

Drury, Jolyon, *Revelation to Revolution: The Legacy of Samuel Palmer. The Revival and Evolution of Pastoral Printmaking by Paul Drury and the Goldsmiths' School in the 20th Century*, Ashford, Kent: Jolyon Drury, 2006.

Guichard, Kenneth M., *British Etchers: 1850–1940*, London: Robin Garton, 1981.

Holloway, Jennifer, *Capel-y-ffin to Ditchling: Watercolours and Drawings by Edgar Holloway*, exhibition catalogue, 2001.

Horne, Alan, *The Dictionary of Twentieth Century British Book Illustrators*, Woodbridge: Antique Collectors' Club, 1999.

Meyrick, Robert, 'Introduction,' *Edgar Holloway at 80*, a retrospective exhibition, Wolesley Fine Art, London 1994, pp. 5-14.

Meyrick, Robert, *Joseph Webb 1908-1962. The light that flits across my brain*, exhibition catalogue, Aberystwyth University, School of Art Gallery and Museum and National Library of Wales, 2007.

Meyrick, Robert, 'In Pursuit of Arcadia: British Print Makers in the 1920s', in Martin, Butlin and Meyrick, *Poets in the Landscape: The Romantic Spirit in British Art*, 2007.

Tanner, Robin, *Double Harness: An Autobiography*, London: Impact Books, 1987.

John Elwyn

Elwyn, John, 'John Elwyn: Four Works with Notes' *Anglo-Welsh Review* Vol. 9, No. 23, 1958.

Meyrick, Robert, *John Elwyn*, an exhibition to celebrate his 80th birthday, National Library of Wales, Aberystwyth, 1996.

F.L. Griggs

Alexander, Russell G., *The engraved work of Frederick Landseer Griggs, etchings and drypoints, 1912–28*, Stratford-Upon-Avon: Shakespeare Head Press, 1928.

Comstock, F.A., *A Gothic Vision: F.L. Griggs and His Work*, Boston and Oxford: Boston Public Library and Ashmolean Museum, 1966, reprinted 1978.

Lister, Raymond, 'F.L. Griggs – an appreciation' in *The Best of Mr F.L.M. Griggs*, exhibition catalogue, Taranman Gallery, 1974.

Northrop Moore, Jerrold, *F. L. Griggs: The Architecture of Dreams*, Oxford: Oxford University Press, 1999.

Wright, Harold J.L., *The Etched Work of F.L. Griggs with a Catalogue by Campbell Dodgson*, London: Print Collectors' Club, 1941.

Neo-Romantics

Collins, Cecil, *The Vision of the Fool*, London: Grey Walls Press, 1947.

Collins, Judith, *Cecil Collins: A Retrospective Exhibition*, exhibition catalogue, Tate Gallery, London, 1989.

Ingrams, Richard and John Piper, *Piper's Places. John Piper in England and Wales*, London: Chatto and Windus, Hogarth Press, 1983.

John Craxton; Paintings and Drawings 1941–1966, exhibition catalogue, Whitechapel Art Gallery, London, 1967.

Martin, Simon 'The Balm of Culture: Romantic Art and Literary Publications of the 1940s', in Martin, Butlin and Meyrick, *Poets in the Landscape*.

Robertson, Byran, *John Craxton: Painting and*

Drawings 1980–1985, exhibition catalogue, London: Christopher Hull Gallery, June–July, 1985.
John Minton 1915–1957: Paintings, Drawings, Illustrations and Stage Designs, exhibition catalogue, Reading Museum and Art Gallery, 1974.
Spalding, Frances, *Dance till the Stars Come Down; A Biography of John Minton*, London: Hodder and Stoughton, 1991.
Yorke, Malcolm, 'English Neo-Romantics', in 'The New Romantics', *Art and Design*, Vol. 4, No. 11/12, 1988, pp. 37-41.
Yorke, Malcolm, *The Spirit of Place: Nine Neo-Romantic Artists and Their Times*, London: Constable, 1988.

Paul Nash

Abbott, C.C. and A. Bertram (eds.), *Poet and Painter: Correspondence between Gordon Bottomley and Paul Nash, 1910–1946*, London and Oxford: Oxford University Press, 1955.
Bertram, Anthony, *Paul Nash. The Portrait of an Artist*, London: Faber, 1955.
Cardinal, Roger, *The Landscape Vision of Paul Nash*, London: Reaktion Books, 1989. Reprinted 1994.
Causey, Andrew, 'Paul Nash and Englishness', in Montagu, *Paul Nash: Modern Artist, Ancient Landscape*, pp. 23-29.
Grant, Simon, 'Paul Nash: War Artist, Landscape Painter' in Montagu, *Modern Artist, Ancient Landscape*, pp. 39-47.
Montagu, Jemima, *Paul Nash. Modern Artist, Ancient Landscape*, exhibition catalogue, London: Tate Britain, 2003.
Nash, Paul, *Monster Field: A Discovery Recorded by Paul Nash*, Oxford: Counterpoint Publications, 1946.
Nash, Paul, *Outline. An Autobiography and Other Writings*, London: Faber, 1949.
Smiles, Sam, 'Ancient Country: Nash and Prehistory' in Montagu, *Paul Nash: Modern Artist, Ancient Landscape*, pp. 31-37.

Samuel Palmer

Alexander, R.G., *A Catalogue of the Etchings of Samuel Palmer*, London: The Print Collectors' Club, 1937.
Binyon, Laurence, *The Followers of William Blake: Edward Calvert, Samuel Palmer, George Richmond and their Circle*, London: Halton & Truscott Smith, 1925.
Butlin, Martin, 'The Pastoral Vision: Blake, Palmer and the Ancients 1805–1850', in Martin, Butlin and Meyrick, *Poets in the Landscape*.
Grigson, Geoffrey, *Samuel Palmer: the Visionary Years*, London: Kegan Paul, 1947.
Harrison, Colin, 'The Artistic Rediscovery of Samuel Palmer', in Vaughan, Barker and Harrison, *Samuel Palmer: Vision and Landscape*, pp. 55-63.
Harrison, Colin 'Later Shoreham (1830–35)', in Vaughan, Barker and Harrison *Samuel Palmer: Vision and Landscape*, pp. 137-168.
Palmer, A.H., *The Life and Letters of Samuel Palmer, Painter and Etcher*, London: Seeley, 1892.
Raine, Kathleen, *William Blake*, London: British Council and Longmans, Green, & Co., 1951.
Sellars, James, *Samuel Palmer*, London: Academy Editions, 1974.
Stephens, F.G., *Notes by Mr F.G. Stephens on a Collection of Drawings, Paintings and Etchings by the Late Samuel Palmer*, London, 1881.
Vaughan, William, Elizabeth E. Barker and Colin Harrison, *Samuel Palmer: Vision and Life*, exhibition catalogue, British Museum, 2005.
Vaughan, William, 'Introduction', in Vaughan, Barker and Harrison, *Samuel Palmer, Vision and Landscape*, pp. 11-16.
Vaughan, William, '"Brothers in art, brothers in love": The Ancients as an Artistic Community', in Vaughan, Barker and Harrison, *Samuel Palmer: Vision and Landscape*, pp. 17-21.
Vaughan, William, 'Shoreham and the Ancients (1825–30)', in Vaughan, Barker and Harrison, *Samuel Palmer, Vision and Landscape*, pp. 105-136.
Vaughan, William, 'The Lonely Tower (*c*.1865–1881)', in Vaughan, Barker and Harrison, *Samuel Palmer: Vision and Life*, pp. 224-244.

Ruralist

Arnold, Ann, 'Graham Arnold and The Brotherhood of Ruralists', in *Graham Arnold; A Retrospective*, pp. 19-20.
Arnold, Graham and Ann, *Exhibition of Work inspired by Gerald Finzi, English Song and Thomas Hardy*, June–July 2001, exhibition leaflet, Silk Top Hat Gallery, Ludlow.
Arwas, Victor, Clive Aslet, Laurie Lee, Robert Melville and Clive Wainwright, *Graham Ovenden*, London: Academy Editions, 1987.
Arwas, Victor, 'Introduction', in Arwas, Aslet, Lee, Melville and Wainwright, *Graham Ovenden*, pp. 13-40.
Cumming, Hugh, 'Post-Modern Landscape: The Art of Graham Ovenden' in 'Post-Avant-Garde: Painting in the Eighties', *Art and Design*, Vol 3, 7/8, August 1987, pp. 77-80.
Dodd, Alan, *Diana Howard-Recent Work*, associate of the Brotherhood of Ruralists, exhibition card, 1991.
Graham Arnold; A Retrospective, exhibition catalogue, The Tabernacle Cultural Centre, Machynlleth, 1992.
James Sellars: Artist-Writer-Teacher, exhibition catalogue, Bodmin: Ruralist Fine Art, 2003.
Lee, Laurie, 'Understanding the Ruralists' in Northrop Moore, Lee, Nahum, *The Ruralists: A Celebration*, pp. 109-112.
Martin, Christopher, *The Ruralists*, London: Academy Editions, 1991.
Martin, Christopher 'In the Secret Garden; Autumn with the Ruralists', *The Ruralist's*, pp. 7-41.
Northrop Moore, Jerrold, Laurie Lee, Peter Nahum, *The Ruralists: A Celebration*, Bodmin: Ruralist Fine Art, 2004.
Nahum, Peter, *The Brotherhood of Ruralists and the Pre-Raphaelites*, The Leicester Galleries, exhibition catalogue, 2005.
Ovenden, Graham, *Satirical Poems and Others*, St Columb, Cornwall: Turangalila Press, 1983.
Ovenden, Graham, *The Marble Mirror: Thirty Poems by Graham Ovenden*, Cornwall: The Einna Press, 1984.
Ovenden, Graham, 'Ruralism and the New Romanticism', 'The New Romantics', *Art and Design*, Vol. 4, No. 11/12, 1988, pp. 51-52.
Ovenden, Graham, 'Viriditas, the greening power of the Divine', *Graham Arnold; A Retrospective*, pp. 13-17.
Rae, Simon, *David Inshaw*, exhibition catalogue, privately printed, 2004.
Ruralist 2001, Barley Splatt, exhibition catalogue, 2001.
Rudd, Natalie, *Peter Blake*, (Modern Artists), London: Tate Modem, 2003.
Usherwood, Nicholas, *David Inshaw: Moments of Vision (Between Fantasy and Reality)*, exhibition catalogue, Agnews, 2004.
Vaizey, Marina, *Peter Blake*, London: Weidenfeld and Nicolson, 1986.
Wainwright, Clive, 'Architecture and Antiquities', Arwas, Aslet, Lee, Melville and Wainwright, *Graham Ovenden*, pp. 97-112.

Graham Sutherland

Berthoud, Roger, *Graham Sutherland: A Biography*, London: Faber and Faber, 1982.
Cooke, Gordon, 'Introduction', *Graham Sutherland Early Etchings*, London: privately printed, 1993.
Cooper, Douglas, *The Work of Graham Sutherland*, London: Lund Humphries 1961.
Hayes, John, *The Art Of Graham Sutherland*, Oxford: Phaidon, 1980.
Sutherland, Graham, 'Thoughts on Painting', *The Listener*, 6 September 1951, pp. 376-78.
Sutherland, Graham, 'Welsh Sketchbook', *Horizon* V, April 1942, pp. 225-335.
Sutherland, Graham, 'Landscape and Figures' Graham Sutherland discusses his art with Andrew Forge, *The Listener*, 26 July 1962, pp. 132-5.
Sutherland, Graham, *The English Vision*, exhibition catalogue, William Weston Gallery, October 1973.
Tassi, Roberto, *Graham Sutherland: The Complete Graphic Work*, London: Thames and Hudson, 1978.

About the Authors

Dr Anne Anderson, BA PhD FSA NADFAS
After graduating in Archaeological Studies, from Leicester University in 1978, Anne worked as an archaeologist for 8 years, being elected to the Society of Antiquaries in 1996. Anne was awarded her PhD in English from Exeter University in 2001. From 1993-2007, she was a senior lecturer on the Fine Arts Valuation degree courses at Southampton Solent University; currently Anne is a Hon. Research Fellow at Exeter University. She has published books on Roman pottery, Art Deco teapots and Octavia Hill, a founder of the National Trust. Her academic papers have appeared in the *Journal of Design History*; *History of Education*; *Women's History Review*; *Journal of the William* Morris *Society* and *The Wildean* the journal of the Oscar Wilde Society. She also writes for *The Antique Collector*. She was the Cumming Ceramics Research Fellow for 2007, researching Chinamania. She is currently working on a book – *Aesthetic Materialities: Constructing Taste from Whistler to Wilde.* As an international speaker, working for NADFAS, Anne has travelled widely – to Australia (twice), New Zealand, Spain, Germany and France.

Robert Meyrick
is Head of School and Keeper of Art at Aberystwyth University's School of Art, Gallery and Museum. He trained in fine art and art history and now writes on twentieth century British art, on printmaking in particular, the history of art in Wales and on collecting. This is reflected in his contribution to teaching at Aberystwyth. In 2001 he was invited to become an Honorary Fellow of the Royal Society of Painter-Printmakers in recognition of his services to the art of printmaking in Britain. He has curated national touring exhibitions and written accompanying publications for leading provincial museums and private art galleries in the UK, including 'Edgar Holloway at 80', a retrospective exhibition, Wolesley Fine Art, London 1994; Joseph Webb 1908-1962; 'The light that flits across my brain', exhibition catalogue, Aberystwyth University, School of Art Gallery and Museum and National Library of Wales 2007; 'In Pursuit of Arcadia: British Print Makers in the 1920s', in Martin, Butlin and Meyrick, *Poets in the Landscape: The Romantic Spirit in British Art*, 2007, Pallant House, Chichester and 'John Elwyn, an exhibition to celebrate his 80th birthday', National Library of Wales, Aberystwyth, 1996.

Peter Nahum, FRSA
Television personality, academic, lecturer, author, frame designer and regular lender of paintings to international exhibitions, Peter Nahum was elected a Fellow of The Royal Society for the Encouragement of Arts, Manufactures and Commerce (FRSA) in 2005. Educated at Sherborne Public School, Nahum began his career at Sotheby's in 1966. During his 17 years with the company he initiated the Victorian Painting Department at the newly opened Sotheby's Belgravia in 1971 and was head of the British Painting Department (1840 to Contemporary) until his departure in 1984. He was also a Senior Director sitting on the chairman's committee and adviser to the British Rail Pension Fund on Victorian Paintings. He has handled a large proportion of the most important Victorian paintings to come on the market.

He left Sotheby's in 1984 to open his own gallery, The Leicester Galleries, in St James's, London, specialising in paintings, drawings and sculptures of the highest quality from the 19th and 20th centuries. From 1981 to 2002 Peter Nahum was a regular contributor to the BBC's *Antiques Roadshow* rediscovering in 1987 Richard Dadd's lost watercolour 'Artists Halt in the Desert' which he later sold to the British Museum.

Photo Credits

Figures

1: Peter Nahum at the Leicester Gallery; © the artist, 2008; 2-4: © Ruralist Fine Art, 2008; 5: Ruralist Fine Art; © of the artist, 2008.

Catalogue

1: SCAG; © the estate of Graham Sutherland, 2008; 2: SCAG; © the artist, 2008; 3: SCAG; 4: Pallant House Gallery, Chichester; 5: Victoria Art Gallery Bath; 6: SCAG; 7: SCAG; © the estate of F.L.M. Griggs, 2008; 8: Pallant House Gallery, Chichester; © the estate of Graham Sutherland, 2008; 9, 9a, 10: Ruralist Fine Art; © the artist, 2008; 11: Graham Ovenden; © estate of John Lefevre, 2008; 12: Peter Nahum at the Leicester Galleries; © the artist, 2008; 13, 14: Graham Ovenden; © the artist, 2008; 15: SCAG; 16: Shell Art Collection; © Tate, London 2008; 17: Graham Ovenden; © the artist, 2008; 18: SCAG; 19: SCAG; © the estate of Graham Sutherland, 2008; 20: SCAG; © the estate of Robin Tanner, Crafts Study Centre, University College for the Creative Arts, Farnham, 2008; 21: SCAG; © Estate of Eric Ravilious/DACS 2008; 22: SCAG; © the estate of Joseph Webb, 2008; 23: SCAG; © the estate of Graham Sutherland, 2008; 24: SCAG; © Chris Beetles Ltd for the S R Badmin Estate, 2008; 25: SCAG; © the estate of Paul Drury; 26: Robert Meyrick; © the estate of William John Elwyn Davies, 2008; 27: University of Wales, Aberystwyth; © the estate of Joseph Webb, 2008; 28: Pallant House Gallery, Chichester; ©: Royal College of Art, 2008; 29: Peter Nahum at the Leicester Galleries; © Royal College of Art, 2008; 31: SCAG; 32: Graham Ovenden; © the artist, 2008; 33: Victoria Art Gallery, Bath; © the artist; 33a: © Ruralist Fine Art, 2008; 34: Peter Nahum at the Leicester Galleries; © the artist, 2008; 35: Diana Morley; © the artist, 2008; 36: SCAG; © the estate of F.L.M. Griggs, 2008; 37, 37a, 37b: SCAG; copyright: the estate of Graham Sutherland, 2008; 38: SCAG; © the estate of Paul Drury; 39, 40: SCAG; © Tate, London 2008; 41: SCAG; © estate of Gilbert Spencer/The Bridgeman Art Library, 2008; 42: SCAG; © The Estate of Stanley Spencer 2008; all rights reserved DACS; 43a: Tullie House, Carlisle; © Tate, London 2008; 44: Ruralist Fine Art; © the artist, 2008; 45: Peter Nahum at the Leicester Gallery; © the artist, 2008; 46: SCAG; © the estate of Graham Sutherland, 2008; 47, 47a: SCAG; © the estate of Edward Bouverie Hoynton or assignee, 2008; 48: SCAG; © Chris Beetles Ltd for the S R Badmin Estate, 2008; 49, 50: John Morley; © the artist, 2008; 51, 52: Ruralist Fine Art; © the artist, 2008; 53: SCAG; © the estate of William Hyde or assignee, 2008; 54: ACC; © estate of Gertrude Hermes, permission of Judith Russell and Simon Hughes-Stanton, 2008; 56, 57, 58: ACC; estate of Agnes Miller Parker or assignee, 2008; 59: ACC; © the artist, 2008; 60: ACC; © J.M. Dent and Daglish family, 2008; 61: SCAG; © Estate of Eric Ravilious/DACS 2008; 62: ACC; estate of Agnes Miller Parker or assignee, 2008; 63: ACC; © the estate of Edward Arthur Wilson or assignee, 2008; 64, 65: Tate; © Tate, London 2008; 66, 66a, 67: ACC; © John Craxton 2008; all Rights Reserved, DACS; 68: ACC; © the artists, 2008; 69: Anne Anderson; © Estate of Eric Ravilious/DACS 2008; 69: Anne Anderson; © estate of Clare Leighton or assignee, 2008; 71, 72: Victoria Art Gallery, Bath; © Tate, London 2008; 73: British Council; © the estate of Graham Sutherland, 2008; 74: SCAG; © the Hitchens Family, 2008; 76: Ruralist Fine Art; © the artist, 2008; 77: Edgar and Jennifer Holloway; © the artist, 2008; 78: ACC; © the artist, 2008; 79: Robert Meyrick; © the estate of William John Elwyn Davies, 2008; 80: Tabretts Fine Art; © the artist, 2008; 81: Edgar and Jennifer Holloway; © the artist, 2008; 83: Graham Ovenden; © the artist, 2008; 84: Ruralist Fine Art; © the artist, 2008; 85: Tabretts Fine Art; © the artist, 2008; 86, 87: SCAG; © the estate of F.L.M. Griggs, 2008; 88, 89: Edgar and Jennifer Holloway; © the artist, 2008; 90: Graham Ovenden; © the artist, 2008; 91: SCAG; © the estate of Graham Sutherland, 2008; 93: SCAG; © John Craxton 2008; all Rights Reserved, DACS; 94: British Council; © Royal College of Art, 2008; 95: © Agnew's, London, UK / The Bridgeman Art Library; © estate of John Piper, 2008; 96: Robert Meyrick; © the estate of William John Elwyn Davies, 2008; 97: Wiltshire Heritage Museum; © the estate of John Piper, 2008; 98, 99: Tabretts Fine Art; © the artist, 2008; 100, 100a: Ovenden, *Sentinels of Silbury*; picture credit: Graham Ovenden; © the artist, 2008; 101: Shell Art Collection; the estate of Edward McKnight-Kauffer, 2008; 102: SCAG; © estate of Gertrude Hermes, permission of Judith Russell and Simon Hughes-Stanton, 2008; 103: Wiltshire Heritage Museum; copyright reproduced by permission of the Henry Moore Foundation, 2008; 104: The Bridgeman Art Library; © estate of John Piper, 2008; 105: Tate; © Tate, London 2008; 107: British Council; © Tate, London, 2008; 108: Graham Ovenden; © the artist, 2008; 109: British Council; © Tate, London 2008; 110: Wiltshire Heritage Museum, Devizes; © the artist, 2008; 111: Shell Art Collection; © the estate of Graham Sutherland, 2008; 112: The Bridgeman Art Library; © the estate of John Piper, 2008; 113-118: Ruralist Fine Art; © the artist, 2008; 120: Pallant House Gallery, Chichester; the estate of John Piper, 2008; 121. Ruralist Fine Art; © the artist, 2008; 122, 122a: Edgar and Jennifer Holloway; © the artist, 2008; 123, 123a: Graham Ovenden; © of the artist, 2008; 124: Peter and Renata Nahum; © the artist, 2008; 125: SCAG; © the estate of Joseph Webb, 2008; 126: University of Wales, Aberystwyth; © the estate of Joseph Webb, 2008; 127: ACC; © of the artist, 2008; 128: Peter and Renata Nahum; © the artist, 2008; 129, 130: Tabretts Fine Art; © the artist, 2008; 131: The Bridgeman Art Library; © Tate, London 2008; 132: Graham Ovenden; © of the artist, 2008; 133: British Council; © Tate, London 2008; 134: Ruralist Fine Art; © of the artist, 2008; 135: Graham Ovenden; © the artist, 2008; 1-14, Sellars: Ruralist Fine Art; © estate of James Sellars, 2008.